Hadoop Real-World Solutions Cookbook
Second Edition

Over 90 hands-on recipes to help you learn and master the intricacies of Apache Hadoop 2.X, YARN, Hive, Pig, Oozie, Flume, Sqoop, Apache Spark, and Mahout

Tanmay Deshpande

[PACKT] open source*
PUBLISHING   community experience distilled

BIRMINGHAM - MUMBAI

Hadoop Real-World Solutions Cookbook
Second Edition

First published: February 2013

Second edition: March 2016

Production reference: 1220316

Published by Packt Publishing Ltd.
Livery Place
35 Livery Street
Birmingham B3 2PB, UK.

ISBN 978-1-78439-550-6

www.packtpub.com

Credits

Authors

Tanmay Deshpande

Jonathan R. Owens

Jon Lentz

Brian Femiano

Reviewer

Shashwat Shriparv

Commissioning Editor

Akram Hussain

Acquisition Editor

Manish Nainani

Content Development Editor

Sumeet Sawant

Technical Editor

Gebin George

Copy Editor

Sonia Cheema

Project Coordinator

Shweta H Birwatkar

Proofreader

Safis Editing

Indexer

Tejal Daruwale Soni

Production Coordinator

Manu Joseph

Cover Work

Manu Joseph

About the Author

Tanmay Deshpande is a Hadoop and big data evangelist. He's interested in a wide range of technologies, such as Apache Spark, Hadoop, Hive, Pig, NoSQL databases, Mahout, Sqoop, Java, cloud computing, and so on. He has vast experience in application development in various domains, such as finance, telecoms, manufacturing, security, and retail. He enjoys solving machine-learning problems and spends his time reading anything that he can get his hands on. He has a great interest in open source technologies and promotes them through his lectures. He has been invited to various computer science colleges to conduct brainstorming sessions with students on the latest technologies. Through his innovative thinking and dynamic leadership, he has successfully completed various projects. Tanmay is currently working with Schlumberger as the lead developer of big data. Before Schlumberger, Tanmay worked with Lumiata, Symantec, and Infosys.

He currently blogs at http://hadooptutorials.co.in.

Acknowledgements

This is my fourth book, and I can't thank the Almighty, enough without whom this wouldn't have been true. I would like to take this opportunity to thank my wife, Sneha, my parents, Avinash and Manisha Deshpande, and my brother, Sakalya Deshpande, for being with me through thick and thin. Without you, I am nothing!

I would like to take this opportunity to thank my colleagues, friends, and family for appreciating my work and making it a grand success so far. I'm truly blessed to have each one of you in my life.

I am thankful to the authors of the first edition of this book, Jonathan R. Owens, Brian Femino, and Jon Lentz for setting the stage for me, and I hope this effort lives up to the expectations you had set in the first edition. I am also thankful to each person in Packt Publishing who has worked to make this book happen! You guys are family to me!

Above all, I am thankful to my readers for their love, appreciation, and criticism, and I assure you that I have tried to give you my best. Hope you enjoy this book! Happy learning!

About the Reviewer

Shashwat Shriparv has 6+ IT experience in industry, and 4+ in BigData technologies. He possesses a master degree in computer application. He has experience in technologies such as Hadoop, HBase, Hive, Pig, Flume, Sqoop, Mongo, Cassandra, Java, C#, Linux, Scripting, PHP,C++,C, Web technologies, and various real life use cases in BigData technologies as a developer and administrator.

He has worked with companies such as CDAC, Genilok, HCL, UIDAI(Aadhaar); he is currently working with CenturyLink Cognilytics. He is the author of *Learning HBase, Packt Publishing* and reviewer *Pig design pattern* book, *Packt Publishing*.

I want to acknowledge everyone I know.

www.PacktPub.com

eBooks, discount offers, and more

Did you know that Packt offers eBook versions of every book published, with PDF and ePub files available? You can upgrade to the eBook version at www.PacktPub.com and as a print book customer, you are entitled to a discount on the eBook copy. Get in touch with us at customercare@packtpub.com for more details.

At www.PacktPub.com, you can also read a collection of free technical articles, sign up for a range of free newsletters and receive exclusive discounts and offers on Packt books and eBooks.

https://www2.packtpub.com/books/subscription/packtlib

Do you need instant solutions to your IT questions? PacktLib is Packt's online digital book library. Here, you can search, access, and read Packt's entire library of books.

Why Subscribe?

- ▸ Fully searchable across every book published by Packt
- ▸ Copy and paste, print, and bookmark content
- ▸ On demand and accessible via a web browser

Table of Contents

Preface

Big Data is the need the day. Many organizations are producing huge amounts of data every day. With the advancement of Hadoop-like tools, it has become easier for everyone to solve Big Data problems with great efficiency and at a very low cost. When you are handling such a massive amount of data, even a small mistake can cost you dearly in terms of performance and storage. It's very important to learn the best practices of handling such tools before you start building an enterprise Big Data Warehouse, which will be greatly advantageous in making your project successful.

This book gives you insights into learning and mastering Big Data recipes. This book not only explores a majority of Big Data tools that are currently being used in the market, but also provides the best practices in order to implement them. This book will also provide you with recipes that are based on the latest version of Apache Hadoop 2.X, YARN, Hive, Pig, Sqoop, Flume, Apache Spark, Mahout, and many more ecosystem tools. This real-world solutions cookbook is packed with handy recipes that you can apply to your own everyday issues. Each chapter talks about recipes in great detail, and these can be referred to easily. This book provides detailed practice on the latest technologies, such as YARN and Apache Spark. This guide is an invaluable tutorial if you are planning to implement Big Data Warehouse for your business.

What this book covers

Chapter 1, Getting Started with Hadoop 2.x, introduces you to the installation details needed for single and multi-node Hadoop clusters. It also contains the recipes that will help you understand various important cluster management techniques, such as decommissioning, benchmarking, and so on.

Chapter 2, Exploring HDFS, provides you with hands-on recipes to manage and maintain the Hadoop Distributed File System (HDFS) in an efficient way. You will learn some important practices, such as transient encryption, saving data in a compressed format, recycling deleted data from HDFS, and so on.

Chapter 3, Mastering Map Reduce Programs, enlightens you about very important recipes for Map Reduce programming, which take you beyond the simple Word Count program. You will learn about various customization techniques in detail.

Chapter 4, Data Analysis Using Hive, Pig, and Hbase, takes you to the analytical world of Hive, Pig, and Hbase. This chapter talks about the use of various file formats, such as RC, ORC, Parquet, and so on. You will also get introduced to the Hbase NoSQL database.

Chapter 5, Advanced Data Analysis Using Hive, provides insights on the usage of serializers and deserializers (SerDe) in Hive for JSON and XML data operations. This chapter will provide you with a detailed explanation for Twitter sentiment analysis using Hive.

Chapter 6, Data Import/Export Using Sqoop and Flume, covers various recipes to import and export data from sources, such as RDBMS, Kafka, web log servers, and so on, using Sqoop and Flume.

Chapter 7, Automation of Hadoop Tasks Using Oozie, introduces you to a very rich scheduling tool called Oozie, which will help you build automated production-ready Big Data applications.

Chapter 8, Machine Learning and Predictive Analytics Using Mahout and R, gives you an end-to-end implementation of predictive analytics applications using Mahout and R. It covers the various visualization options available in R as well.

Chapter 9, Integration with Apache Spark, introduces you to a very important distributed computing framework called Apache Spark. It covers basic to advanced topics such as installation, Spark application development and execution, usage of the Spark Machine Learning Library, MLib, and graph processing using Spark.

Chapter 10, Hadoop Use Cases, provides you with end-to-end implementations of Hadoop use cases from various domains, such as telecom, finance, e-commerce, and so on.

What you need for this book

To get started with this hands-on recipe-driven book, you should have a laptop/desktop with any OS, such as Windows, Linux, or Mac. It's good to have an IDE, such as Eclipse or IntelliJ, and of course, you need a lot of enthusiasm to learn.

Who this book is for

This book is for those of you who have basic knowledge of Big Data systems and want to advance your knowledge with hands-on recipes.

Conventions

In this book, you will find a number of text styles that distinguish between different kinds of information. Here are some examples of these styles and an explanation of their meaning.

Code words in text, database table names, folder names, filenames, file extensions, pathnames, dummy URLs, user input, and Twitter handles are shown as follows: " Spark MLib provides a huge list of supported algorithms."

A block of code is set as follows:

```
$jps
2184 DataNode
2765 NodeManager
2835 Jps
2403 SecondaryNameNode
2025 NameNode
2606 ResourceManager
```

When we wish to draw your attention to a particular part of a code block, the relevant lines or items are set in bold:

```
    // The results of SQL queries are themselves RDDs and support all
normal RDD functions.  The
    // items in the RDD are of type Row, which allows you to access
each column by ordinal.
valrddFromSql = sql("SELECT id, name FROM empSpark WHERE id < 20 ORDER
BY id")
```

Any command-line input or output is written as follows:

```
# cp /usr/src/asterisk-addons/configs/cdr_mysql.conf.sample
    /etc/asterisk/cdr_mysql.conf
```

New terms and **important words** are shown in bold. Words that you see on the screen, for example, in menus or dialog boxes, appear in the text like this: "Click on **Create your Twitter application** to save your application."

Warnings or important notes appear in a box like this.

Tips and tricks appear like this.

Reader feedback

Feedback from our readers is always welcome. Let us know what you think about this book—what you liked or disliked. Reader feedback is important for us as it helps us develop titles that you will really get the most out of.

To send us general feedback, simply e-mail feedback@packtpub.com, and mention the book's title in the subject of your message.

If there is a topic that you have expertise in and you are interested in either writing or contributing to a book, see our author guide at www.packtpub.com/authors.

Customer support

Now that you are the proud owner of a Packt book, we have a number of things to help you to get the most from your purchase.

Downloading the example code

You can download the example code files for this book from your account at http://www.packtpub.com. If you purchased this book elsewhere, you can visit http://www.packtpub.com/support and register to have the files e-mailed directly to you.

You can download the code files by following these steps:

1. Log in or register to our website using your e-mail address and password.
2. Hover the mouse pointer on the **SUPPORT** tab at the top.
3. Click on **Code Downloads & Errata**.
4. Enter the name of the book in the **Search** box.
5. Select the book for which you're looking to download the code files.
6. Choose from the drop-down menu where you purchased this book from.
7. Click on **Code Download**.

Once the file is downloaded, please make sure that you unzip or extract the folder using the latest version of:

► WinRAR / 7-Zip for Windows
► Zipeg / iZip / UnRarX for Mac
► 7-Zip / PeaZip for Linux

Downloading the color images of this book

We also provide you with a PDF file that has color images of the screenshots/diagrams used in this book. The color images will help you better understand the changes in the output. You can download this file from `https://www.packtpub.com/sites/default/files/downloads/HadoopRealWorldSolutionsCookbookSecondEdition_ColoredImages.pdf`.

Errata

Although we have taken every care to ensure the accuracy of our content, mistakes do happen. If you find a mistake in one of our books—maybe a mistake in the text or the code—we would be grateful if you could report this to us. By doing so, you can save other readers from frustration and help us improve subsequent versions of this book. If you find any errata, please report them by visiting `http://www.packtpub.com/submit-errata`, selecting your book, clicking on the **Errata Submission Form** link, and entering the details of your errata. Once your errata are verified, your submission will be accepted and the errata will be uploaded to our website or added to any list of existing errata under the Errata section of that title.

To view the previously submitted errata, go to `https://www.packtpub.com/books/content/support` and enter the name of the book in the search field. The required information will appear under the **Errata** section.

Piracy

Piracy of copyrighted material on the Internet is an ongoing problem across all media. At Packt, we take the protection of our copyright and licenses very seriously. If you come across any illegal copies of our works in any form on the Internet, please provide us with the location address or website name immediately so that we can pursue a remedy.

Please contact us at `copyright@packtpub.com` with a link to the suspected pirated material.

We appreciate your help in protecting our authors and our ability to bring you valuable content.

Questions

If you have a problem with any aspect of this book, you can contact us at `questions@packtpub.com`, and we will do our best to address the problem.

1
Getting Started with Hadoop 2.X

This chapter covers the following topics:

- ▶ Installing a single-node Hadoop cluster
- ▶ Installing a multi-node Hadoop cluster
- ▶ Adding new nodes to existing Hadoop clusters
- ▶ Executing the balancer command for uniform data distribution
- ▶ Entering and exiting from the safe mode in a Hadoop cluster
- ▶ Decommissioning `DataNodes`
- ▶ Performing benchmarking on a Hadoop cluster

Introduction

Hadoop has been the primary platform for many people who deal with big data problems. It is the heart of big data. Hadoop was developed way back between 2003 and 2004 when Google published research papers on **Google File System (GFS)** and **Map Reduce**. Hadoop was structured around the crux of these research papers, and thus derived its shape. With the advancement of the Internet and social media, people slowly started realizing the power that Hadoop had, and it soon became the top platform used to handle big data. With a lot of hard work from dedicated contributors and open source groups to the project, Hadoop 1.0 was released and the IT industry welcomed it with open arms.

A lot of companies started using Hadoop as the primary platform for their Data Warehousing and **Extract-Transform-Load** (**ETL**) needs. They started deploying thousands of nodes in a Hadoop cluster and realized that there were scalability issues beyond the 4000+ node clusters that were already present. This was because JobTracker was not able to handle that many Task Trackers, and there was also the need for high availability in order to make sure that clusters were reliable to use. This gave birth to Hadoop 2.0.

In this introductory chapter, we are going to learn interesting recipes such as installing a single/multi-node Hadoop 2.0 cluster, its benchmarking, adding new nodes to existing clusters, and so on. So, let's get started.

Installing a single-node Hadoop Cluster

In this recipe, we are going to learn how to install a single-node Hadoop cluster, which can be used for development and testing.

Getting ready

To install Hadoop, you need to have a machine with the UNIX operating system installed on it. You can choose from any well known UNIX OS such as Red Hat, CentOS, Ubuntu, Fedora, and Amazon Linux (this is in case you are using Amazon Web Service instances).

Here, we will be using the Ubuntu distribution for demonstration purposes.

How to do it...

Let's start installing Hadoop:

1. First of all, you need to download the required installers from the Internet. Here, we need to download Java and Hadoop installers. The following are the links to do this:

   For the Java download, choose the latest version of the available JDK from `http://www.oracle.com/technetwork/java/javase/downloads/jdk8-downloads-2133151.html`.

   You can also use Open JDK instead of Oracle.

   For the Hadoop 2.7 Download, go to

   `http://www.eu.apache.org/dist/hadoop/common/hadoop-2.7.0/hadoop-2.7.0.tar.gz`.

2. We will first install Java. Here, I am using `/usr/local` as the installation directory and the `root` user for all installations. You can choose a directory of your choice.

Extract `tar.gz` like this:

```
tar -xzf java-7-oracle.tar.gz
```

Rename the extracted folder to give the shorter name Java instead of java-7-oracle. Doing this will help you remember the folder name easily.

Alternately, you can install Java using the `apt-get` package manager if your machine is connected to the Internet:

```
sudo apt-get update

sudo apt-get install openjdk-7-jdk
```

3. Similarly, we will extract and configure Hadoop. We will also rename the extracted folder for easier accessibility. Here, we will extract Hadoop to `path /usr/local`:

```
tar -xzf hadoop-2.7.0.tar.gz

mv hadoop-2.7.0 hadoop
```

4. Next, in order to use Java and Hadoop from any folder, we would need to add these paths to the `~/.bashrc` file. The contents of the file get executed every time a user logs in:

```
cd ~

vi .bashrc
```

Once the file is open, append the following environment variable settings to it. These variables are used by Java and Hadoop at runtime:

```
export JAVA_HOME=/usr/local/java
export PATH=$PATH:$JAVA_HOME/bin
export HADOOP_INSTALL=/usr/local/hadoop
export PATH=$PATH:$HADOOP_INSTALL/bin
export PATH=$PATH:$HADOOP_INSTALL/sbin
export HADOOP_MAPRED_HOME=$HADOOP_INSTALL
export HADOOP_COMMON_HOME=$HADOOP_INSTALL
export HADOOP_HDFS_HOME=$HADOOP_INSTALL
export YARN_HOME=$HADOOP_INSTALL
export HADOOP_COMMON_LIB_NATIVE_DIR=$HADOOP_INSTALL/lib/native
export HADOOP_OPTS="-Djava.library.path=$HADOOP_INSTALL/lib"
```

5. In order to verify whether our installation is perfect, close the terminal and restart it again. Also, check whether the Java and Hadoop versions can be seen:

```
$java -version
java version "1.7.0_45"
Java(TM) SE Runtime Environment (build 1.7.0_45-b18)
Java HotSpot(TM) Server VM (build 24.45-b08, mixed mode)
```

```
$ hadoop version
Hadoop 2.7.0
Subversion https://git-wip-us.apache.org/repos/asf/hadoop.git -r
d4c8d4d4d203c934e8074b31289a28724c0842cf
Compiled by jenkins on 2015-04-10T18:40Z
Compiled with protoc 2.5.0
From source with checksum a9e90912c37a35c3195d23951fd18f
```

This command was run using `/usr/local/hadoop/share/hadoop/common/hadoop-common-2.7.0.jar`.

6. Now that Hadoop and Java are installed and verified, we need to install `ssh` (Secure Shell) if it's not already available by default. If you are connected to the Internet, execute the following commands. `SSH` is used to secure data transfers between nodes:

   `sudo apt-get install openssh-client`

   `sudo apt-get install openssh-server`

7. Once the `ssh` installation is done, we need to execute the `ssh` configuration in order to avail a passwordless access to remote hosts. Note that even though we are installing Hadoop on a single node, we need to perform an `ssh` configuration in order to securely access the localhost.

   First of all, we need to generate public and private keys by executing the following command:

   `ssh-keygen -t rsa -P ""`

   This will generate the private and public keys by default in the `$HOME/.ssh` folder. In order to provide passwordless access, we need to append the public key to `authorized_keys` file:

   `cat $HOME/.ssh/id_rsa.pub >> $HOME/.ssh/authorized_keys`

   Let's check whether the `ssh` configuration is okay or not. To test it, execute and connect to the localhost like this:

   `ssh localhost`

   This will prompt you to confirm whether to add this connection to the `known_hosts` file. Type `yes`, and you should be connected to `ssh` without prompting for the password.

8. Once the `ssh` configuration is done and verified, we need to configure Hadoop. The Hadoop configuration begins with adding various configuration parameters to the following default files:

   ❑ `hadoop-env.sh`: This is where we need to perform the Java environment variable configuration.

   ❑ `core-site.xml`: This is where we need to perform `NameNode`-related configurations.

- ❏ `yarn-site.xml`: This is where we need to perform configurations related to **Yet Another Resource Negotiator (YARN)**.
- ❏ `mapred-site.xml`: This is where we need to the map reduce engine as YARN.
- ❏ `hdfs-site.xml`: This is where we need to perform configurations related to **Hadoop Distributed File System (HDFS)**.

These configuration files can be found in the `/usr/local/hadoop/etc/hadoop` folder. If you install Hadoop as the root user, you will have access to edit these files, but if not, you will first need to get access to this folder before editing.

So, let's take a look at the configurations one by one.

Configure `hadoop-env.sh` and update the Java path like this:

1. Export `JAVA_HOME=/usr/local/java`.

2. Edit `core-site.xml`, and add the host and port on which you wish to install `NameNode`. Here is the single node installation that we would need in order to add the localhost:

```
<configuration>
  <property>
    <name>fs.default.name</name>
    <value>hdfs://localhost:9000/</value>
  </property>
</configuration>
```

3. Edit `yarn-site.xml`, add the following properties to it:

```
<configuration>
    <property>
        <name>yarn.nodemanager.aux-services</name>
        <value>mapreduce_shuffle</value>
    </property>
    <property>
        <name>yarn.nodemanager.aux-services.mapreduce.shuffle.
class</name>
        <value>org.apache.hadoop.mapred.ShuffleHandler</value>
    </property>
</configuration>
```

The `yarn.nodemanager.aux-services` property tells `NodeManager` that an auxiliary service named `mapreduce.shuffle` is present and needs to be implemented. The second property tells `NodeManager` about the class by which means it needs to implement the shuffle auxiliary service. This specific configuration is needed as the `MapReduce` job involves shuffling of key value pairs.

4. Next, edit `mapred-site.xml` to set the map reduce processing engine as YARN:

```
<configuration>
    <property>
        <name>mapreduce.framework.name</name>
        <value>yarn</value>
    </property>
</configuration>
```

5. Edit `hdfs-site.xml` to set the folder paths that can be used by `NameNode` and `datanode`:

```
<configuration>
    <property>
        <name>yarn.nodemanager.aux-services</name>
        <value>mapreduce_shuffle</value>
    </property>
    <property>
        <name>yarn.nodemanager.aux-services.mapreduce.shuffle.
class</name>
        <value>org.apache.hadoop.mapred.ShuffleHandler</value>
    </property>
</configuration>
```

6. I am also setting the HDFS block replication factor to `1` as this is a single node cluster installation.

   We also need to make sure that we create the previously mentioned folders and change their ownership to suit the current user. To do this, you can choose a folder path of your own choice:

```
sudo mkdir -p /usr/local/store/hdfs/namenode

sudo mkdir -p /usr/local/store/hdfs/datanode

sudo chown root:root -R /usr/local/store
```

7. Now, it's time to format `namenode` so that it creates the required folder structure by default:

```
hadoop namenode -format
```

8. The final step involves starting Hadoop daemons; here, we will first execute two scripts to start HDFS daemons and then start YARN daemons:

```
/usr/local/hadoop/sbin/start-dfs.sh
```

This will start `NameNode`, the secondary `NameNode`, and then `DataNode` daemons:

```
/usr/local/hadoop/sbin/start-yarn.sh
```

This will start `NodeManager` and `ResourceManager`. You can execute the `jps` command to take a look at the running daemons:

```
$jps
2184 DataNode
2765 NodeManager
2835 Jps
2403 SecondaryNameNode
2025 NameNode
2606 ResourceManager
```

We can also access the web portals for HDFS and YARN by accessing the following URLs:

- For HDFS: `http://<hostname>:50070/`
- For YARN: `http://<hostname>:8088/`

How it works...

Hadoop 2.0 has been majorly reformed in order to solve issues of scalability and high-availability. Earlier in Hadoop 1.0, Map Reduce was the only means of processing data stored in HDFS. With advancement of YARN, Map Reduce is one of the ways of processing data on Hadoop. Here is a pictorial difference between Hadoop 1.x and Hadoop 2.x:

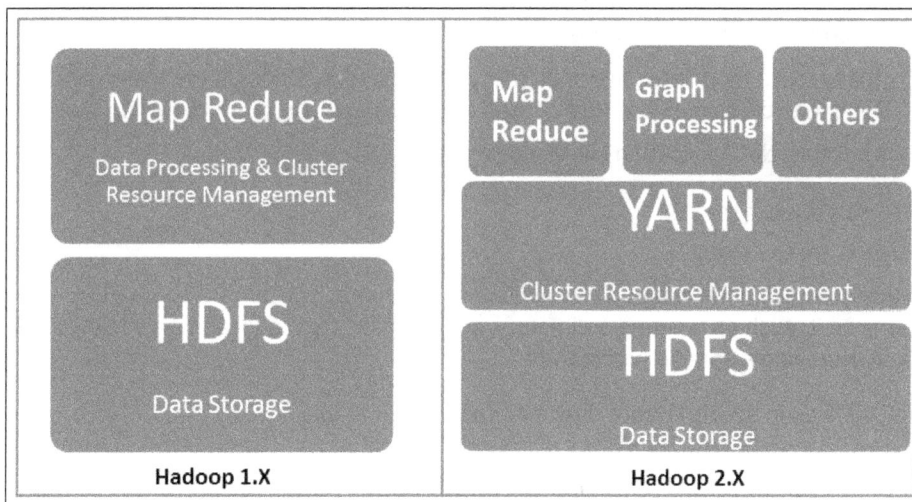

Now, let's try to understand how HDFS and YARN works.

Hadoop Distributed File System (HDFS)

HDFS is a redundant, reliable storage for Hadoop. It consists of three important parts: NameNode, the secondary NameNode, and DataNodes. When a file needs to be processed on Hadoop, it first needs to be saved on HDFS. HDFS distributes the file in chunks of 64/128 MB data blocks across the data nodes. The blocks are replicated across data nodes for reliability. NameNode stores the metadata in the blocks and replicas. After a certain period of time, the metadata is backed up on the secondary NameNode. The default time is 60 seconds. We can modify this by setting a property called dfs.namenode.checkpoint.check.period in hdfs-site.xml.

Yet Another Resource Negotiator (YARN)

YARN has been developed to address scalability issues and for the better management of jobs in Hadoop; till date, it has proved itself to be the perfect solution. It is responsible for the management of resources available in clusters. It consists of two important components: ResouceManager(Master) and NodeManager(Worker). NodeManager provides a node-level view of the cluster, while ResourceManager takes a view of a cluster. When an application is submitted by an application client, the following things happen:

- The application talks to ResourceManager and provides details about it.
- ResourceManager makes a container request on behalf of an application to any of the worker nodes and ApplicationMaster starts running within that container.
- ApplicationMaster then makes subsequent requests for the containers to execute tasks on other nodes.
- These tasks then take care of all the communication. Once all the tasks are complete, containers are deallocated and ApplicationMaster exits.
- After this, the application client also exits.

There's more

Now that your single node Hadoop cluster is up and running, you can try some HDFS file operations on it, such as creating a directory, copying a file from a local machine to HDFS, and so on. Here some sample commands.

To list all the files in the HDFS root directory, take a look at this:

```
hadoop fs -ls /
```

To create a new directory, take a look at this:

```
hadoop fs -mkdir /input
```

To copy a file from the local machine to HDFS, take a look at this:

```
hadoop fs -copyFromLocal /usr/local/hadoop/LICENSE.txt /input
```

In order to access all the command options that are available, go to `https://hadoop.apache.org/docs/current/hadoop-project-dist/hadoop-common/FileSystemShell.html`.

Installing a multi-node Hadoop cluster

Now that we are comfortable with a single-node Hadoop installation, it's time to learn about a multi-node Hadoop installation.

Getting ready

In the previous recipe, we used a single Ubuntu machine for installation; in this recipe, we will be using three Ubuntu machines. If you are an individual trying to install Hadoop for your own purposes and you don't have three machines to try this recipe, I would suggest that you get three AWS EC2 Ubuntu machines. I am using the `t2.small` type of EC2 instances. For more information on this, go to `https://aws.amazon.com/ec2/`.

Apart from this, I've also performed the following configurations on all the EC2 instances that I have been using:

1. Create an AWS security group to allow access to traffic to EC2 instances, and add EC2 instances to this security group.

2. Change the hostname of EC2 instances to their public hostnames like this:

   ```
   sudo hostname ec2-52-10-22-65.us-west-2.compute.amazonaws.com
   ```

3. Disable firewalls for EC2 Ubuntu instances:

   ```
   sudo ufw disable
   ```

How to do it...

There are a lot of similarities between single node and multi-node Hadoop installations, so instead of repeating the steps, I would suggest that you refer to earlier recipes as and when they're mentioned. So, let's start installing a multi-node Hadoop cluster:

1. Install Java and Hadoop, as discussed in the previous recipe, on the master and slave nodes. Refer to steps 1-5 in the previous recipe.

2. AWS EC2 has a built-in installation of `ssh` so there's no need to install it again. To configure it, we need to perform the following steps.

First, copy the PEM key with which you initiated EC2 instances to the master node. Next, you need to execute the following set of commands that will add an identity into the master's `ssh` configurations, which can be used to perform passwordless logins to slave machines:

```
eval `ssh-agent -s`
chmod 644 $HOME/.ssh/authorized_keys
chmod 400 <my-pem-key>.pem
ssh-add <my-pem-key>.pem
```

But if you are NOT using AWS EC2, then you need to generate the `ssh` key on the master, and this key needs to be copied to slave machines. Here is a sample command to do this:

```
ssh-keygen -t rsa -P ""
ssh-copy-id -i $HOME/.ssh/id_rsa.pub ubuntu@slave1
ssh-copy-id -i $HOME/.ssh/id_rsa.pub ubuntu@slave2
```

3. Next, we need to perform the Hadoop configurations—most of the configuration files will be same as they were in the case of the single-node installation. These configurations are the same for all the nodes in the cluster. Refer to step 8 from the previous recipe for `hadoop-env.sh`, `mapred-site.xml`, and `hdfs-site.xml`. For `core-site.xml` and `yarn-site.xml`, we need to add some more properties, as shown here:

Edit `core-site.xml` and add the host and port on which you wish to install `NameNode`. As this is a multi-node Hadoop cluster installation, we will add the master's hostname instead of the localhost:

```
<configuration>
<property>
    <name>fs.default.name</name>
    <value>hdfs://<master's-host-name>:9000/</value>
</property>
</configuration>
```

Edit `yarn-site.xml` and add the following properties. As this is a multi-node installation, we also need to provide the address of the machine where `ResourceManager` is running:

```
<configuration>
    <property>
      <name>yarn.nodemanager.aux-services</name>
      <value>mapreduce_shuffle</value>
    </property>
    <property>
```

```
        <name>yarn.nodemanager.aux-services.mapreduce.shuffle.
class</name>
        <value>org.apache.hadoop.mapred.ShuffleHandler</value>
    </property>
    <property>
        <name>yarn.resourcemanager.hostname</name>
        <value><master's-host-name></value>
    </property>
</configuration>
```

In the case of `hdfs-site.xml`, in the previous recipe, we set the replication factor to 1. As this is a multi-node cluster, we set it to 3. Don't forget to create storage folders configured in `hdfs-site.xml`.

These configurations need to be made on all the machines of the cluster.

4. Now that we are done with configurations, execute the `namenode` format command so that it creates the required subfolder structure:

    `hadoop namenode -format`

5. Now, we need to start specific services on specific nodes in order to start the cluster.

    On the master node, execute following:

    `/usr/local/hadoop/sbin/hadoop-daemon.sh start namenode`

    `/usr/local/hadoop/sbin/hadoop-daemon.sh start secondarynamenode`

    `/usr/local/hadoop/sbin/yarn-daemon.sh start resourcemanager`

    On all slave nodes, execute following:

    `/usr/local/hadoop/sbin/hadoop-daemon.sh start datanode`

    `/usr/local/hadoop/sbin/yarn-daemon.sh start nodemanager`

If everything goes well, you should be able to see the cluster running properly. You can also check out the web interfaces for `NameNode` and Resource Managers, for example, by going to `http://<master-ip-hostname>:50070/`.

For `ResourceManager`, go to `http://<master-ip-hostname>/8088`

How it works...

Refer to the *How it works* section from the previous recipe.

Adding new nodes to existing Hadoop clusters

Sometimes, it may happen that an existing Hadoop cluster's capacity is not adequate enough to handle all the data you may want to process. In this case, you can add new nodes to the existing Hadoop cluster without any downtime for the existing cluster. Hadoop supports horizontal scalability.

Getting ready

To perform this recipe, you should have a Hadoop cluster running. Also, you will need one more machine. If you are using AWS EC2, then you can launch an EC2 instance that's similar to what we did in the previous recipes. You will also need the same security group configurations in order to make the installation process smooth.

How to do it...

To add a new instance to an existing cluster, simply install and configure Hadoop the way we did for the previous recipe. Make sure that you put the same configurations in `core-site.xml` and `yarn-site.xml`, which will point to the correct master node.

Once all the configurations are done, simply execute commands to start the newly added `datanode` and `nodemanager`:

```
/usr/local/hadoop/sbin/hadoop-daemon.sh start datanode
```

```
/usr/local/hadoop/sbin/yarn-daemon.sh start nodemanager
```

If you take a look at the cluster again, you will find that the new node is registered. You can use the `dfsadmin` command to take a look at the number of nodes and amount of capacity that's been used:

```
hdfs dfsadmin -report
```

Here is a sample output for the preceding command:

```
ubuntu@ec2-52-10-22-65:~$ hdfs dfsadmin -report
15/10/08 08:57:24 WARN util.NativeCodeLoader: Unable to load native-hadoop library for your platform... using builtin-java classes where applicable
Configured Capacity: 33239728128 (30.96 GB)
Present Capacity: 23809320097 (22.17 GB)
DFS Remaining: 23605534720 (21.98 GB)
DFS Used: 203785377 (194.34 MB)
DFS Used%: 0.86%
Under replicated blocks: 0
Blocks with corrupt replicas: 0
Missing blocks: 0
Missing blocks (with replication factor 1): 0

-------------------------------------------------
Live datanodes (4):

Name: 172.31.18.55:50010 (ip-172-31-18-55.us-west-2.compute.internal)
Hostname: ip-172-31-18-55.us-west-2.compute.internal
Decommission Status : Normal
Configured Capacity: 8309932032 (7.74 GB)
DFS Used: 1127585 (1.08 MB)
Non DFS Used: 2372033375 (2.21 GB)
DFS Remaining: 5936771072 (5.53 GB)
DFS Used%: 0.01%
DFS Remaining%: 71.44%
Configured Cache Capacity: 0 (0 B)
Cache Used: 0 (0 B)
Cache Remaining: 0 (0 B)
Cache Used%: 100.00%
Cache Remaining%: 0.00%
Xceivers: 1
Last contact: Thu Oct 08 08:57:25 UTC 2015


Name: 172.31.0.9:50010 (ip-172-31-0-9.us-west-2.compute.internal)
Hostname: ip-172-31-0-9.us-west-2.compute.internal
Decommission Status : Normal
Configured Capacity: 8309932032 (7.74 GB)
DFS Used: 67551232 (64.42 MB)
Non DFS Used: 2193256448 (2.04 GB)
```

How it works...

Hadoop supports horizontal scalability. If the resources that are being used are not enough, we can always go ahead and add new nodes to the existing cluster without hiccups. In Hadoop, it's always the slave that reports to the master. So, while making configurations, we always configure the details of the master and do nothing about the slaves. This architecture helps achieve horizontal scalability as at any point of time, we can add new nodes by only providing the configurations of the master, and everything else is taken care of by the Hadoop cluster. As soon as the daemons start, the master node realizes that a new node has been added and it becomes part of the cluster.

Executing the balancer command for uniform data distribution

Data in HDFS may not always be placed uniformly. There can be numerous reasons for this. One of the major reasons is the addition of new nodes to the cluster. In such a case, it's the Hadoop administrator's job to make sure that they execute the balancer command to rebalance the data load.

Getting ready

To perform this recipe, you should have performed earlier recipes.

How to do it...

In the previous recipe, we added a new node to the cluster while the other three nodes were already part of the cluster. When you execute the `dfsadmin report` command, you would have noticed that the data is not uniformly balanced because of the addition of a new node. In my case, here is the state of the new node versus the old node.

This is the code for the old node:

```
Name: 172.31.0.9:50010 (ip-172-31-0-9.us-west-2.compute.internal)
Hostname: ip-172-31-0-9.us-west-2.compute.internal
Decommission Status : Normal
Configured Capacity: 8309932032 (7.74 GB)
DFS Used: 67551232 (64.42 MB)
Non DFS Used: 2193256448 (2.04 GB)
DFS Remaining: 6049124352 (5.63 GB)
DFS Used%: 0.81%
DFS Remaining%: 72.79%
Configured Cache Capacity: 0 (0 B)
Cache Used: 0 (0 B)
Cache Remaining: 0 (0 B)
Cache Used%: 100.00%
Cache Remaining%: 0.00%
Xceivers: 1
Last contact: Thu Oct 08 08:57:23 UTC 2015
```

This is the code for the new node:

```
Name: 172.31.18.55:50010 (ip-172-31-18-55.us-west-2.compute.internal)
Hostname: ip-172-31-18-55.us-west-2.compute.internal
Decommission Status : Normal
Configured Capacity: 8309932032 (7.74 GB)
DFS Used: 1127585 (1.08 MB)
Non DFS Used: 2372033375 (2.21 GB)
DFS Remaining: 5936771072 (5.53 GB)
DFS Used%: 0.01%
DFS Remaining%: 71.44%
Configured Cache Capacity: 0 (0 B)
Cache Used: 0 (0 B)
```

```
Cache Remaining: 0 (0 B)

Cache Used%: 100.00%

Cache Remaining%: 0.00%

Xceivers: 1

Last contact: Thu Oct 08 08:57:25 UTC 2015
```

This means that the load on the cluster is not uniform. In this case, we can execute the balancer command to distribute the data uniformly throughout the data nodes:

```
hdfs balancer
```

This will initiate the block balancing activity across the cluster. By default, it will run the balancing activity to make sure that the block storage in the nodes does not differ by more than 10%. You can also decide on the threshold limit by setting an optional parameter called threshold:

```
hdfs balancer -threshold 5
```

This will execute the balancer command with 5% threshold. This is how the sample execution looks:

How it works...

The balancer command provides instructions to namenode so that it can rebalance the data uniformly across datanode. This balancing is done by repositioning the blocks placed in datanode. So, if a data node is over utilized, some the blocks from that node would be repositioned to the node that is underutilized.

There's more...

There are some options you can provide as arguments to this command:

```
Usage: hdfs balancer
        [-policy <policy>]        the balancing policy: datanode or
blockpool
        [-threshold <threshold>]        Percentage of disk capacity
```

```
        [-exclude [-f <hosts-file> | <comma-separated list of hosts>]]
Excludes the specified datanodes.

        [-include [-f <hosts-file> | <comma-separated list of hosts>]]
Includes only the specified datanodes.

        [-idleiterations <idleiterations>]        Number of consecutive
idle iterations (-1 for Infinite) before exit.
```

Entering and exiting from the safe mode in a Hadoop cluster

Sometimes, due to an unclear filesystem image state, the Hadoop cluster goes into `safemode`. In this recipe, we will see how to enter and exit from `safemode`.

How to do it...

`Safemode` is an HDFS state that does not allow any new writes to the filesystem. It also does not replicate or delete any blocks from the filesystem. In case you want to make any configuration changes to your cluster, you can put the system into `safemode`. Here is a command to enter the system into `safemode`:

hdfs dfsadmin -safemode enter

Now, if you try to make any writes to HDFS, it will not allow you do so. You can perform cluster maintenance and once this is done, you can switch off `safemode`:

hdfs dfsadmin -safemode leave

In case you are not aware of whether `safemode` is ON or OFF, you can get its status by executing the following command:

hdfs dfsadmin -safemode get

How it works...

Generally, `safemode` is enabled automatically for `NameNode` on startup. It then tries to get the state of the filesystem from `FSImage` and `EditLogs`. `Namenode` waits until `datanodes` start reporting the block status of individual nodes. `safemode` is automatically disabled when `datanodes` report the availability of most of the blocks.

If we enter into `safemode` manually, we need to disable it manually. It won't be disabled automatically.

Decommissioning DataNodes

The Hadoop framework provides us with the option to remove certain nodes from the cluster if they are not needed any more. Here, we cannot simply shutdown the nodes that need to be removed as we might lose some of our data. They need to be decommissioned properly. In this recipe, we are going to learn how to decommission nodes from the Hadoop cluster.

Getting ready

To perform this recipe, you should have a Hadoop cluster, and you should have decided which node to decommission.

How to do it...

To decommission a node from the HDFS cluster, we need to perform the following steps:

1. Create a `dfs.exclude` file in a folder, say `/usr/local/hadoop/etc/hadoop`, and add the hostname of the node you wish to decommission.

2. Edit `hdfs-site.xml` on `NameNode` to append the following property:

   ```
   <property>
       <name>dfs.hosts.exclude</name>
       <value>/usr/local/hadoop/etc/hadoop/dfs.exclude</value>
   </property>
   ```

3. Next, we need to execute the `refreshNodes` command so that it rereads the HDFS configuration in order to start the decommissioning:

   ```
   hdfs dfsadmin -refreshNodes
   ```

This will start the decommissioning, and once successful execution of the `dfsadmin` report command, you will see that the node's status is changed to `Decommissioned` from `Normal`:

```
hdfs dfsadmin -report
Name: 172.31.18.55:50010 (ip-172-31-18-55.us-west-2.compute.internal)
Hostname: ip-172-31-18-55.us-west-2.compute.internal
Decommission Status : Decommissioned
Configured Capacity: 8309932032 (7.74 GB)
DFS Used: 1179648 (1.13 MB)
Non DFS Used: 2371989504 (2.21 GB)
DFS Remaining: 5936762880 (5.53 GB)
DFS Used%: 0.01%
```

```
DFS Remaining%: 71.44%

Configured Cache Capacity: 0 (0 B)

Cache Used: 0 (0 B)

Cache Remaining: 0 (0 B)

Cache Used%: 100.00%

Cache Remaining%: 0.00%

Xceivers: 1

Last contact: Thu Oct 08 10:56:49 UTC 2015
```

Generally, the decommissioning takes time as it requires block replications on other nodes. Once the decommissioning is complete, the node will be added to the decommissioned nodes list.

How it works...

HDFS/Namenode reads the configurations from hdfs-site.xml. You can configure a file with the list of nodes to decommission and execute the refreshNodes command; it then rereads the configuration file. While doing this, it reads the configuration about the decommissioned nodes and will start rereplicating blocks to other available datanode. Depending on the size of datanode getting decommissioned, the time varies. Unless the completed decommissioning is not completed, it advisable for you to touch datanode.

Performing benchmarking on a Hadoop cluster

The Hadoop framework supports built-in libraries so that we can perform benchmarking in order to take a look at how the Hadoop cluster configurations/hardware are performing. There are plenty of tests available that will perform the benchmarking of various aspects of the Hadoop cluster. In this recipe, we are going to take a look at how to perform benchmarking and read the results.

Getting ready

To perform this recipe, you should have a Hadoop cluster up and running.

How to do it...

The Hadoop framework supports built-in support to benchmark various aspects. These tests are written in a library called hadoop-mapreduce-client-jobclient-2.7.0-tests.jar

To know the list of all the supported tests, you can execute the following command:

```
hadoop jar /usr/local/hadoop/share/hadoop/mapreduce/hadoop-mapreduce-
client-jobclient-2.7.0-tests.jar
```

The result of the command will be similar to what is shown in this screenshot:

TestDFSIO

This is one the major tests that you may want to do in order to see how DFS is performing. So, we are now going to take a look at how to use these tests to know how efficiently HDFS is able to write and read data.

As seen in the preceding screenshot, the library provides tools to test DFS through an option called `TestDFSIO`. Now, let's execute the write test in order to understand how efficiently HDFS is able to write big files. The following is the command to execute the write test:

```
hadoop jar /usr/local/hadoop/share/hadoop/mapreduce/hadoop-mapreduce-
client-jobclient-2.7.0-tests.jar TestDFSIO -write -nrFiles 2 -fileSize
1GB -resFile /tmp/TestDFSIOwrite.txt
```

Once you initiate the preceding command, a map reduce job will start, which will write two files to HDFS that are 1GB in size . You can choose any numbers based on your cluster size. These tests create data in HDFS under the `/benchmarks` directory. Once the execution is complete, you will see these results:

```
15/10/08 11:37:23 INFO fs.TestDFSIO: ----- TestDFSIO ----- : write
15/10/08 11:37:23 INFO fs.TestDFSIO:            Date & time: Thu Oct 08
11:37:23 UTC 2015
15/10/08 11:37:23 INFO fs.TestDFSIO:         Number of files: 2
15/10/08 11:37:23 INFO fs.TestDFSIO: Total MBytes processed: 2048.0
15/10/08 11:37:23 INFO fs.TestDFSIO:       Throughput mb/sec:
26.637185406776354
```

```
15/10/08 11:37:23 INFO fs.TestDFSIO: Average IO rate mb/sec:
26.63718605041504

15/10/08 11:37:23 INFO fs.TestDFSIO:  IO rate std deviation:
0.00829867575568246

15/10/08 11:37:23 INFO fs.TestDFSIO:    Test exec time sec: 69.023
```

The preceding data is calculated from the RAW data generated by the Map Reduce program. You can also view the raw data as follows:

```
hdfs dfs -cat /benchmarks/TestDFSIO/io_read/part*
f:rate   53274.37
f:sqrate          1419079.2
l:size   2147483648
l:tasks 2
l:time   76885
```

> The following formulae are used to calculate throughput, the average IO rate, and standard deviation.
>
> *Throughput = size * 1000/time * 1048576*
>
> *Average IO rate = rate/1000/tasks*
>
> *Standard deviation = square root of (absolute value(sqrate/1000/tasks – Average IO Rate * Average IO Rate))*

Similarly, you can perform benchmarking of HDFS read operations as well:

```
hadoop jar /usr/local/hadoop/share/hadoop/mapreduce/hadoop-mapreduce-
client-jobclient-2.7.0-tests.jar TestDFSIO -read -nrFiles 2 -fileSize 1GB
-resFile /tmp/TestDFSIOread.txt
```

At the end of the execution, a reducer will collect the data from the RAW results, and you will see calculated numbers for the DFSIO reads:

```
15/10/08 11:41:01 INFO fs.TestDFSIO: ----- TestDFSIO ----- : read
15/10/08 11:41:01 INFO fs.TestDFSIO:             Date & time: Thu Oct 08
11:41:01 UTC 2015
15/10/08 11:41:01 INFO fs.TestDFSIO:         Number of files: 2
15/10/08 11:41:01 INFO fs.TestDFSIO: Total MBytes processed: 2048.0
15/10/08 11:41:01 INFO fs.TestDFSIO:       Throughput mb/sec:
33.96633220001659
15/10/08 11:41:01 INFO fs.TestDFSIO: Average IO rate mb/sec:
33.968116760253906
15/10/08 11:41:01 INFO fs.TestDFSIO:  IO rate std deviation:
0.24641533955938721
15/10/08 11:41:01 INFO fs.TestDFSIO:    Test exec time sec: 59.343
```

Here, we can take a look at the RAW data as well:

```
hdfs dfs -cat /benchmarks/TestDFSIO/io_read/part*
f:rate    67936.234
f:sqrate           2307787.2
l:size   2147483648
l:tasks  2
l:time   60295
```

The same formulae are used to calculate the throughput, average IO rate, and standard deviation.

This way, you can benchmark the DFSIO reads and writes.

NNBench

Similar to DFS IO, we can also perform benchmarking for `NameNode`:

```
hadoop jar /usr/local/hadoop/share/hadoop/mapreduce/hadoop-mapreduce-
client-jobclient-2.7.0-tests.jar nnbench -operation create_write
```

MRBench

MRBench helps us understand the average time taken for a job to execute for a given number of mappers and reducers. The following is a sample command to execute MRBench with default parameters:

```
hadoop jar /usr/local/hadoop/share/hadoop/mapreduce/hadoop-mapreduce-
client-jobclient-2.7.0-tests.jar mrbench
```

How it works...

Hadoop benchmark tests use the parameters and conditions provided by users. For every test, it executes a map reduce job and once complete, it displays the results on the screen. Generally, it is recommended that you run the benchmarking tests as soon as you have installed the Hadoop cluster in order to predict the performance of HDFS/Map Reduce and so on.

Most of the tests require a sequence in which they should be executed, for example, all write tests should be executed first, then read/delete, and so on.

Once the complete execution is done, make sure you clean up the data in the `/benchmarks` directory in HDFS.

Here is an example command to clean up the data generated by the `TestDFSIO` tests:

```
hadoop jar /usr/local/hadoop/share/hadoop/mapreduce/hadoop-mapreduce-
client-jobclient-2.7.0-tests.jar TestDFSIO -clean
```

2
Exploring HDFS

In this chapter, we'll take a look at the following recipes:

- ▸ Loading data from a local machine to HDFS
- ▸ Exporting HDFS data to a local machine
- ▸ Changing the replication factor of an existing file in HDFS
- ▸ Setting the HDFS block size for all the files in a cluster
- ▸ Setting the HDFS block size for a specific file in a cluster
- ▸ Enabling transparent encryption for HDFS
- ▸ Importing data from another Hadoop cluster
- ▸ Recycling deleted data from trash to HDFS
- ▸ Saving compressed data in HDFS

Introduction

In the previous chapter, we discussed the installation and configuration details of a Hadoop cluster. In this chapter, we are going to explore the details of HDFS. As we know, Hadoop has two important components:

- ▸ **Storage**: This includes HDFS
- ▸ **Processing**: This includes Map Reduce

HDFS takes care of the storage part of Hadoop. So, let's explore the internals of HDFS through various recipes.

Loading data from a local machine to HDFS

In this recipe, we are going to load data from a local machine's disk to HDFS.

Getting ready

To perform this recipe, you should have an already Hadoop running cluster.

How to do it...

Performing this recipe is as simple as copying data from one folder to another. There are a couple of ways to copy data from the local machine to HDFS.

- Using the `copyFromLocal` command
    - To copy the file on HDFS, let's first create a directory on HDFS and then copy the file. Here are the commands to do this:

        ```
        hadoop fs -mkdir /mydir1
        hadoop fs -copyFromLocal /usr/local/hadoop/LICENSE.txt /
        mydir1
        ```

- Using the `put` command
    - We will first create the directory, and then put the local file in HDFS:

        ```
        hadoop fs -mkdir /mydir2
        hadoop fs -put /usr/local/hadoop/LICENSE.txt /mydir2
        ```

You can validate that the files have been copied to the correct folders by listing the files:

```
hadoop fs -ls /mydir1
hadoop fs -ls /mydir2
```

How it works...

When you use HDFS `copyFromLocal` or the `put` command, the following things will occur:

1. First of all, the HDFS client (the command prompt, in this case) contacts `NameNode` because it needs to copy the file to HDFS.
2. `NameNode` then asks the client to break the file into chunks of different cluster block sizes. In Hadoop 2.X, the default block size is 128MB.
3. Based on the capacity and availability of space in `DataNodes`, `NameNode` will decide where these blocks should be copied.

4. Then, the client starts copying data to specified `DataNodes` for a specific block. The blocks are copied sequentially one after another.

5. When a single block is copied, the block is sent to `DataNode` in packets that are 4MB in size. With each packet, a checksum is sent; once the packet copying is done, it is verified with checksum to check whether it matches. The packets are then sent to the next `DataNode` where the block will be replicated.

6. The HDFS client's responsibility is to copy the data to only the first node; the replication is taken care by respective `DataNode`. Thus, the data block is pipelined from one `DataNode` to the next.

7. When the block copying and replication is taking place, metadata on the file is updated in `NameNode` by `DataNode`.

Exporting HDFS data to a local machine

In this recipe, we are going to export/copy data from HDFS to the local machine.

Getting ready

To perform this recipe, you should already have a running Hadoop cluster.

How to do it...

Performing this recipe is as simple as copying data from one folder to the other. There are a couple of ways in which you can export data from HDFS to the local machine.

▸ Using the `copyToLocal` command, you'll get this code:

```
hadoop fs -copyToLocal /mydir1/LICENSE.txt /home/ubuntu
```

▸ Using the `get` command, you'll get this code:

```
hadoop fs -get/mydir1/LICENSE.txt /home/ubuntu
```

How it works...

When you use HDFS `copyToLocal` or the `get` command, the following things occur:

1. First of all, the client contacts `NameNode` because it needs a specific file in HDFS.

2. `NameNode` then checks whether such a file exists in its `FSImage`. If the file is not present, the error code is returned to the client.

3. If the file exists, `NameNode` checks the metadata for blocks and replica placements in `DataNodes`.

4. NameNode then directly points DataNode from where the blocks would be given to the client one by one. The data is directly copied from DataNode to the client machine. and it never goes through NameNode to avoid bottlenecks.

5. Thus, the file is exported to the local machine from HDFS.

Changing the replication factor of an existing file in HDFS

In this recipe, we are going to take a look at how to change the replication factor of a file in HDFS. The default replication factor is 3.

Getting ready

To perform this recipe, you should already have a running Hadoop cluster.

How to do it...

Sometimes. there might be a need to increase or decrease the replication factor of a specific file in HDFS. In this case, we'll use the setrep command.

This is how you can use the command:

```
hadoop fs -setrep [-R] [-w] <noOfReplicas><path> ...
```

In this command, a path can either be a file or directory; if its a directory, then it recursively sets the replication factor for all replicas.

  ▸ The w option flags the command and should wait until the replication is complete
  ▸ The r option is accepted for backward compatibility

First, let's check the replication factor of the file we copied to HDFS in the previous recipe:

```
hadoop fs -ls /mydir1/LICENSE.txt
-rw-r--r--   3 ubuntu supergroup      15429 2015-10-29 03:04 /mydir1/
LICENSE.txt
```

Once you list the file, it will show you the read/write permissions on this file, and the very next parameter is the replication factor. We have the replication factor set to 3 for our cluster, hence, you the number is 3 .

Let's change it to 2 using this command:

```
hadoop fs -setrep -w 2 /mydir1/LICENSE.txt
```

It will wait till the replication is adjusted. Once done, you can verify this again by running the ls command:

```
hadoop fs -ls /mydir1/LICENSE.txt

-rw-r--r--   2 ubuntu supergroup       15429 2015-10-29 03:04 /mydir1/
LICENSE.txt
```

How it works...

Once the `setrep` command is executed, NameNode will be notified, and then NameNode decides whether the replicas need to be increased or decreased from certain DataNode. When you are using the `-w` command, sometimes, this process may take too long if the file size is too big.

Setting the HDFS block size for all the files in a cluster

In this recipe, we are going to take a look at how to set a block size at the cluster level.

Getting ready

To perform this recipe, you should already have a running Hadoop cluster.

How to do it...

The HDFS block size is configurable for all files in the cluster or for a single file as well. To change the block size at the cluster level itself, we need to modify the `hdfs-site.xml` file.

By default, the HDFS block size is 128MB. In case we want to modify this, we need to update this property, as shown in the following code. This property changes the default block size to 64MB:

```
<property>
<name>dfs.block.size</name>
    <value>67108864</value>
    <description>HDFS Block size</description>
</property>
```

If you have a multi-node Hadoop cluster, you should update this file in the nodes, that is, NameNode and DataNode. Make sure you save these changes and restart the HDFS daemons:

```
/usr/local/hadoop/sbin/stop-dfs.sh
```

```
/usr/local/hadoop/sbin/start-dfs.sh
```

This will set the block size for files that will now get added to the HDFS cluster. Make sure that this does not change the block size of the files that are already present in HDFS. There is no way to change the block sizes of existing files.

How it works...

By default, the HDFS block size is 128MB for Hadoop 2.X. Sometimes, we may want to change this default block size for optimization purposes. When this configuration is successfully updated, all the new files will be saved into blocks of this size. Ensure that these changes do not affect the files that are already present in HDFS; their block size will be defined at the time being copied.

Setting the HDFS block size for a specific file in a cluster

In this recipe, we are going to take a look at how to set the block size for a specific file only.

Getting ready

To perform this recipe, you should already have a running Hadoop cluster.

How to do it...

In the previous recipe, we learned how to change the block size at the cluster level. But this is not always required. HDFS provides us with the facility to set the block size for a single file as well. The following command copies a file called `myfile` to HDFS, setting the block size to 1MB:

```
hadoop fs -Ddfs.block.size=1048576  -put /home/ubuntu/myfile /
```

Once the file is copied, you can verify whether the block size is set to 1MB and has been broken into exact chunks:

```
hdfs fsck -blocks /myfile
    Connecting to namenode via
    http://localhost:50070/fsck?ugi=ubuntu&blocks=1&path=%2Fmyfile
    FSCK started by ubuntu (auth:SIMPLE) from /127.0.0.1 for path
    /myfile at Thu Oct 29 14:58:00 UTC 2015
    .Status: HEALTHY
    Total size:     17276808 B
    Total dirs:     0
```

```
Total files:    1
Total symlinks:            0
Total blocks (validated):  17 (avg. block size 1016282 B)
Minimally replicated blocks: 17 (100.0 %)
Over-replicated blocks:    0 (0.0 %)
Under-replicated blocks:   0 (0.0 %)
Mis-replicated blocks:     0 (0.0 %)
Default replication factor: 1
Average block replication: 1.0
Corrupt blocks:            0
Missing replicas:          0 (0.0 %)
Number of data-nodes:      3
Number of racks:           1
FSCK ended at Thu Oct 29 14:58:00 UTC 2015 in 2 milliseconds


The filesystem under path '/myfile' is HEALTHY
```

How it works...

When we specify the block size at the time of copying a file, it overwrites the default block size and copies the file to HDFS by breaking the file into chunks of a given size. Generally, these modifications are made in order to perform other optimizations. Make sure you make these changes, and you are aware of their consequences. If the block size isn't adequate enough, it will increase the parallelization, but it will also increase the load on NameNode as it would have more entries in `FSImage`. On the other hand, if the block size is too big, then it will reduce the parallelization and degrade the processing performance.

Enabling transparent encryption for HDFS

When handling sensitive data, it is always important to consider the security measures. Hadoop allows us to encrypt sensitive data that's present in HDFS. In this recipe, we are going to see how to encrypt data in HDFS.

Getting ready

To perform this recipe, you should already have a running Hadoop cluster.

How to do it...

For many applications that hold sensitive data, it is very important to adhere to standards such as PCI, HIPPA, FISMA, and so on. To enable this, HDFS provides a utility called encryption zone in which we can create a directory so that data is encrypted on writes and decrypted on read.

To use this encryption facility, we first need to enable Hadoop **Key Management Server** (**KMS**):

```
/usr/local/hadoop/sbin/kms.sh start
```

This would start KMS in the Tomcat web server.

Next, we need to append the following properties in `core-site.xml` and `hdfs-site.xml`.

In `core-site.xml`, add the following property:

```
<property>
    <name>hadoop.security.key.provider.path</name>
    <value>kms://http@localhost:16000/kms</value>
</property>
```

In `hds-site.xml`, add the following property:

```
<property>
    <name>dfs.encryption.key.provider.uri</name>
    <value>kms://http@localhost:16000/kms</value>
</property>
```

Restart the HDFS daemons:

```
/usr/local/hadoop/sbin/stop-dfs.sh
/usr/local/hadoop/sbin/start-dfs.sh
```

Now, we are all set to use KMS. Next, we need to create a key that will be used for the encryption:

```
hadoop key create mykey
```

This will create a key, and then, save it on KMS. Next, we have to create an encryption zone, which is a directory in HDFS where all the encrypted data is saved:

```
hadoop fs -mkdir /zone
hdfs crypto -createZone -keyName mykey -path /zone
```

We will change the ownership to the current user:

```
hadoop fs -chown ubuntu:ubuntu /zone
```

If we put any file into this directory, it will encrypt and would decrypt at the time of reading:

```
hadoop fs -put myfile /zone
hadoop fs -cat /zone/myfile
```

How it works...

There can be various types of encryptions one can do in order to comply with security standards, for example, application-level encryption, database-level, file-level, and disk-level encryption.

The HDFS transparent encryption sits between the database and file-level encryptions. KMS acts like a proxy between HDFS clients and HDFS's encryption provider via HTTP REST APIs. There are two types of keys used for encryption: **Encryption Zone Key(EZK)** and **Data Encryption Key (DEK)**. EZK is used to encrypt DEK, which is also called **Encrypted Data Encryption Key(EDEK)**. This is then saved on NameNode.

When a file needs to be written to the HDFS encryption zone, the client gets EDEK from NameNode and EZK from KMS to form DEK, which is used to encrypt data and store it in HDFS (the encrypted zone).

When an encrypted file needs to be read, the client needs DEK, which is formed by combining EZK and EDEK. These are obtained from KMS and NameNode, respectively. Thus, encryption and decryption is automatically handled by HDFS. and the end user does not need to worry about executing this on their own.

> You can read more on this topic at http://blog.cloudera. com/blog/2015/01/new-in-cdh-5-3-transparent- encryption-in-hdfs/.

Importing data from another Hadoop cluster

Sometimes, we may want to copy data from one HDFS to another either for development, testing, or production migration. In this recipe, we will learn how to copy data from one HDFS cluster to another.

Getting ready

To perform this recipe, you should already have a running Hadoop cluster.

How to do it...

Hadoop provides a utility called `DistCp`, which helps us copy data from one cluster to another. Using this utility is as simple as copying from one folder to another:

```
hadoop distcp hdfs://hadoopCluster1:9000/source hdfs://
hadoopCluster2:9000/target
```

This would use a Map Reduce job to copy data from one cluster to another. You can also specify multiple source files to be copied to the target. There are a couple of other options that we can also use:

- ▶ `-update`: When we use `DistCp` with the update option, it will copy only those files from the source that are not part of the target or differ from the target.
- ▶ `-overwrite`: When we use `DistCp` with the overwrite option, it overwrites the target directory with the source.

How it works...

When `DistCp` is executed, it uses map reduce to copy the data and also assists in error handling and reporting. It expands the list of source files and directories and inputs them to map tasks. When copying from multiple sources, collisions are resolved in the destination based on the option (update/overwrite) that's provided. By default, it skips if the file is already present at the target. Once the copying is complete, the count of skipped files is presented.

> You can read more on `DistCp` at `https://hadoop.apache.org/docs/current/hadoop-distcp/DistCp.html`.

Recycling deleted data from trash to HDFS

In this recipe, we are going to see how to recover deleted data from the trash to HDFS.

Getting ready

To perform this recipe, you should already have a running Hadoop cluster.

How to do it...

To recover accidently deleted data from HDFS, we first need to enable the trash folder, which is not enabled by default in HDFS. This can be achieved by adding the following property to `core-site.xml`:

```
<property>
    <name>fs.trash.interval</name>
    <value>120</value>
</property>
```

Then, restart the HDFS daemons:

/usr/local/hadoop/sbin/stop-dfs.sh

/usr/local/hadoop/sbin/start-dfs.sh

This will set the deleted file retention to 120 minutes.

Now, let's try to delete a file from HDFS:

hadoop fs -rmr /LICENSE.txt

```
15/10/30 10:26:26 INFO fs.TrashPolicyDefault: Namenode trash
configuration: Deletion interval = 120 minutes, Emptier interval
= 0 minutes.

Moved: 'hdfs://localhost:9000/LICENSE.txt' to trash at:
hdfs://localhost:9000/user/ubuntu/.Trash/Current
```

We have 120 minutes to recover this file before it is permanently deleted from HDFS. To restore the file to its original location, we can execute the following commands.

First, let's confirm whether the file exists:

hadoop fs -ls /user/ubuntu/.Trash/Current

```
Found 1 items

-rw-r--r--   1 ubuntu supergroup      15429 2015-10-30 10:26
/user/ubuntu/.Trash/Current/LICENSE.txt
```

Now, restore the deleted file or folder; it's better to use the `distcp` command instead of copying each file one by one:

hadoop `distcp` hdfs

//localhost:9000/user/ubuntu/.Trash/Current/LICENSE.txt hdfs://localhost:9000/

This will start a map reduce job to restore data from the trash to the original HDFS folder. Check the HDFS path; the deleted file should be back to its original form.

How it works...

Enabling trash enforces the file retention policy for a specified amount of time. So, when trash is enabled, HDFS does not execute any blocks deletions or movements immediately but only updates the metadata of the file and its location. This way, we can accidently stop deleting files from HDFS; make sure that trash is enabled before experimenting with this recipe.

Saving compressed data in HDFS

In this recipe, we are going to take a look at how to store and process compressed data in HDFS.

Getting ready

To perform this recipe, you should already have a running Hadoop.

How to do it...

It's always good to use compression while storing data in HDFS. HDFS supports various types of compression algorithms such as LZO, BIZ2, Snappy, GZIP, and so on. Every algorithm has its own pros and cons when you consider the time taken to compress and decompress and the space efficiency. These days people prefer Snappy compression as it aims to achieve a very high speed and a reasonable amount of compression.

We can easily store and process any number of files in HDFS. To store compressed data, we don't need to specifically make any changes to the Hadoop cluster. You can simply copy the compressed data in the same way it's in HDFS. Here is an example of this:

```
hadoop fs -mkdir /compressed
hadoop fs -put file.bz2 /compressed
```

Now, we'll run a sample program to take a look at how Hadoop automatically uncompresses the file and processes it:

```
hadoop jar /usr/local/hadoop/share/hadoop/mapreduce/hadoop-mapreduce-
examples-2.7.0.jar wordcount /compressed /compressed_out
```

Once the job is complete, you can verify the output.

How it works...

Hadoop explores native libraries to find the support needed for various codecs and their implementations. Native libraries are specific to the platform that you run Hadoop on. You don't need to make any configuration changes to enable compression algorithms. As mentioned earlier, Hadoop supports various compression algorithms that are already familiar to the computer world. Based on your needs and requirements (more space or more time), you can choose your compression algorithm.

Take a look at `http://comphadoop.weebly.com/` for more information on this.

Downloading the example code

You can download the example code files for this book from your account at `http://www.packtpub.com`. If you purchased this book elsewhere, you can visit `http://www.packtpub.com/support` and register to have the files e-mailed directly to you.

You can download the code files by following these steps:

- ▸ Log in or register to our website using your e-mail address and password
- ▸ Hover the mouse pointer on the SUPPORT tab at the top.
- ▸ Click on Code Downloads & Errata
- ▸ Enter the name of the book in the Search box
- ▸ Select the book for which you're looking to download the code files
- ▸ Choose from the drop-down menu where you purchased this book from
- ▸ Click on Code Download

Once the file is downloaded, please make sure that you unzip or extract the folder using the latest version of:

- ▸ WinRAR / 7-Zip for Windows
- ▸ Zipeg / iZip / UnRarX for Mac
- ▸ 7-Zip / PeaZip for Linux

3
Mastering Map Reduce Programs

In this chapter, we'll cover the following recipes:

- ▶ Writing the Map Reduce program in Java to analyze web log data
- ▶ Executing the Map Reduce program in a Hadoop cluster
- ▶ Adding support for a new writable data type in Hadoop
- ▶ Implementing a user-defined counter in a Map Reduce program
- ▶ Map Reduce program to find the top X
- ▶ Map Reduce program to find distinct values
- ▶ Map Reduce program to partition data using a custom partitioner
- ▶ Writing Map Reduce results to multiple output files
- ▶ Performing Reduce side Joins using Map Reduce
- ▶ Unit testing the Map Reduce code using MRUnit

Introduction

Hadoop consists of two important components: HDFS and Map Reduce. In the previous chapter, we talked about various recipes one can perform to use and maintain HDFS in a good state. In this chapter, we are going to explore the details of the Map Reduce framework. Hadoop itself is written in Java, and Java is, of course, a preferred way to write Map Reduce programs, but this does not restrict you to only using Java. It provides libraries, such as Hadoop-Streaming, Hadoop Pipes, and so on so that you can write map reduce programs in most popular languages. These include C++, C#, Shell Scripting using Hadoop-Streaming, and so on.

Writing the Map Reduce program in Java to analyze web log data

In this recipe, we are going to take a look at how to write a map reduce program to analyze web logs. Web logs are data that is generated by web servers for requests they receive. There are various web servers such as Apache, Nginx, Tomcat, and so on. Each web server logs data in a specific format. In this recipe, we are going to use data from the Apache Web Server, which is in combined access logs.

> To read more on combined access logs, refer to
> `http://httpd.apache.org/docs/1.3/logs.html#combined`.

Getting ready

To perform this recipe, you should already have a running Hadoop cluster as well as an eclipse similar to an IDE.

How to do it...

We can write map reduce programs to analyze various aspects of web log data. In this recipe, we are going to write a map reduce program that reads a web log file, results pages, views, and their counts. Here is some sample web log data we'll consider as input for our program:

```
106.208.17.105 - - [12/Nov/2015:21:20:32 -0800] "GET /tutorials/
mapreduce/advanced-map-reduce-examples-1.html HTTP/1.1" 200 0
"https://www.google.co.in/" "Mozilla/5.0 (Windows NT 6.3; WOW64)
AppleWebKit/537.36 (KHTML, like Gecko) Chrome/46.0.2490.86 Safari/537.36"

60.250.32.153 - - [12/Nov/2015:21:42:14 -0800] "GET /tutorials/
elasticsearch/install-elasticsearch-kibana-logstash-on-windows.html
HTTP/1.1" 304 0 - "Mozilla/5.0 (Windows NT 6.1; WOW64) AppleWebKit/537.36
(KHTML, like Gecko) Chrome/46.0.2490.86 Safari/537.36"

49.49.250.23 - - [12/Nov/2015:21:40:56 -0800] "GET /tutorials/hadoop/
images/internals-of-hdfs-file-read-operations/HDFS_Read_Write.png
HTTP/1.1" 200 0 "http://hadooptutorials.co.in/tutorials/spark/install-
apache-spark-on-ubuntu.html" "Mozilla/5.0 (Windows NT 10.0; WOW64;
Trident/7.0; Touch; LCTE; rv:11.0) like Gecko"

60.250.32.153 - - [12/Nov/2015:21:36:01 -0800] "GET /tutorials/
elasticsearch/install-elasticsearch-kibana-logstash-on-windows.html
HTTP/1.1" 200 0 - "Mozilla/5.0 (Windows NT 6.1; WOW64) AppleWebKit/537.36
(KHTML, like Gecko) Chrome/46.0.2490.86 Safari/537.36"
```

```
91.200.12.136 - - [12/Nov/2015:21:30:14 -0800] "GET /tutorials/hadoop/
hadoop-fundamentals.html HTTP/1.1" 200 0 "http://hadooptutorials.co.in/
tutorials/hadoop/hadoop-fundamentals.html" "Mozilla/5.0 (Windows NT 6.1)
AppleWebKit/537.36 (KHTML, like Gecko) Chrome/45.0.2454.99 Safari/537.36"
```

These combined Apache Access logs are in a specific format. Here is the sequence and meaning of each component in each access log:

- **%h**: This is the remote host (that is, the IP client)
- **%l**: This is the identity of the user determined by an identifier (this is not usually used since it's not reliable)
- **%u**: This is the username determined by the HTTP authentication
- **%t**: This is the time the server takes to finish processing a request
- **%r**: This is the request line from the client ("GET / HTTP/1.0")
- **%>s**: This is the status code sent from a server to a client (200, 404, and so on)
- **%b**: This is the size of the response given to a client (in bytes)
- **Referrer**: This is the page that is linked to this URL
- **User agent**: This is the browser identification string

Now, let's start a writing program in order to get to know the page views of each unique URL that we have in our web logs.

First, we will write a mapper class where we will read each and every line and parse it to the extract page URL. Here, we will use a Java pattern that matches a utility in order to extract information:

```
public static class PageViewMapper extends Mapper<Object, Text, Text,
IntWritable> {
        public static String APACHE_ACCESS_LOGS_PATTERN = "^(\\S+) (\\
S+) (\\S+) \\[([\\w:/]+\\s[+\\-]\\d{4})\\] \"(\\S+) (\\S+) (\\S+)\"
(\\d{3}) (\\d+) (.+?) \"([^\"]+|(.+?))\"";

        public static Pattern pattern = Pattern.compile(APACHE_ACCESS_
LOGS_PATTERN);

        private static final IntWritable one = new IntWritable(1);
        private Text url = new Text();

        public void map(Object key, Text value, Mapper<Object, Text,
Text, IntWritable>.Context context)
                throws IOException, InterruptedException {
        Matcher matcher = pattern.matcher(value.toString());
            if (matcher.matches()) {
                // Group 6 as we want only Page URL
```

```
                url.set (matcher.group(6));
                System.out.println(url.toString());
                context.write(this.url, one);
            }


        }
    }
```

In the preceding mapper class, we read key value pairs from the text file. By default, the key is a byte offset (the number of characters in a line), and the value is an actual line in a text file. Next, we match the line with the Apache Access Log regex pattern so that we can extract the exact information we need. For a page view counter, we only need a URL. Mapper outputs the URL as a key and 1 as the value. So, we can count these URL in reducer.

Here is the reducer class that sums up the output values of the mapper class:

```
public static class IntSumReducer extends Reducer<Text, IntWritable,
Text, IntWritable> {
        private IntWritable result = new IntWritable();

        public void reduce(Text key, Iterable<IntWritable> values,
                Reducer<Text, IntWritable, Text, IntWritable>.Context
context)
                        throws IOException, InterruptedException {
            int sum = 0;
            for (IntWritable val : values) {
                sum += val.get();
            }
            this.result.set(sum);
            context.write(key, this.result);
        }
    }
```

Now, we just need a driver class to call these mappers and reducers:

```
public class PageViewCounter {

    public static void main(String[] args) throws Exception {
        Configuration conf = new Configuration();
        if (args.length != 2) {
            System.err.println("Usage: PageViewCounter <in><out>");
            System.exit(2);
        }
```

```
        Job job = Job.getInstance(conf, "Page View Counter");
        job.setJarByClass(PageViewCounter.class);
        job.setMapperClass(PageViewMapper.class);
        job.setCombinerClass(IntSumReducer.class);
        job.setReducerClass(IntSumReducer.class);
        job.setOutputKeyClass(Text.class);
        job.setOutputValueClass(IntWritable.class);
        FileInputFormat.addInputPath(job, new Path(args[0]));

        FileOutputFormat.setOutputPath(job, new Path(args[1]));
        System.exit(job.waitForCompletion(true) ? 0 : 1);
    }
}
```

As the operation we are performing is aggregation, we can also use a combiner here to optimize the results. Here, the same reducer logic is being used as the one used for the combiner.

To compile your program properly, you need to add two external JARs, `hadoop-common-2.7.jar`, which can be found in the `/usr/local/hadoop/share/hadoop/common` folder and `hadoop-mapreduce-client-core-2.7.jar`, which can be found in the `/usr/local/hadoop/share/hadoop/mapreduce` path.

Make sure you add these two JARs in your build path so that your program can be compiled easily.

How it works...

The page view counter program helps us find the most popular pages, least accessed pages, and so on. Such information helps us make decisions about the ranking of pages, frequency of visits, and the relevance of a page. When a program is executed, each line of the HDFS block is read individually and then sent to Mapper. Mapper matches the input line with the log format and extracts its page URL. Mapper emits the (URL,1) type of key value pairs. These pairs are shuffled across nodes and partitioners to make sure that a similar URL goes to only one reducer. Once received by the reducers, we add up all the values for each key and emit them. This way, we get results in the form of a URL and the number of times it was accessed.

Executing the Map Reduce program in a Hadoop cluster

In the previous recipe, we took a look at how to write a map reduce program for a page view counter. In this recipe, we will explore how to execute this in a Hadoop cluster.

Getting ready

To perform this recipe, you should already have a running Hadoop cluster as well as an eclipse similar to an IDE.

How to do it

To execute the program, we first need to create a JAR file of it. JAR stands for Java Archive file, which contains compiled class files. To create a JAR file in eclipse, we need to perform the following steps:

1. Right-click on the project where you've written your Map Reduce Program. Then, click on **Export**.

2. Select **Java->Jar File** and click on the **Next** button. Browse through the path where you wish to export the JAR file, and provide a proper name to the jar file. Click on **Finish** to complete the creation of the JAR file.

3. Now, copy this file to the Hadoop cluster. If you have your Hadoop cluster running in the AWS EC2 instance, you can use the following command to copy the JAR file:

   ```
   scp -i mykey.pem logAnalyzer.jar ubuntu@ec2-52-27-157-247.us-
   west-2.compute.amazonaws.com:/home/ubuntu
   ```

4. If you don't already have your input log files in HDFS, use following commands:

   ```
   hadoop fs -mkdir /logs

   hadoop fs -put web.log /logs
   ```

5. Now, it's time to execute the map reduce program. Use the following command to start the execution:

   ```
   hadoop jar logAnalyzer.jar com.demo.PageViewCounter /logs /
   pageview_output
   ```

6. This will start the Map Reduce execution on your cluster. If everything goes well, you should be able to see output in the pageview_output folder in HDFS. Here, logAnalyzer is the name of the JAR file we created through eclipse. logs is the folder we have our input data in, while pageview_output is the folder that will first be created, and then results will be saved into. It is also important to provide a fully qualified name to the class along with its package name.

How it works...

Once the job is submitted, it first creates the Application Client and Application Master in the Hadoop cluster. The application tasks for Mapper are initiated in each node where data blocks are present in the Hadoop cluster. Once the Mapper phase is complete, the data is locally reduced by a combiner. Once the combiner finishes, the data is shuffled across the nodes in the cluster. Unless all the mappers have finished, reducers cannot be started. Output from the reducers is also written to HDFS in a specified folder.

> The output folder to be specified should be a nonexisting folder in HDFS. If the folder is already present, then the program will give you an error.

When all the tasks are finished for the application, you can take a look at the output in HDFS. The following are the commands to do this:

```
hadoop fs -ls /pageview_output
hadoop fs -cat /pageview_output/part-m-00000
```

This way, you can write similar programs for the following:

- Most number of referral sites (hint: use a referral group from the matcher)
- Number of client errors (with the Http status of 4XX)
- Number of of server errors (with the Http status of 5XX)

Adding support for a new writable data type in Hadoop

In this recipe, we are going to learn how to introduce a new data type in Map Reduce programs and then use it.

Getting ready

To perform this recipe, you should have a running Hadoop cluster as well as an eclipse that's similar to an IDE.

How to do it...

Hadoop allows us to add new custom data types ,which are made up of one or more primary data types. In the previous recipe, you must have noticed that when you handled the log data structure, you had to remember the sequence in which each data component was placed. This can get very nasty when it comes to complex programs. To avoid this, we will introduce a new data type in which `WritableComparable` can be used efficiently.

To add a new data type, we need to implement the `WritableComparable` interface, which is provided by Hadoop. This interface provides three methods, `readFields(DataInput in)`, `write(DataOut out)`, and `compareTo(To)`, which we will need to override with our own custom implementation. Here, we are going to abstract the log parsing and pattern matching logic from the user of this data type by providing a method that returns parsed objects:

```
public class ApacheAccessLogWritable implements WritableComparable<Apa
cheAccessLogWritable> {

    public static String APACHE_ACCESS_LOGS_PATTERN = "^(\\S+) (\\
S+) (\\S+) \\[([\\w:/]+\\s[+\\-]\\d{4})\\] \"(\\S+) (\\S+) (\\S+)\"
(\\d{3}) (\\d+) (.+?) \"([^\"]+|(.+?))\"";
    public static Pattern pattern = Pattern.compile(APACHE_ACCESS_
LOGS_PATTERN);

    private Text clientIp, id, username, dateString, httpMethod, url,
httpVersion, referral, browserString;
    private IntWritable httpStatus, requestSize;

    @Override
    public void readFields(DataInput in) throws IOException {
        clientIp.readFields(in);
        id.readFields(in);
        username.readFields(in);
        dateString.readFields(in);
        httpMethod.readFields(in);
        url.readFields(in);
        httpVersion.readFields(in);
        referral.readFields(in);
        browserString.readFields(in);
        httpStatus.readFields(in);
        requestSize.readFields(in);

    }
```

```java
    @Override
    public void write(DataOutput out) throws IOException {
        clientIp.write(out);
        id.write(out);
        username.write(out);
        dateString.write(out);
        httpMethod.write(out);
        url.write(out);
        httpVersion.write(out);
        referral.write(out);
        browserString.write(out);
        httpStatus.write(out);
        requestSize.write(out);

    }


    private ApacheAccessLogWritable(Text clientIp, Text id, Text
username, Text dateString, Text httpMethod, Text url,
            Text httpVersion, IntWritable httpStatus, IntWritable
requestSize, Text referral, Text browserString) {

        this.clientIp = clientIp;
        this.id = id;
        this.username = username;
        this.dateString = dateString;
        this.httpMethod = httpMethod;
        this.url = url;
        this.httpVersion = httpVersion;
        this.referral = referral;
        this.browserString = browserString;
        this.httpStatus = httpStatus;
        this.requestSize = requestSize;
    }


    public static ApacheAccessLogWritable parseFromLogLine(String
logline) {
        Matcher m = pattern.matcher(logline);
        if (!m.find()) {

            throw new RuntimeException("Error parsing logline");
        }

        return new ApacheAccessLogWritable(new Text(m.group(1)), new
Text(m.group(2)), new Text(m.group(3)),
```

```
                  new Text(m.group(4)), new Text(m.group(5)), new
Text(m.group(6)), new Text(m.group(7)),
                  new IntWritable(Integer.parseInt(m.group(8))), new
IntWritable(Integer.parseInt(m.group(9))),
                  new Text(m.group(10)), new Text(m.group(11)));
    }

    @Override
    public int compareTo(ApacheAccessLogWritable o) {
        // TODO Auto-generated method stub
        return 0;
    }
    // Getter and Setter methods
    ..

}
```

The following piece of code shows us how we can use the data type in our map reduce program; here, I am going to update the same program that we used in the previous recipe. So, the mapper code will be updated as follows:

```
public static class PageViewMapper extends Mapper<Object, Text, Text,
IntWritable> {

        private static final IntWritable one = new IntWritable(1);

        public void map(Object key, Text value, Mapper<Object, Text,
Text, IntWritable>.Context context)
                    throws IOException, InterruptedException {
            ApacheAccessLogWritable log = ApacheAccessLogWritable.
parseFromLogLine(value.toString());
            context.write(log.getUrl(), one);


        }
    }
```

The highlighted code shows you where we have used our own custom data type. Here, the reducer and driver code remain as it is. Refer to the previous recipe to know more about these two.

To execute this code, we need to bundle the datatype class and map reduce program into a single JAR itself so that at runtime the map reduce code is able to find our newly introduced data type.

How it works...

We know that when we execute the map reduce code, a lot of data gets transferred over the network when this shuffle takes place. Sometimes, the size of the keys and values that are transferred can be huge, which might affect network traffic. To avoid congestion, it's very important to send the data in a serialized format. To abstract the pain of serialization and deserialization from the map reduce programmer, Hadoop has introduced a set of box/wrapper classes such as `IntWritable`, `LongWritable`, `Text`, `FloatWritable`, `DoubleWritable`, and so on. These are wrapper classes on top of primitive data types, which can be serialized and deserialized easily. The keys need to be `WritableComparable`, while the values need to be `Writable`. Technically, both keys and values are `WritableComparable`.

Apart from the set of built-in data types, Hadoop also supports the introduction of custom and new data types that are `WritableComparable`. This is done so that the handling of complex data becomes easy and serialization and deserialization is taken care of automatically. `WritableComparable` are data types that are easy to serialize and deserialize and can be compared in order to decide what their order is.

Implementing a user-defined counter in a Map Reduce program

In this recipe, we are going to learn how to add a user-defined counter so that we can keep track of certain events easily.

Getting ready

To perform this recipe, you should have a running Hadoop cluster as well as an eclipse that's similar to an IDE.

How to do it...

After every map reduce execution, you will see a set of system defined counters getting published, such as File System counters, Job counters, and Map Reduce Framework counters. These counters help us understand the execution in detail. They give very detailed information about the number of bytes written to HDFS, read from HDFS, the input given to a map, the output received from a map, and so on. Similar to this information, we can also add our own user-defined counters, which will help us track the execution in a better manner.

In earlier recipes, we considered the use case of log analytics. There can be chances that the input we receive might always not be in the same format as we expect it to be. So, its very important to track such bad records and also avoid any failures because of them. In order to achieve this, in this recipe, we are going to add one custom counter that keeps track of such bad records without failing the task.

First of all, we have to define the counter as enum in our program:

```
private enum COUNTERS {
        INVALID_RECORD_COUNT
    }
```

Next, we will update our mapper code to use the defined counter, as shown here:

```
public static class PageViewMapper extends Mapper<Object, Text, Text,
IntWritable> {

        private static final IntWritable one = new IntWritable(1);

        public void map(Object key, Text value, Mapper<Object, Text,
Text, IntWritable>.Context context)
                throws IOException, InterruptedException {
            ApacheAccessLogWritable log = null;
            try {
                // If record is in expected format, do normal
processing
                log = ApacheAccessLogWritable.parseFromLogLine(value.
toString());
                context.write(log.getUrl(), one);
            } catch (Exception e) {
                // if not, increment the invalid record counter
                System.out.println("Invalid record found");
                context.getCounter(COUNTERS.INVALID_RECORD_COUNT).
increment(1L);

            }

        }
    }
```

The reducer code will remain as it is while we will update the driver code to print the final count of invalid records, as shown here:

```
public static void main(String[] args) throws Exception {
        Configuration conf = new Configuration();
        if (args.length != 2) {
            System.err.println("Usage: PageViewCounter <in><out>");
            System.exit(2);
        }
        Job job = Job.getInstance(conf, "Page View Counter");
        job.setJarByClass(PageViewCounter.class);
        job.setMapperClass(PageViewMapper.class);
```

```
      job.setCombinerClass(IntSumReducer.class);
      job.setReducerClass(IntSumReducer.class);
      job.setOutputKeyClass(Text.class);
      job.setOutputValueClass(IntWritable.class);
      FileInputFormat.addInputPath(job, new Path(args[0]));

      FileOutputFormat.setOutputPath(job, new Path(args[1]));
      System.exit(job.waitForCompletion(true) ? 0 : 1);
      org.apache.hadoop.mapreduce.Counters counters = job.
getCounters();
        System.out.println("No. of Invalid Records :" + counters.
findCounter(COUNTERS.INVALID_RECORD_COUNT).getValue());
    }
```

Now, to demonstrate, I've added a few invalid records (records with fewer columns than expected) and added the log file to HDFS. So, when I execute the program, I can see the invalid record count getting printed at the end of the execution:

```
$hadoop jar logAnalyzer.jar com.demo.PageViewCounter /log-input /log-
output
15/11/15 08:44:37 INFO client.RMProxy: Connecting to ResourceManager
at /0.0.0.0:8032
15/11/15 08:44:37 WARN mapreduce.JobResourceUploader: Hadoop command-
line option parsing not performed. Implement the Tool interface and
execute your application with ToolRunner to remedy this.
15/11/15 08:44:37 INFO input.FileInputFormat: Total input paths to
process : 2
15/11/15 08:44:37 INFO mapreduce.JobSubmitter: number of splits:2
15/11/15 08:44:38 INFO mapreduce.JobSubmitter: Submitting tokens for
job: job_1447554086128_0003
15/11/15 08:44:38 INFO impl.YarnClientImpl: Submitted application
application_1447554086128_0003
15/11/15 08:44:38 INFO mapreduce.Job: The url to track the job:
http://admin1:8088/proxy/application_1447554086128_0003/
15/11/15 08:44:38 INFO mapreduce.Job: Running job:
job_1447554086128_0003
15/11/15 08:44:43 INFO mapreduce.Job: Job job_1447554086128_0003
running in uber mode : false
15/11/15 08:44:43 INFO mapreduce.Job:  map 0% reduce 0%
15/11/15 08:44:50 INFO mapreduce.Job:  map 100% reduce 0%
15/11/15 08:44:55 INFO mapreduce.Job:  map 100% reduce 100%
15/11/15 08:44:55 INFO mapreduce.Job: Job job_1447554086128_0003
completed successfully
15/11/15 08:44:55 INFO mapreduce.Job: Counters: 50
    File System Counters
        FILE: Number of bytes read=580
```

```
            FILE: Number of bytes written=345070
            FILE: Number of read operations=0
            FILE: Number of large read operations=0
            FILE: Number of write operations=0
            HDFS: Number of bytes read=3168
            HDFS: Number of bytes written=271
            HDFS: Number of read operations=9
            HDFS: Number of large read operations=0
            HDFS: Number of write operations=2
    Job Counters
            Launched map tasks=2
            Launched reduce tasks=1
            Data-local map tasks=2
            Total time spent by all maps in occupied slots (ms)=8542
            Total time spent by all reduces in occupied slots (ms)=3046
            Total time spent by all map tasks (ms)=8542
            Total time spent by all reduce tasks (ms)=3046
            Total vcore-seconds taken by all map tasks=8542
            Total vcore-seconds taken by all reduce tasks=3046
            Total megabyte-seconds taken by all map tasks=8747008
            Total megabyte-seconds taken by all reduce tasks=3119104
    Map-Reduce Framework
            Map input records=13
            Map output records=10
            Map output bytes=724
            Map output materialized bytes=586
            Input split bytes=201
            Combine input records=10
            Combine output records=8
            Reduce input groups=4
            Reduce shuffle bytes=586
            Reduce input records=8
            Reduce output records=4
            Spilled Records=16
            Shuffled Maps =2
            Failed Shuffles=0
            Merged Map outputs=2
            GC time elapsed (ms)=69
            CPU time spent (ms)=1640
            Physical memory (bytes) snapshot=591077376
            Virtual memory (bytes) snapshot=1219731456
            Total committed heap usage (bytes)=467140608
    Shuffle Errors
            BAD_ID=0
```

```
        CONNECTION=0
        IO_ERROR=0
        WRONG_LENGTH=0
        WRONG_MAP=0
        WRONG_REDUCE=0
com.demo.PageViewCounter$COUNTERS
        INVALID_RECORD_COUNT=3
    File Input Format Counters
        Bytes Read=2967
    File Output Format Counters
        Bytes Written=271
```

How it works...

Custom counters are helpful in various situations such as keeping track of bad records, count outliers in the form of maximum and minimum values, summations, and so on. The Hadoop framework imposes an upper limit on using these counters. They can be incremented/decremented globally, or you may also update them in mappers or reducers. In either case, they are referred to using the group and counter names. All the counters are managed at the Application Master level. Information about each increment or decrement is passed to the Application Master via heartbeat messages between the containers that run mappers and reducers.

It is better to keep the counters to a limited number as this causes an overhead on the processing framework. The best thing to do is to remember a thumb rule: do not let the number of counters go beyond 100.

Map Reduce program to find the top X

In this recipe, we are going to learn how to write a map reduce program to find the top X records from the given set of values.

Getting ready

To perform this recipe, you should have a running Hadoop cluster as well as an eclipse that's similar to an IDE.

How to do it...

A lot of the time, we might need to find the top X values from the given set of values. A simple example could be to find the top 10 trending topics from a Twitter dataset. In this case, we will need to use two map reduce jobs. First of all, find out all the words that start with # and the number of times each hashtag has occurred in a given set of data. The first map reduce program is quite simple, which is pretty similar to the word count program. But for the second program, we need to use some logic. In this recipe, we'll explore how we can write a map reduce program to find the top X values from the given set. Now, though, lets try to understand the logic behind this.

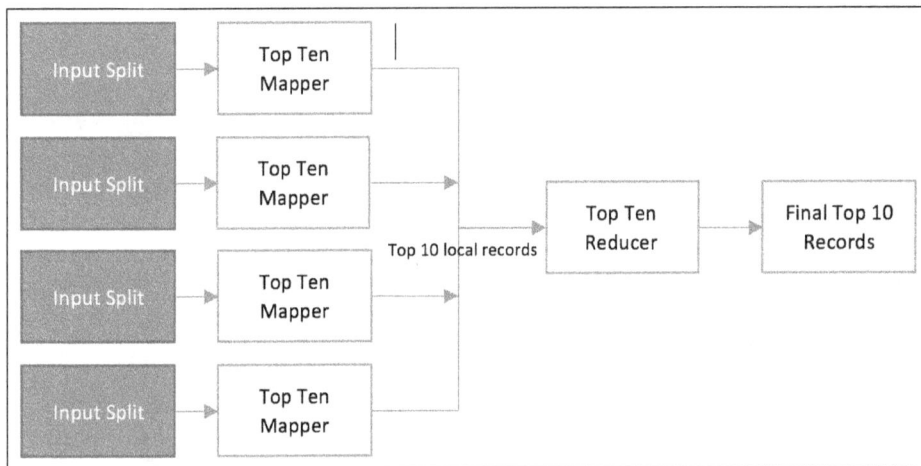

As shown in the preceding figure, our logic includes finding the top 10 words from each input split and then sending these records to only one reducer. In the reducer, we will again find the top 10 words to get the final result of the top 10 records. Now, let's understand the execution.

First, let's prepare the input. Here, we will use the word count program provided along with Hadoop binaries:

First of all, let's put data in HDFS to be processed.

```
hadoop fs -mkdir /input
```

```
hadoop fs -put /usr/local/hadoop/LICENSE.txt /input
```

```
hadoop jar /usr/local/hadoop/share/hadoop/mapreduce/hadoop-mapreduce-
examples-2.7.0.jar /input /word_count_output
```

This will execute the word count program and store the output in the HDFS folder called `/word_count_output`. This output will be used as the input for our top 10 map reduce program.

Let's take a look at the mapper code:

```java
public static class TopTenMapper extends Mapper<Object, Text, Text,
IntWritable> {

        // Tree map keeps records sorted by key
        private TreeMap<Integer, String> countWordMap = new
TreeMap<Integer, String>();

        public void map(Object key, Text value, Mapper<Object, Text,
Text, IntWritable>.Context context)
                throws IOException, InterruptedException {

            String[] words = value.toString().split("[\t]");
            int count = Integer.parseInt(words[1]);
            String word = words[0];
            countWordMap.put(count, word);
            if (countWordMap.size() > 10) {

                countWordMap.remove(countWordMap.firstKey());
            }

        }

        @Override
        protected void cleanup(Context context) throws IOException,
InterruptedException {
            for (Entry<Integer, String> entry : countWordMap.
entrySet()) {
                context.write(new Text(entry.getValue()), new
IntWritable(entry.getKey()));

            }

        }
    }
```

In the preceding code, we are using `TreeMap` to store the words and their count. `TreeMap` helps store keys and values sorted order by the key. Here, we are using the count as the key and words as values. In each Mapper iteration, we check whether the size is greater than 10. If it is, we remove the first key from the key map, which would be the lowest count of the set. This way, at the end of each mapper, we will emit the top 10 words of the reducer.

You can read more about `TreeMap` at `http://docs.oracle.com/javase/7/docs/api/java/util/TreeMap.html`.

Now, let's take a look at the reducer code:

```
public static class TopTenReducer extends Reducer<Text, IntWritable,
Text, IntWritable> {

        // Tree map keeps records sorted by key
        private TreeMap<IntWritable, Text> countWordMap = new
TreeMap<IntWritable, Text>();

        public void reduce(Text key, Iterable<IntWritable> values,
                Reducer<Text, IntWritable, Text, IntWritable>.Context
context)
                        throws IOException, InterruptedException {

            for (IntWritable value : values) {

                countWordMap.put(value, key);

            }
            if (countWordMap.size() > 10) {

                countWordMap.remove(countWordMap.firstKey());
            }
            for (Entry<IntWritable, Text> entry : countWordMap.
descendingMap().entrySet()) {
                    context.write(entry.getValue(), entry.getKey());

            }

        }

    }
```

In the reducer, we will again use `TreeMap` to find the top 10 of all the collected records from each Mapper. Here, is it very important to use only one reducer for the complete processing; hence, we need to set this in the Driver class, as shown here:

```
public class TopTenWordsByOccurence {
    public static void main(String[] args) throws Exception {
        Configuration conf = new Configuration();
        if (args.length != 2) {
            System.err.println("Usage: toptencounter <in><out>");
            System.exit(2);
        }
        Job job = Job.getInstance(conf, "Top Ten Word By Occurence
Counter");
            job.setJarByClass(TopTenWordsByOccurence.class);
```

```
job.setMapperClass(TopTenMapper.class);
job.setCombinerClass(TopTenReducer.class);
job.setReducerClass(TopTenReducer.class);
job.setOutputKeyClass(Text.class);
job.setOutputValueClass(IntWritable.class);
job.setNumReduceTasks(1);
FileInputFormat.addInputPath(job, new Path(args[0]));

FileOutputFormat.setOutputPath(job, new Path(args[1]));

System.exit(job.waitForCompletion(true) ? 0 : 1);
    }
  }
```

Now, when you execute the preceding code, as a result, you will see the output in the form of the top 10 words due to their frequencies in the document.

You can modify the same program to get the top 5, 20, or any number.

How it works

Here, the logic is quite straightforward, as shown in the preceding diagram. The trick is using `TreeMap`, which stores data in a sorted key order. It is also important to use only one reducer, and if we can't, we will again get the number of sets of the top records from each reducer, which will not show you the correct output.

Map Reduce program to find distinct values

In this recipe, we are going to learn how to write a map reduce program to find distinct values from a given set of data.

Getting ready

To perform this recipe, you should have a running Hadoop cluster as well as an eclipse that is similar to an IDE.

How to do it

Sometimes, there may be a chance that the data you have contains some duplicate values. In SQL, we have something called a distinct function, which helps us get distinct values. In this recipe, we are going to take a look at how we can get distinct values using map reduce programs.

Let's consider a use case where we have some user data with us, which contains two columns: `userId` and `username`. Let's assume that the data we have contains duplicate records, and for our processing needs, we only need distinct records through user IDs. Here is some sample data that we have where columns are separated by '|':

```
1|Tanmay
2|Ramesh
3|Ram
1|Tanmay
2|Ramesh
6|Rahul
6|Rahul
4|Sneha
4|Sneha
```

The idea here is to use the default reducer behavior where the same keys are sent to one reducer. In this case, we will make `userId` the key and emit it to the reducer. In the reducer, the same keys will be reduced together, which will avoid duplicates.

Let's look at the Mapper Code.

```java
public static class DistinctUserMapper extends Mapper<Object, Text,
Text, NullWritable> {
        private Text userId = new Text();

        public void map(Object key, Text value, Context context)
throws IOException, InterruptedException {

                String words[] = value.toString().split("[|]");
                userId.set(words[0]);
                context.write(userId, NullWritable.get());
        }
    }
```

We only want distinct user IDs, hence, we emit only user IDs as keys and nulls as values.

Now, let's look at the reducer code:

```java
public static class DistinctUserReducer extends Reducer<Text,
NullWritable, Text, NullWritable> {
        public void reduce(Text key, Iterable<NullWritable> values,
Context context)
                throws IOException, InterruptedException {
            context.write(key, NullWritable.get());
        }
    }
```

Here, we only emit user IDs as they come. This step removes duplicates as the reducer only treats the records by their keys and only one record per key is kept.

The driver code remains simple, as shown here:

```
public class DistinctValues {

    public static void main(String[] args) throws Exception {
        Configuration conf = new Configuration();
        if (args.length != 2) {
            System.err.println("Usage: DistinctValues <in><out>");
            System.exit(2);
        }
        Job job = Job.getInstance(conf, "Distinct User Id finder");
        job.setJarByClass(DistinctValues.class);
        job.setMapperClass(DistinctUserMapper.class);
        job.setReducerClass(DistinctUserReducer.class);
        job.setOutputKeyClass(Text.class);
        job.setOutputValueClass(NullWritable.class);
        FileInputFormat.addInputPath(job, new Path(args[0]));
        FileOutputFormat.setOutputPath(job, new Path(args[1]));
        System.exit(job.waitForCompletion(true) ? 0 : 1);

    }
}
```

Now, when we execute the code, we will see the following output:

```
hadoop jar distinct.jar com.demo.DistinctValues /users /distinct_user_ids
hadoop fs -cat /distinct_user_ids/part-r-00000
    1
    2
    3
    4
    6
```

How it works...

When mapper emits keys and values, the output is shuffled across the nodes in the cluster. Here, the partitioner decides which keys should be reduced and on which node. On all the nodes, the same partitioning logic is used, which makes sure that the same keys are grouped together. In the preceding code, we use this default behavior to find distinct user IDs.

Map Reduce program to partition data using a custom partitioner

In this recipe, we are going to learn how to write a map reduce program to partition data using a custom partitioner.

Getting ready

To perform this recipe, you should have a running Hadoop cluster running as well as an eclipse that's similar to an IDE.

How to do it...

During the shuffle and sort, if it's not specified, Hadoop by default uses a hash partitioner. We can also write our own custom partitioner with custom partitioning logic, such that we can partition the data into separate files.

Let's consider one example where we have user data with us along with the year of joining. Now, assume that we have to partition the users based on the year of joining that's specified in the record. The sample input data looks like this:

```
User_id|user_name|yoj
1|Tanmay|2010
2|Sneha|2015
3|Sakalya|2020
4|Manisha|2011
5|Avinash|2012
6|Vinit|2022
```

To get this data partitioned based on YOJ, we will have to write a custom partitioner:

```
public class YearOfJoiningPartitioner extends Partitioner<IntWritable,
Text> implements Configurable {

    private Configuration conf = null;

    @Override
    public int getPartition(IntWritable key, Text value, int
numPartitions) {
        return key.get() % 10;
    }
```

```
    @Override
    public Configuration getConf() {

        return conf;

    }

    @Override
    public void setConf(Configuration conf) {
        this.conf = conf;

    }
}
```

In the custom partitioner, we need to override the getPartition() method where we will write our own custom partitioning logic. Here, we will be using YOJ as the key and partition the data based on the modulo 10 value of year. The value given by this method will be in the form of a reducer where the key will be reduced.

Now, to use this partitioner, we need to set this in the driver class, as shown here:

```
public class YOJPartitioner {

    public static void main(String[] args) throws Exception {
        Configuration conf = new Configuration();
        if (args.length != 2) {
            System.err.println("Usage: YOJPartitioner <in><out>");
            System.exit(2);
        }
        Job job = Job.getInstance(conf, "YOJPartitioner");
        job.setJarByClass(YOJPartitioner.class);
        job.setMapperClass(YOJPartitionerMapper.class);
        job.setReducerClass(YOJReducer.class);
        job.setOutputKeyClass(IntWritable.class);
        job.setOutputValueClass(Text.class);
        job.setPartitionerClass(YearOfJoiningPartitioner.class);
        FileInputFormat.addInputPath(job, new Path(args[0]));

        FileOutputFormat.setOutputPath(job, new Path(args[1]));
        System.exit(job.waitForCompletion(true) ? 0 : 1);

    }
}
```

Now that we want to partition the data based on YOJ, we will have to set YOJ as the key while emitting data from the mapper, as shown here:

```
public static class YOJPartitionerMapper extends Mapper<Object, Text,
IntWritable, Text> {

        public void map(Object key, Text value, Mapper<Object, Text,
IntWritable, Text>.Context context)
                throws IOException, InterruptedException {
            String words[] = value.toString().split("[|]");
            context.write(new IntWritable(Integer.parseInt(words[2])),
value);

        }
    }
```

Next, we will write the identity reducer, which emits keys and values as they come:

```
public static class YOJReducer extends Reducer<IntWritable, Text,
Text, NullWritable> {
        protected void reduce(IntWritable key, Iterable<Text> values,
Context context)
                throws IOException, InterruptedException {
            for (Text t : values) {
                context.write(t, NullWritable.get());
            }
        }
    }
```

When we execute this code in a multimode cluster, the records will be partitioned into different files based on the logic we wrote.

How it works...

When we provide the custom partitioner to the map reduce code and the mappers have finished their work, the custom partitioner will come into the picture. The keys are sent through the getPartition() method and the resultant value will be in the form of the reducer number where the keys are sent. Here, we are executing modulo 10 to the year value which would partition the data into 10 partitions. This way, by controlling the logic of the getPartition() method, we can decide which partitioning strategy to use.

Writing Map Reduce results to multiple output files

In this recipe, we are going to learn how to write a map reduce output to multiple output files. This will be useful when we need to use classified output for different purposes.

Getting ready

To perform this recipe, you should have a running Hadoop cluster as well as an eclipse similar to an IDE.

How to do it...

Hadoop supports a class called `MultipleOutputs`, which allows us to write out of a map reduce program to multiple files. We can write output to different files, file types, and different locations with it. You can also choose the filename with this API. To use this, we will take a look at a simple word count program and write out of this program to multiple output files.

To do so, we need to add the named output files and their types in our Driver code, as shown here:

```
public class WordCount {
    public static void main(String[] args) throws Exception {
        Configuration conf = new Configuration();
        if (args.length != 2) {
            System.err.println("Usage: wordcount <in><out>");
            System.exit(2);
        }
        Job job = Job.getInstance(conf, "WordCount");
        job.setJarByClass(WordCount.class);
        job.setMapperClass(TokenizerMapper.class);
        job.setCombinerClass(IntSumReducer.class);
        job.setReducerClass(IntSumReducer.class);
        job.setOutputKeyClass(Text.class);
        job.setOutputValueClass(IntWritable.class);
        MultipleOutputs.addNamedOutput(job, "text", TextOutputFormat.
class, Text.class, IntWritable.class);
        MultipleOutputs.addNamedOutput(job, "seq",
SequenceFileOutputFormat.class, Text.class, IntWritable.class);
        FileInputFormat.addInputPath(job, new Path(args[0]));

        FileOutputFormat.setOutputPath(job, new Path(args[1]));
        System.exit(job.waitForCompletion(true) ? 0 : 1);
    }
}
```

The highlighted code shows that we have two named output files, that is, the text and seq. This will generate two more files in addition to the default output files. Next, we need to update the reducer code to write output key values to these new files as well:

```
public static class IntSumReducer extends Reducer<Text, IntWritable,
Text, IntWritable> {
        private MultipleOutputs mos;
        private IntWritable result = new IntWritable();

        public void setup(Context context) {

            mos = new MultipleOutputs(context);
        }

        public void reduce(Text key, Iterable<IntWritable> values,
                Reducer<Text, IntWritable, Text, IntWritable>.Context
context)
                        throws IOException, InterruptedException {
            int sum = 0;
            for (IntWritable val : values) {
                sum += val.get();
            }
            this.result.set(sum);
            mos.write("text", key, this.result);
            mos.write("seq", key, this.result);

            context.write(key, this.result);
        }

        public void cleanup(Context context) throws IOException,
InterruptedException {
            mos.close();

        }
    }
```

In the setup method, we need to initiate the object of the `MultipleOutputs` class. In the reduce method, we have to add the `write` method, which would write the desired key values to two files, one of the text type and the other of the sequence file type.

Additionally, you can also specify the complete path apart from the default output path in the reducer code where you wish to see to your file:

```
mos.write(key, this.result, "/my_new_output_path_up/file");
```

It is very important to close the `MultipleOutputs` stream in the `cleanup` method.

How it works...

`MulitpleOutputs` is a great help in two conditions: when you wish to see multiple output files in different file formats and when you wish to write the output of your map reduce program in order to use specified files. `MultipleOutputs` supports counters but they are disabled by default. Once specified, `MultipleOutputs` will first create a file with a specific name, and then it will start writing any data if available. If no data is generated, it will still create zero-sized files. To avoid this, we can use `LazyOutputFormat`, as shown in the following. Details on `LazyOutputFormat` are available at `https://hadoop.apache.org/docs/r2.6.1/api/org/apache/hadoop/mapreduce/lib/output/LazyOutputFormat.html`. Here is the code for `LazyOutputFormat`:

```
LazyOutputFormat.setOutputFormatClass(job, TextOutputFormat.class);
```

Performing Reduce side Joins using Map Reduce

In this recipe, we are going to learn how to write a map reduce, which will join records from two tables.

Getting ready

To perform this recipe, you should have a running Hadoop cluster as well as an eclipse that's similar to an IDE.

How to do it

We are aware of the various types of joins that are available in SQL—Inner Join, Left outer join, right outer join, full outer join, and so on. Performing joins in SQL is quite easy, but when it comes to MapReduce, this is a little tricky. In this recipe, we will be try to perform various join operations using the Map Reduce program in the following dataset.

Consider two datasets: the `Users` table, which has information about `userId`, username, and `deptId`. We also have data on the `Department` table where we have `deptId` and `deptName` as columns. If we place our data in a table, it would look like this:

Users' table:

User ID	Username	Department ID
1	Tanmay	1
2	Sneha	1
3	Sakalya	2

User ID	Username	Department ID
4	Manisha	2
5	Avinash	3

Department table:

Department ID	Department name
1	Engineering
2	Sales
3	Production

Here, `deptId` is the foreign key between two tables, and we will join the two tables based on this key.

To start with, we need to have a driver code where we will use the `MultipleInputs` API, which allows us to take the two input paths where the users and department table is stored in HDFS. We also need to accept the join type from the user, and lastly, we need to accept the output path where we will save our final result:

```
public class ReduceSideJoin {
    public static void main(String[] args) throws Exception {
        Configuration conf = new Configuration();
        if (args.length != 4) {
            System.err.println("Usage: join <input-table1><input-table
2><jointype:inner|leftouter|rightouter|fullouter><out>");
            System.exit(2);
        }
        Job job = Job.getInstance(conf, "Reduce Side Join");
        job.setJarByClass(ReduceSideJoin.class);

        job.setReducerClass(DeptJoinReducer.class);
        job.setOutputKeyClass(Text.class);
        job.setOutputValueClass(Text.class);
        MultipleInputs.addInputPath(job, new Path(args[0]),
TextInputFormat.class, UserJoinMapper.class);
        MultipleInputs.addInputPath(job, new Path(args[1]),
TextInputFormat.class, DeptJoinMapper.class);
        job.getConfiguration().set("join.type", args[2]);
        FileOutputFormat.setOutputPath(job, new Path(args[3]));
        System.exit(job.waitForCompletion(true) ? 0 : 1);
    }
}
```

Next, we need to write two mappers that deal with each table. We'll first look at the users table. We'll join the records with `deptId`, hence we need to emit keys as `deptIds`. Also, we are going to append an identifier, which will help us classify records based on the table that they are from:

```
public static class UserJoinMapper extends Mapper<Object, Text, Text,
Text> {
        private Text outkey = new Text();
        private Text outvalue = new Text();

        public void map(Object key, Text value, Context context)
throws IOException, InterruptedException {
            String attrs[] = value.toString().split("[\t]");
            String deptId = attrs[2];
            // The foreign join key is the dept ID
            outkey.set(deptId);
            // flag this each record with prefixing it with 'A'
            outvalue.set("A" + value.toString());
            context.write(outkey, outvalue);
        }
    }
```

Similarly, we'll write a mapper class for the department table as well:

```
public static class DeptJoinMapper extends Mapper<Object, Text, Text,
Text> {
        private Text outkey = new Text();
        private Text outvalue = new Text();

        public void map(Object key, Text value, Context context)
throws IOException, InterruptedException {
            String attrs[] = value.toString().split("[\t]");
            String deptId = attrs[0];
            // The foreign join key is the dept ID
            outkey.set(deptId);
            // flag this each record with prefixing it with 'B'
            outvalue.set("B" + value.toString());
            context.write(outkey, outvalue);
        }
    }
```

Next, we need to write a reducer class where we will write our logic to join the records:

```
public static class DeptJoinReducer extends Reducer<Text, Text, Text,
Text> {
        private static final Text EMPTY_TEXT = new Text("");
        private Text tmp = new Text();
        private ArrayList<Text> listA = new ArrayList<Text>();
        private ArrayList<Text> listB = new ArrayList<Text>();
        private String joinType = null;

        public void setup(Context context) {
            // set up join configuration based on input
            joinType = context.getConfiguration().get("join.type");
        }

        public void reduce(Text key, Iterable<Text> values, Context
context) throws IOException, InterruptedException {
            // Clear the lists
            listA.clear();
            listB.clear();
            // Put records from each table into correct lists, remove
the prefix
            for (Text t : values) {
                tmp = t;
                if (tmp.charAt(0) == 'A') {
                    listA.add(new Text(tmp.toString().substring(1)));
                } else if (tmp.charAt(0) == 'B') {
                    listB.add(new Text(tmp.toString().substring(1)));
                }
            }
            // Execute joining logic based on its type
            executeJoinLogic(context);
        }
    ...
}
```

In the preceding code, we first initialize the two empty lists where we keep our records. There's one list for each table. We segregate the records based on their prefix. In the setup method, we also set up the join type that's been provided by the user in the job configuration.

Next, we need to write the join logic based on the join type. The following code shows the logic for the inner, left outer, right outer, and the full outer join:

```
private void executeJoinLogic(Context context) throws IOException,
InterruptedException {
        if (joinType.equalsIgnoreCase("inner")) {

            if (!listA.isEmpty() && !listB.isEmpty()) {
                for (Text A : listA) {
                    for (Text B : listB) {
                        context.write(A, B);
                    }
                }
            }
        } else if (joinType.equalsIgnoreCase("leftouter")) {

            for (Text A : listA) {

                if (!listB.isEmpty()) {
                    for (Text B : listB) {
                        context.write(A, B);
                    }
                } else {

                    context.write(A, EMPTY_TEXT);
                }
            }
        } else if (joinType.equalsIgnoreCase("rightouter")) {

            for (Text B : listB) {

                if (!listA.isEmpty()) {
                    for (Text A : listA) {
                        context.write(A, B);
                    }
                } else {

                    context.write(EMPTY_TEXT, B);
                }
            }
        } else if (joinType.equalsIgnoreCase("fullouter")) {

            if (!listA.isEmpty()) {
```

```
                    for (Text A : listA) {

                        if (!listB.isEmpty()) {
                            for (Text B : listB) {
                                context.write(A, B);
                            }
                        } else {

                            context.write(A, EMPTY_TEXT);
                        }
                    }
                } else {

                    for (Text B : listB) {
                        context.write(EMPTY_TEXT, B);
                    }
                }
            }
        }
    }
```

Now, when we compile this code and bundle it into jar, it is ready for execution. Before the execution, we need to prepare our input:

```
hadoop fs -mkdir /users
hadoop fs -put users.txt /users
hadoop fs -mkdir /dept
hadoop fs -put dept.txt /dept
hadoop jar join.jar com.demo.ReduceSideJoin /users /dept inner /inner-join-output
```

Once the execution is complete, you can take a look at the output file:

```
hadoop fs -cat /inner-join-output/part-r-00000
    2    Sneha  1     1      Engineering
    1    Tanmay 1     1      Engineering
    4    Manisha      2     2      Sales
    3    Sakalya      2     2      Sales
    5    Avinash      3     3      Production
```

How it works...

MulitpleInputs works with each mapper and sends data from the respective directories. Inside mappers, the keys and values are emitted based on the joining foreign key. When it comes to reducers, the actual join logic is executed based on the join type. Generally, reduce side joins consume a lot of resources and take more time than map side joins. But when you have huge data at hand, reduce side joins are the only options we have. Reduce side joins also cause huge network traffic as each and every record is sent to the reducers. Based on the foreign key to join, the keys should be changed. This way, you can update the code in the preceding section to join any two datasets easily.

Unit testing the Map Reduce code using MRUnit

In this recipe, we are going to learn how to unit test the map reduce code using a library called MRUnit.

Getting ready

To perform this recipe, you should have a running Hadoop cluster as well as an eclipse similar to an IDE.

How to do it...

Sometimes, it is very difficult to develop, compile, deploy and execute the map reduce program and then figure out whether the code is correct or not. In order to avoid this deploying and testing technique, we can use a unit testing framework that's been built specially for Map Reduce called, MRUnit.

Let's assume that we have a map reduce program that emits and counts words starting with '#', such as a Twitter hashtag counter. The Mapper code for this hashtag counter looks like this:

```
public static class TokenizerMapper extends
        Mapper<Object, Text, Text, IntWritable> {
    private static final IntWritable one = new IntWritable(1);
    private Text word = new Text();

    public void map(Object key, Text value,
        Mapper<Object, Text, Text, IntWritable>.Context context)
            throws IOException, InterruptedException {
```

```
                StringTokenizer itr = new StringTokenizer(value.
    toString());
            while (itr.hasMoreTokens()) {
                this.word.set(itr.nextToken());
                if (word.toString().startsWith("#"))
                    context.write(this.word, one);
            }
        }
    }
```

The Reduce code is a simple sum reducer code:

```
    public static class IntSumReducer extends
            Reducer<Text, IntWritable, Text, IntWritable> {
        private IntWritable result = new IntWritable();

        public void reduce(Text key, Iterable<IntWritable> values,
            Reducer<Text, IntWritable, Text, IntWritable>.Context
    context)
            throws IOException, InterruptedException {
            int sum = 0;
            for (IntWritable val : values) {
                sum += val.get();
            }
            this.result.set(sum);
            if (result.get() >= 2)
                context.write(key, this.result);
        }
    - }
```

Now, to unit test this code, we will first add dependencies that are required for MRUnit. We need the following dependencies to be added to POM.xml:

```
            <dependency>
                <groupId>junit</groupId>
                <artifactId>junit</artifactId>
                <version>4.12</version>
            </dependency>
            <dependency>
                <groupId>org.mockito</groupId>
                <artifactId>mockito-all</artifactId>
                <version>2.0.2-beta</version>
            </dependency>
            <dependency>
                <groupId>org.apache.mrunit</groupId>
```

```
              <artifactId>mrunit</artifactId>
              <version>1.1.0</version>
              <classifier>hadoop1</classifier>
          </dependency>
          <dependency>
              <groupId>org.apache.hadoop</groupId>
              <artifactId>hadoop-mapreduce-client-core</artifactId>
              <version>2.7.1</version>
          </dependency>
          <dependency>
              <groupId>org.apache.hadoop</groupId>
              <artifactId>hadoop-common</artifactId>
              <version>2.7.1</version>
          </dependency>
```

We need to write a test class that would test the methods from our Map Reduce code:

First we write a setup method which would initialize the objects:

```
    MapDriver<Object, Text, Text, IntWritable> mapDriver;
        ReduceDriver<Text, IntWritable, Text, IntWritable> reduceDriver;
        MapReduceDriver<Object, Text, Text, IntWritable, Text,
    IntWritable> mapReduceDriver;

        @Before
        public void setUp() {
            TokenizerMapper mapper = new TokenizerMapper();
            IntSumReducer reducer = new IntSumReducer();
            mapDriver = MapDriver.newMapDriver(mapper);
            reduceDriver = ReduceDriver.newReduceDriver(reducer);
            mapReduceDriver = MapReduceDriver.newMapReduceDriver(mapper,
    reducer);
        }
```

Here, we are initiating the mapper, reducer, and drivers so that they can be accessed in test cases.

Now, let's write a test case for the mapper class:

```
    @Test
        public void testMapper() throws IOException {
                mapDriver.withInput(new LongWritable(), new Text("Hello
    World #mrunit"));
            mapDriver.withOutput(new Text("#mrunit"), new IntWritable(1));
            mapDriver.runTest();
        }
```

Here, we are testing whether the mapper only emits words starting with '#'.

Next, we will write a test case to check whether the reducer properly sums up the values:

```
@Test
    public void testReducer() throws IOException {
        List<IntWritable> values = new ArrayList<IntWritable>();
        values.add(new IntWritable(1));
        values.add(new IntWritable(1));
        reduceDriver.withInput(new Text("#mrunit"), values);
        reduceDriver.withOutput(new Text("#mrunit"), new
IntWritable(2));
        reduceDriver.runTest();
    }
```

We can also write a combined test for the mapper and reducer:

```
@Test
    public void testMapReduce() throws IOException {
        mapReduceDriver.withInput(new LongWritable(), new Text("Hello
World #mrunit"));
        List<IntWritable> values = new ArrayList<IntWritable>();
        values.add(new IntWritable(1));
        values.add(new IntWritable(1));
        mapReduceDriver.withOutput(new Text("#mrunit"), new
IntWritable(2));
        mapReduceDriver.runTest();
    }
```

This way, you can test any important logic that you have written in your map reduce code.

How it works...

MRUnit works exactly like any other testing framework, such as JUnit/TestNG. It only unit tests the logic. Mockito is a framework that helps mocking up an object, which is a part of the Hadoop/Map Reduce framework.

It is always good practice to unit test your code and only then deploy your map reduce jobs in production clusters. This also helps us with continuous integration to get to know any braking changes because any code update.

4
Data Analysis Using Hive, Pig, and Hbase

- ▸ Storing and processing Hive data in a sequential file format
- ▸ Storing and processing Hive data in the RC file format
- ▸ Storing and processing Hive data in the ORC file format
- ▸ Storing and processing Hive data in the Parquet file format
- ▸ Performing `FILTER By` queries in Pig
- ▸ Performing Group By queries in Pig
- ▸ Performing Order By queries in Pig
- ▸ Performing JOINS in Pig
- ▸ Writing a user-defined function in Pig
- ▸ Analyzing web log data using Pig
- ▸ Performing the Hbase operation in CLI
- ▸ Performing Hbase operations in Java
- ▸ Executing the MapReduce programming Hbase Table

Introduction

In the previous chapter, we discussed how to write MapReduce programs in various ways in order to analyze data. Earlier, MapReduce was the only means of processing data in Hadoop, but with the passage of time, growing popularity, and the ease of using the Hadoop platform, various subprojects joined its league, which helps users write logic in SQL, scripts, and so on, and analyze the data. Projects, such as Apache Hive, Apache Pig, and Apache Hbase, are well accepted by users, so the majority of development these days takes place using any of these. In this chapter, we are going to take a look at how to use these tools to perform various advanced operations. If you are new to these terms, I would recommend that you read through these links first.

- ▸ For Hive resources, take a look a these links:
- ▸ `https://hive.apache.org/`
- ▸ `http://hadooptutorials.co.in/tutorials/hive/introduction-to-apache-hive.html`
- ▸ `http://hadooptutorials.co.in/tutorials/hive/hive-data-units.html`
- ▸ `http://hadooptutorials.co.in/tutorials/hive/hive-best-practices.html`

For Pig resources, take a look at these links:

- ▸ `https://pig.apache.org/`

For Hbase resources, take a look at these links:

- ▸ `https://hbase.apache.org/`

We won't be going through the installations of the above in this book as the installations are quite easy if your Hadoop cluster is already installed; just download the binaries and set the installation paths with few or no configurations as you'll have to use all of them.

Let's get started with our first recipe now.

Storing and processing Hive data in a sequential file format

I'm sure that most of the time, you would have created Hive tables and stored data in a text format; in this recipe, we are going to store data in sequential files.

Getting ready

To perform this recipe, you should have a running Hadoop cluster as well as the latest version of Hive installed on it. Here, I am going to use Hive 1.2.1.

How to do it...

Hive 1.2.1 supports various different types of files, which help process data in a faster manner. In this recipe, we are going to use sequential files to store data in Hive. To store data in sequential files, we first need to create a Hive table that stores the data in a textual format:

```
create table employee(
id int, name string)
row format delimited
fields terminated by '|'
 stored as textfile;
```

The preceding statement will create a table in Hive along with the employee name. Now, let's load data into this table:

```
load data local inpath '/usr/local/hive/examples/files/employee.dat'
into table employee;
```

Here, I am using an example data file that's been provided by the Hive distribution itself. The location where Hive is installed is `/usr/local/hive`.

Now, we can execute a select query to check whether the data is correct:

```
select * from employee;
```

You should see this output:

```
16      john
17      robert
18      andrew
19      katty
21      tom
22      tim
```

23	james
24	paul
27	edward
29	alan
31	kerry
34	terri

Now, to store data in a sequential file format, we will create one more table and insert data from this table to the new table:

```
create table employee_seq(
id int, name string)
row format delimited
fields terminated by '|'
stored as SEQUENCEFILE;
```

This will create a table in Hive that will read data in the sequential file format. Let's insert data into this table:

```
insert into employee_seq
select * from employee;
```

This will start a MapReduce program, which will read the data from the text table and write it to files in the sequential file format.

We can again verify that it's been stored properly by executing this code:

```
select * from employee_seq;
```

This will give you all the records from the sequential file.

Just to check whether the data is stored in sequential files, you can check the HDFS file directly, which gives you unreadable text on your screen:

```
hadoop fs -cat /user/hive/warehouse/employee_seq/000000_0
```

How it works...

A sequential file is a flat file consisting of key value pairs. It is one of the most commonly used file formats in the Hadoop ecosystem. It's worth noting that the temporary output of maps is stored in the sequential file format. The sequential file provides a writer, reader, and sorter classes to read, write, and sort data. There are three types of sequential files:

▸ Uncompressed key value records

▸ Record compressed key value records, where only values are compressed

▶ Block compressed key value records, where keys and values are stored in blocks, and the blocks are compressed.

You can select the type of sequential file you want by setting the following property in either `mapred-site.xml`, `hive-site.xml`, or setting it before a job or query execution:

```
<property>
    <name>mapred.output.compression.type</name>
    <value>BLOCK</value>
    <description>If the job outputs are to compressed as
SequenceFiles, how should they be compressed? Should be one of NONE,
RECORD or BLOCK.
    </description>
</property>
```

This way, you can use sequential files to store your data. Processing these files is the same as processing any other Hive query.

Storing and processing Hive data in the RC file format

I'm sure that most of the time, you would have created Hive tables and stored data in a text format; in this recipe, we are going to store data in RC files.

Getting ready

To perform this recipe, you should have a running Hadoop cluster as well as the latest version of Hive installed on it. Here, I am going to use Hive 1.2.1.

How to do it...

Hive 1.2.1 supports different types of files, which help process data in a fast manner. In this recipe, we are going to use RC files to store data in Hive. To store data in RC files, we first need to create a Hive table that stores this data in a textual format. We will use the same table that we created in the first recipe.

Creating a table to store `RCFILE` is very easy, as shown here:

```
create table employee_rc(
id int, name string)
row format delimited
fields terminated by '|'
stored as RCFILE;
```

To insert data into the table from our text table, we need to execute the following query, which would start the MapReduce program that reads the data from one table in order to write it using the `RCFILE` writer:

```
insert into table employee_rc
select * from employee;
```

We can verify the data import by selecting the records from the table and displaying it on the console:

```
select * from employee_rc;
```

We can also look at the actual file stored in the Hive warehouse folder, which won't be as readable:

```
hadoop fs -cat /user/hive/warehouse/employee_rc/000000_0
```

How it works...

RC files are Record Columnar files that are flat and store the data in binary key value pairs, which is similar to sequence files. An RC file stores records in a columnar manner. Let's assume that we have the following table data:

C1	C2	C3	C4
1	2	3	4
5	6	7	8
9	10	11	12
13	14	15	16
17	18	19	20

To serialize this data, it first horizontally partitions the data into multiple row groups, which looks like this:

Row group 1:

C1	C2	C3	C4
1	2	3	4
5	6	7	8
9	10	11	12

Row group 2:

C1	C2	C3	C4
13	14	15	16
17	18	19	20

Next, it partitions the data within the row group vertically similar to a column store:

Row group 1:

1;5;9

2;6;10

3;7;11

4;8;12

Row group 2

13;17

14;18

15;19

16;20

Within row groups, columns are compressed to reduce the storage.

These file storages are more efficient when a query only requires a subset of columns as the output at which time, it only reads the required output, whereas in a row store, it needs to scan the complete row itself, which consumes more I/O. This way, we can store the retrieved data more efficiently using the RC file.

Storing and processing Hive data in the ORC file format

I'm sure that most of the time, you would have created Hive tables and stored data in a text format; in this recipe, we are going store data in ORC files.

Getting ready

To perform this recipe, you should have a running Hadoop cluster as well as the latest version of Hive installed on it. Here, I am going to use Hive 1.2.1.

How to do it...

Hive 1.2.1 supports different types of files, which help process data in a fast manner. In this recipe, we are going to use ORC files to store data in Hive. To store the data in ORC files, we first need to create a Hive table that stores the data in a textual format. We will use the same table that we created in the first recipe.

Creating a table to store ORCFILE is very easy, as shown here:

```
create table employee_orc(
id int, name string)
row format delimited
fields terminated by '|'
stored as ORC;
```

To insert data into the table from our text table, we need to execute the following query, which would start the Map Reduce program that reads the data from one table in order to write it using the ORC writer:

```
insert into table employee_orc
select * from employee;
```

We can verify the data import by selecting the records from the table and displaying it in the console:

```
select * from employee_orc;
```

We can also look at the actual file stored in the Hive warehouse folder, which won't be as readable:

```
hadoop fs -cat /user/hive/warehouse/employee_orc/000000_0
```

How it works...

ORC files stand for Optimized Record Columnar files, which are specially designed to improve data reading, writing, and processing in Hadoop-based systems. An ORC file will give you the following advantages over other file formats such as RC and sequential:

- ▶ A single file as the output of each task
- ▶ Supports data types such as date and time, decimals and complex types, and so on
- ▶ Lightweight indexes that are included in the file itself
- ▶ Concurrent reads of the same file using individual RecordReaders
- ▶ It's able to scan files without scanning for markers
- ▶ Metadata is stored using Protocol Buffers, which help add and remove fields

The data storage, partitions, and so on are the same as the RC file, but apart from this, it also contains additional fields/information that help achieve the preceding advantages over other files.

The ORC file contains groups of row data, which are called stripes. The default size of each stripe is 250MB; this size enables the efficient reading of data from HDFS. The auxiliary information is kept in a file footer. It contains information like the number of stripes in a file, rows per stripe, and each column's data type. It also contains column-level aggregations such as count, min, max, and sum.

Here's the ORC file structure:

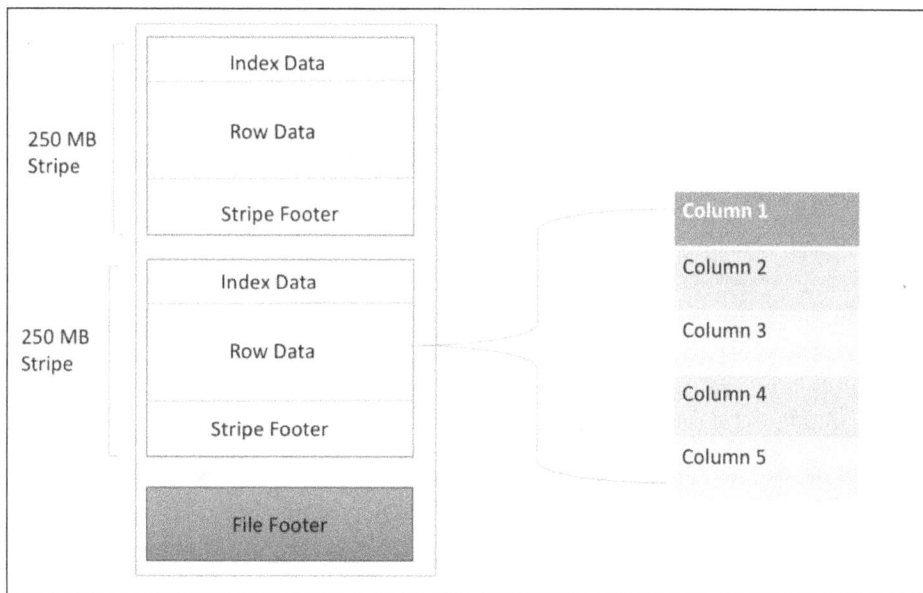

Storing and processing Hive data in the Parquet file format

I'm sure that most of the time, you would have created Hive tables and stored data in a text format; in this recipe, we are going to learn how to store data in PARQUET files.

Getting ready

To perform this recipe, you should have a running Hadoop cluster as well as the latest version of Hive installed on it. Here, I am going to use Hive 1.2.1.

How to do it...

Hive 1.2.1 supports various types of files, which help process data more efficiently. Parquet is an ecosystem-wide accepted file format and can be used in Hive, Map Reduce, Pig, Impala, and so on. To store the data in Parquet files, we first need to create one Hive table, which will store the data in a textual format. We will use the same table that we created in the first recipe.

Creating a table to store Parquet is very easy, as shown here:

```
create table employee_par(
id int, name string)
row format delimited
fields terminated by '|'
stored as PARQUET;
```

To insert data into the table from our text table, we need to execute the following query, which would start the Map Reduce program so that it reads the data from one table in order to write it using the ORC writer:

```
insert into table employee_par
select * from employee;
```

We can verify the data import by selecting the records from the table and displaying it in the console:

```
select * from employee_par;
```

We can also take a look at the actual file stored in the Hive warehouse folder, which will not be as readable:

```
hadoop fs -cat /user/hive/warehouse/employee_par/000000_0
```

How it works...

Parquet files were designed keeping in mind the best compressed and columnar data files. They are built to support very efficient compressions and encoding schemes. A lot of projects have demonstrated the impact of efficient encoding and compression schemes. Parquet allows us to specify the compressions scheme per column level. It is also built to accommodate new compression and encoding schemes for future needs and extensibility. A detailed description of the Parquet storage format is available at https://parquet.apache.org/documentation/latest/.

Performing FILTER By queries in Pig

After going through the various file formats that we can use to store data in HDFS, it's time to take a look at how to execute various operations in Pig. Pig is a data flow language and works in the same way as Hive by transforming the instructions given in Pig Latin to Map Reduce programs.

Getting ready

To perform this recipe, you should have a running Hadoop cluster as well as the latest version of Pig installed on it. Here, I am going to use Pig 0.15. In case you don't have the installation already, you can refer to `https://pig.apache.org/docs/r0.15.0/start.html#Pig+Setup`.

How to do it...

In this recipe, you will learn how to use `FILTER BY` in the Pig script. To do so, let's assume that we have an employee dataset that is stored in the following format (ID, name, department, and salary):

```
1       Tanmay ENGINEERING    5000
2       Sneha  PRODUCTION     8000
3       Sakalya        ENGINEERING   7000
4       Avinash        SALES  6000
5       Manisha        SALES  5700
6       Vinit  FINANCE        6200
```

Here the columns are delimited by \+t (*Tab*).

Now, let's put this data into HDFS and load it into Pig bag:

```
hadoop fs -mkdir /pig/emps_data
hadoop fs -put emps.txt /pig/emps_data
```

Apart from regular daemons, Pig needs one more daemon to be running on Hadoop called a Job History Server. If you have not started it earlier, execute the following command:

```
/usr/local/hadoop/sbin/mr-jobhistory-daemon.sh start historyserver
```

Start the Pig interactive shell to perform the processing. Pig's shell is called grunt. Now, let's load the data we have put in HDFS into one bag, say `emps`:

```
emps = LOAD '/pig/emps_data/emps.txt' AS (id, name, dept, salary);
```

This will load the data into the `emps` bag through the columns, as shown in the preceding command. The default delimiter is \+t (*Tab*).

Next, we filter some databases on the basis of salary and load into a new bag called `rich`:

```
rich = FILTER emps BY salary > 6000;
```

Pig scripts are lazy executors, which means that unless they don't get any actionable command, Pig will keep on stacking up the instructions. In order to perform the processing, we need to provide an actionable command, such as DUMP, which asks Pig to print the tuples of the bag in the terminal:

```
DUMP rich;
```

This will invoke the Map Reduce job as long as all the commands are received by grunt. On completion, you should be able to see results on your screen like this:

```
(2,Sneha,PRODUCTION,8000)

(3,Sakalya,ENGINEERING,7000)

(6,Vinit,FINANCE,6200)
```

How it works...

Pig has some very interesting terminology. In Pig, an item is called an Atom. A collection of Atoms is called a tuple. Collections of tuples are called bags. When we load data into a bag, we don't always need to provide data types for the atoms unlike Hive. Depending on the actions submitted by users, grunt explicitly casts the data into specific data types. It also informs the user that it has performed the type casting. When we use the FILTER BY command in a Pig script, it converts it into a Map Reduce program where the filtering logic is mostly applied in a mapper function.

After map, only those records are sent to reducers that are in line with the filter criteria. This way, we can filter out things we wish to.

Performing Group By queries in Pig

In this recipe, we will use the Group By operator in Pig scripts to get the desired output.

Getting ready

To perform this recipe, you should have a running Hadoop cluster as well as the latest version of Pig installed on it.

How to do it...

Group By is a very useful operator for data analysis. Pig supports this operator so that we can perform aggregations at the group level. Take the same data that we used in the previous recipe where we have this employee dataset:

```
1       Tanmay ENGINEERING    5000
2       Sneha  PRODUCTION     8000
3       Sakalya      ENGINEERING   7000
4       Avinash      SALES  6000
5       Manisha      SALES  5700
6       Vinit  FINANCE        6200
```

First of all, load the data into HDFS:

```
hadoop fs -mkdir /pig/emps_data
hadoop fs -put emps.txt /pig/emps_data
```

Next, we load the data into a bag called emps, and then perform the Group By operation on this data by the department:

```
emps = LOAD '/pig/emps_data/emps.txt' AS (id, name, dept, salary);
by_dept = GROUP emps BY dept;
DUMP by_dept;
```

This will start a MapReduce job, which groups tuples by the department. As a result, you will see these details on your screen:

```
(SALES,{(5,Manisha,SALES,5700),(4,Avinash,SALES,6000)})
(FINANCE,{(6,Vinit,FINANCE,6200)})
(PRODUCTION,{(2,Sneha,PRODUCTION,8000)})
(ENGINEERING,{(3,Sakalya,ENGINEERING,7000),(1,Tanmay,ENGINEERI
NG,5000)})
```

We can also get the count of the employees by executing the following query:

```
dept_counts = FOREACH by_dept GENERATE
group as dept,
COUNT(emps);
DUMP dept_counts;
```

Use the `aggregation` function called `count` to count the number of employees per department. You will see the following results on completion:

```
(SALES,2)
(FINANCE,1)
(PRODUCTION,1)
(ENGINEERING,2)
```

We can also perform Group By on multiple attributes together. We just need to specify the attribute name one by one after the `by` clause.

How it works...

Pig converts the actions provided in the pig script form into MapReduce jobs. To perform Group By, it first maps the data by the key and then reduces the records with the help of this key. The group operator groups together all the tuples by the key. If the `by` clause has multiple keys, then the group key will be a tuple. You can get more information about the Group operator at `https://pig.apache.org/docs/r0.7.0/piglatin_ref2.html#GROUP`.

Performing Order By queries in Pig

In this recipe, we will use the Order By operator in Pig scripts to get the desired output.

Getting ready

To perform this recipe, you should have a running Hadoop cluster as well as the latest version of Pig installed on it.

How to do it..

Order By is a very useful operator for data analysis when it comes to sequencing data records based on their values for certain attributes. In order to sequence the records in the proper order, Pig supports Order By.

To learn its usage, we will use the dataset that we took a look at in the previous recipe; in case you don't have the employee dataset, you can perform the following actions.

First of all, load the data in HDFS:

```
hadoop fs -mkdir /pig/emps_data
hadoop fs -put emps.txt /pig/emps_data
```

Next, we load data into a bag called `emps`, and then perform the Order By operation on this data on the basis of salary:

```
emps = LOAD '/pig/emps_data/emps.txt' AS (id, name, dept, salary);
```

Next, we will sequence the data by salary. We can also specify the order type, that is, whether it should be in ascending or descending form:

```
sorted_emps = ORDER emps by salary DESC;
DUMP sorted_emps;
```

At the end of the execution, you will see the following results:

```
(2,Sneha,PRODUCTION,8000)
```

```
(3,Sakalya,ENGINEERING,7000)
```

```
(6,Vinit,FINANCE,6200)
```

```
(4,Avinash,SALES,6000)
```

```
(5,Manisha,SALES,5700)
```

```
(1,Tanmay,ENGINEERING,5000)
```

How it works...

Pig converts the actions provided in the Pig script form into MapReduce jobs. When we execute the order through this command, a MapReduce job will get invoked in order to sort the data on the basis of the provided attribute. Pig performs a natural sort on the attribute, that is, here, we need to order employees by their salary. Therefore, the MapReduce job will get triggered so that it can sort the salary, which is of the data type integer. Similarly, if we order the record by a string, it sequences the string by its natural order.

Performing JOINS in Pig

In this recipe, we will learn how to perform various joins in Pig in order to join datasets.

Getting ready

To perform this recipe, you should have a running Hadoop cluster as well as the latest version of Pig installed on it.

How to do it...

JOIN operations are very famous in SQL. Pig Latin also supports joining datasets based on a common attribute between them. Pig supports both Inner and Outer joins. Let's understand these syntaxes one by one.

In order to learn about Joins in Pig, we'll need two datasets. The first one is the employee dataset, which we have been using in earlier recipes, the second is the ID location dataset, which contains information about the ID of an employee and their location.

The employee dataset will look like this:

```
1       Tanmay ENGINEERING   5000
2       Sneha  PRODUCTION    8000
3       Sakalya        ENGINEERING   7000
4       Avinash        SALES  6000
5       Manisha        SALES  5700
6       Vinit  FINANCE       6200
```

The ID location dataset will look like this:

```
1       Pune
2       London
3       Mumbai
4       Pune
```

Like the emps data, we also loaded the ID locations data in HDFS and then into the id_locations bag:

hadoop fs -put id_locations /pig/emps_data

On grunt:

```
id_location = load '/pig/emps_data/id_locations' AS (emp_id,
location);
```

Now, to perform inner joins on these datasets, we'll execute the following command:

```
emps_location = JOIN emps BY id, id_location BY emp_id;
DUMP emps_location;
```

As result, you will get the following displayed on your screen:

```
(1,Tanmay,ENGINEERING,5000,1,Pune)
(2,Sneha,PRODUCTION,8000,2,London)
(3,Sakalya,ENGINEERING,7000,3,Mumbai)
(4,Avinash,SALES,6000,4,Pune)
```

As this is the inner join, only matching ID records will make it to the final results.

Next, we can execute OUTER Joins on the same dataset; to perform the LEFT OUTER join, we execute the following command:

```
emps_location_left_outer = JOIN emps BY id LEFT OUTER, id_location BY
emp_id;
DUMP emps_location_left_outer;
```

On successful execution, you will see the following results:

```
(1,Tanmay,ENGINEERING,5000,1,Pune)

(2,Sneha,PRODUCTION,8000,2,London)

(3,Sakalya,ENGINEERING,7000,3,Mumbai)

(4,Avinash,SALES,6000,4,Pune)

(5,Manisha,SALES,5700,,)

(6,Vinit,FINANCE,6200,,)
```

Here, all records from the LHS of the command will make it to the final table, and all the nonmatching records will be kept blank.

Similarly, we can perform RIGHT OUTER and FULL OUTER joins as well.

We can also specify the type of specialized joins supported by Pig, that is, Replicated Joins, Skewed Joins, and Merge Joins:

```
emps_location_left_outer = JOIN emps BY id LEFT OUTER, id_location BY
emp_id using 'replicated';

DUMP emps_location_left_outer;
```

The results are the same but Pig performs certain optimizations when we mention these types. Similarly, we can use skewed and merge joins as well.

How it works

Pig converts the actions provided in the Pig script form into Map Reduce jobs. In the previous chapter, we spoke about how to write a Map Reduce program to perform joins. When we execute the JOIN operation, Pig converts it into a Map Reduce job.

To perform optimizations while executing JOINS in pig, we can specify the join type as a replicated, skewed, or merge join. Let's understand what these joins mean.

Replicated Joins

Replicated joins are fragmented joins in which a piece of data is taken in memory and joined with other sets of data in a map function. These joins can only be performed on the Left Outer join. Having data in the memory helps reduce IO disk seeks and provides optimization during executions.

> You can read more about Replicated Joins at `https://pig.apache.org/docs/r0.11.1/perf.html#replicated-joins`.

Skewed Joins

Parallel joins can be vulnerable to any skews in data. If the data is skewed enough, it might encounter some issues when balancing data parts during executions. To avoid this, skewed joins compute a histogram of key spaces and use this information to allocate reducers for a given key. Skewed joins only have certain conditions: first, currently, a skewed join can only be performed on two tables and not more than that at one go, second, it does not address uneven data balancing across reducers; it makes sure that tasks are executed slowly rather than failing them.

> You can read more about skewed joins at `https://pig.apache.org/docs/r0.11.1/perf.html#skewed-joins`.

Merge Joins

Joins are beneficial when they are performed in the map phase of a Map Reduce program. Pig supports merge joins, which work with presorted data. Here, the idea is to gain performance benefits by performing joins in the map phase and avoid sending huge amounts of data through the sort and shuffle phase.

> You can read more about merge joins at
> `https://pig.apache.org/docs/r0.11.1/perf.html#merge-joins`.

Writing a user-defined function in Pig

In this recipe, we will learn how to write user-defined functions (UDFs) in order to have our own custom filters.

Getting ready

To perform this recipe, you should have a running Hadoop cluster as well as the latest version of Pig installed on it. We will also need an IDE, such as Eclipse, to write the Java class.

How to do it...

In this recipe, we are going to write user-defined functions for the dataset we have been considering in this chapter. Our dataset is an employee dataset, so let's assume that we want to convert all the names present in our dataset into uppercase. To do this, we will write a user-defined function to convert the lowercase letters into uppercase letters.

Writing a UDF is very simple: we need to write a class that extends the `EvalFunc` Pig class. In order to have this and other Hadoop classes in our class path, first of all, we need to create a maven project, and add the following dependencies to the `POM.xml` project:

```xml
<dependency>
    <groupId>org.apache.pig</groupId>
    <artifactId>pig</artifactId>
    <version>0.15.0</version>
</dependency>
<dependency>
    <groupId>org.apache.hadoop</groupId>
    <artifactId>hadoop-mapreduce-client-core</artifactId>
    <version>2.7.1</version>
</dependency>
<dependency>
    <groupId>org.apache.hadoop</groupId>
    <artifactId>hadoop-common</artifactId>
    <version>2.7.1</version>
</dependency>
```

Now, we write a class that extends the `EvalFunc` class and overwrites the `exec` method in it:

```java
package com.demo.pig.udf;

import java.io.IOException;

import org.apache.pig.EvalFunc;
import org.apache.pig.data.DataByteArray;
import org.apache.pig.data.Tuple;


/**
 * Used Defined Function in Pig to covert given string argument into
Upper Case
 *
 */
public class ToUpper extends EvalFunc<String> {
```

```
        /**
         * Pig hands over the tuple instead of specific arguement, we need
    to get
         * the specific attribute from tuple by calling tuple.get() method
         *
         */
        @Override
        public String exec(Tuple input) throws IOException {
            if (null == input || input.size() == 0) {
                return null;
            }
            try {
                DataByteArray name = (DataByteArray) input.get(1);
                return name.toString().toUpperCase();

            } catch (Exception e) {
                throw new IOException("Caught exception while processing
    ", e);
            }

        }

    }
```

In the `exec` method, we get a complete tuple, and we need to convert the name column, which is at index 1 in our tuple. By default, if we don't specify any data type while loading data into the bag, the data type is assumed to be `DataByteArray`. So, we simply extract it and convert it into uppercase and return the converted string.

Now, we build our maven project to create a JAR of this implementation. Once the JAR is ready, we copy it to the Hadoop cluster and do the following things in order to use this UDF:

REGISTER ToUpperUDF-1.0.jar;

emps_upper = FOREACH emps GENERATE com.demo.pig.udf.ToUpper(*);

DUMP emps_upper;

In the first statement, we register the UDF jar with Pig. Next, we create a new bag, which would have converted the uppercase names from our previous `emps` bag. To start the execution, we DUMP the values in `emps_upper`.

Once the execution is complete, we will see the following results:

(TANMAY)

(SNEHA)

(SAKALYA)

(AVINASH)

(MANISHA)

(VINIT)

How it works...

Whenever we register a function in Pig, we include the implementation in the Pig class path. So, whenever the UDF class is mentioned, Pig looks for this class in its class path. If the proper name is provided at the time of execution, Pig will send the tuples to the respective implementation and get back the returned results.

There's more...

Similar to EvalFunc, we can also write FilterFunc, which can be used to filter out tuples based on certain values of the tuple. Here is an example function that filters out ENGINEERING department employees from the dataset:

```
package com.demo.pig.udf;

import java.io.IOException;

import org.apache.pig.FilterFunc;
import org.apache.pig.data.DataByteArray;
import org.apache.pig.data.Tuple;

public class EngFilter extends FilterFunc {

    @Override
    public Boolean exec(Tuple input) throws IOException {
        if (null == input || input.size() == 0) {
            return false;
        }
        try {
            DataByteArray name = (DataByteArray) input.get(2);
            if (name.toString().equalsIgnoreCase("ENGINEERING")) {
                return true;
            } else {
                return false;
            }

        } catch (Exception e) {
            throw new IOException("Caught exception while processing
", e);
        }
    }

}
```

Here, we check whether the department is engineering and only then return `true`, else we return `false`. Now, we build the jar and execute it using this filter in the following way:

```
REGISTER udfs-1.0.jar;
emps_eng = FILTER emps BY com.demo.pig.udf.EngFilter(*);
DUMP emps_eng;
```

At the end of the execution, you will see results like these:

```
(1,Tanmay,ENGINEERING,5000)
```

```
(3,Sakalya,ENGINEERING,7000)
```

Analyzing web log data using Pig

In this recipe, we will learn how to use Pig scripts to analyze web log data.

Getting ready

To perform this recipe, you should have a running Hadoop cluster as well as the latest version of Pig installed on it.

How to do it...

In the previous chapter, we saw how to analyze web logs using the MapReduce program. In this recipe, we are going to take a look at how to use Pig scripts to analyze web log data. Let's consider two use cases:

Here is a sample of web log data:

```
106.208.17.105 - - [12/Nov/2015:21:20:32 -0800] "GET /tutorials/
mapreduce/advanced-map-reduce-examples-1.html HTTP/1.1" 200 0
"https://www.google.co.in/" "Mozilla/5.0 (Windows NT 6.3; WOW64)
AppleWebKit/537.36 (KHTML, like Gecko) Chrome/46.0.2490.86 Safari/537.36"

60.250.32.153 - - [12/Nov/2015:21:42:14 -0800] "GET /tutorials/
elasticsearch/install-elasticsearch-kibana-logstash-on-windows.html
HTTP/1.1" 304 0 - "Mozilla/5.0 (Windows NT 6.1; WOW64) AppleWebKit/537.36
(KHTML, like Gecko) Chrome/46.0.2490.86 Safari/537.36"

49.49.250.23 - - [12/Nov/2015:21:40:56 -0800] "GET /tutorials/hadoop/
images/internals-of-hdfs-file-read-operations/HDFS_Read_Write.png
HTTP/1.1" 200 0 "http://hadooptutorials.co.in/tutorials/spark/install-
apache-spark-on-ubuntu.html" "Mozilla/5.0 (Windows NT 10.0; WOW64;
Trident/7.0; Touch; LCTE; rv:11.0) like Gecko"
```

```
60.250.32.153 - - [12/Nov/2015:21:36:01 -0800] "GET /tutorials/
elasticsearch/install-elasticsearch-kibana-logstash-on-windows.html
HTTP/1.1" 200 0 - "Mozilla/5.0 (Windows NT 6.1; WOW64) AppleWebKit/537.36
(KHTML, like Gecko) Chrome/46.0.2490.86 Safari/537.36"

91.200.12.136 - - [12/Nov/2015:21:30:14 -0800] "GET /tutorials/hadoop/
hadoop-fundamentals.html HTTP/1.1" 200 0 "http://hadooptutorials.co.in/
tutorials/hadoop/hadoop-fundamentals.html" "Mozilla/5.0 (Windows NT 6.1)
AppleWebKit/537.36 (KHTML, like Gecko) Chrome/45.0.2454.99 Safari/537.36"
```

These logs are formatted in the following manner:

- %h is the remote host (that is, the IP client)
- %l is the identity of the user determined by an identifier (this is not usually used since it's not reliable)
- %u is the username determined by the HTTP authentication
- %t is the time taken by the server to finish processing a request
- %r is the request line from a client ("GET / HTTP/1.0")
- %>s is the status code sent from a server to a client (200, 404, and so on)
- %b is the size of the response to a client (in bytes)
- The referrer is the page that is linked to the URL
- The user agent is a browser identification string

Now, let's load this data into the bag and start analyzing it:

```
hadoop fs -mkdir /data
hadoop fs -put web_log.tx /data
```

In grunt, we start loading this data into a bag:

```
raw_logs = LOAD '/data/web_log.txt' USING TextLoader AS (line:chararray);
```

This way, we can load each web load as a single line. Next, we write regex, which parses the data into respective attributes:

```
logs_base = FOREACH raw_logs GENERATE FLATTEN (REGEX_EXTRACT_
ALL(line,'^(\\S+) (\\S+) (\\S+) \\[([\\w:/]+\\s[+\\-]\\d{4})\\] "(.+?)"
(\\S+) (\\S+) "([^"]*)" "([^"]*)"') ) AS (ip: chararray, id: chararray,
user: chararray, time: chararray, request: chararray, status: int, bytes_
string: chararray, referrer: chararray, browser: chararray);
```

Now, we need to find the referrer sites from which we are getting the most traffic. To do this, we execute the following commands:

```
by_referrer = GROUP logs_base BY referrer

referrer_counts = FOREACH by_referrer GENERATE
group as referrer,
COUNT(logs_base);

DUMP referrer_counts;
```

On successful completion, we will see these results:

```
(https://www.google.co.in/,1)
(http://hadooptutorials.co.in/tutorials/hadoop/hadoop-fundamentals.
html,1)
(http://hadooptutorials.co.in/tutorials/spark/install-apache-spark-on-
ubuntu.html,1)
(,0)
```

Next, we can find the requests that have resulted into some errors. Here, an error could be any request whose status is 4XX or 5XX. Now, we write a filter function to execute this:

```
package com.demo.pig.udf;

import java.io.IOException;

import org.apache.pig.FilterFunc;
import org.apache.pig.data.Tuple;

public class ErrorFilter extends FilterFunc {

    @Override
    public Boolean exec(Tuple input) throws IOException {
        if (null == input || input.size() == 0) {
            return false;
        }
        try {
            String statusStr = (String) input.get(5);
            if (null == statusStr){
                return false;
            }
            int status = Integer.parseInt(statusStr);
            if (status <= 400 && status >= 505) {
                return true;
```

```
            } else {
                return false;
            }

        } catch (Exception e) {
            throw new IOException("Caught exception while processing
    ", e);
        }
      }
    }
```

We create a jar of this class and copy it in the Hadoop cluster. We'll execute the following to get the web logs with errors:

```
REGISTER udfs-1.0.jar ;
log_base_error = FILTER logs_base BY com.demo.pig.udf.ErrorFilter(*);
DUMP log_base_error;
```

How it works...

Here, we use various things that we have already taken a look at in the earlier recipes. The important thing is to parse the logs using the correct regex. If you get this right, the next few things will be a cakewalk for you.

Performing the Hbase operation in CLI

Now that we have gone through various operations in Pig and Hive, it's time to learn about some operations in Hbase. Hbase is a NoSQL database and runs on top of HDFS. In this recipe, we are going to take a look at how to perform various Hbase command-line operations.

Getting ready

To perform this recipe, you should have a Hadoop cluster running as well as the latest version of Hbase installed on it. In case you don't know how to install Hbase, here is a link you can refer to http://hbase.apache.org/book.html#quickstart.

How to do it

Once the installation is complete, execute the following command to start daemons that are related to Hbase such as Zookeeper, Hbase Master, and Hbase region server:

```
/usr/local/hbase/bin/start-hbase.sh
```

Once all the daemons are up and running, you can start the Hbase shell by executing the following code:

hbase shell

You can also open the Hbase UI in a browser. You can hit the following URL to view the Hbase UI:

`http://<hostname>:16010.`

Let's start with a command in Hbase.

1. List:

```
hbase(main):001:0> list
TABLE
test_table
1 row(s) in 0.3730 seconds

=> ["test_table"]
```

This lists the tables that are present in the key space.

2. Status:

This returns the status of the system and the number of servers:

```
hbase(main):002:0> status
1 servers, 0 dead, 3.0000 average load
```

3. Version:

This prints the running version of Hbase:

```
hbase(main):003:0> version
1.0.1.1, re1dbf4df30d214fca14908df71d038081577ea46, Sun May 17
12:34:26 PDT 2015
```

4. table_help:

This provides help for table-related operations:

```
hbase(main):004:0> table_help
```

Help for table-reference commands.

You can either create a table via `create` and then manipulate the table via commands like `put`, `get`, and so on.

See the standard help information for how to use each of these commands.

However, as of 0.96, you can also get a reference to a table, on which you can invoke commands.

For instance, you can get create a table and keep around a reference to it via:

```
hbase> t = create 't', 'cf'
```

Or, if you have already created the table, you can get a reference to it:

```
hbase> t = get_table 't'
```

You can do things like call `put` on the table:

```
hbase> t.put 'r', 'cf:q', 'v'
```

which puts a row 'r' with column family 'cf', qualifier 'q' and value 'v' into table `t`. To read the data out, you can scan the table:

```
hbase> t.scan
```

which will read all the rows in table 't'.

Essentially, any command that takes a table name can also be done via table reference. Other commands include things like: `get`, `delete`, `deleteall.`, `get_all_columns`, `get_counter`, `count`, `incr`. These functions, along with the standard `JRuby` object methods are also available via tab completion.

For more information on how to use each of these commands, you can also just type:

```
hbase> t.help 'scan'
```

which will output more information on how to use that command.

You can also perform general admin actions directly on `table`; `things` such as `enable`, `disable`, `flush`, and `drop` just by typing this:

```
hbase> t.enable
hbase> t.flush
hbase> t.disable
hbase> t.drop
```

Note that after dropping a table, your reference to it becomes useless and further usage is undefined (and not recommended).

5. Creating a table:

   Now, let's create a table called `employee`, which contains two column families: one to store `personal details` and the other to store `professional details`:

   ```
   hbase(main):005:0> create 'emp', 'personal details', 'professional details';
   ```

6. Describe the table:

   We can describe the created table to know about its details:

   ```
   hbase(main):017:0> describe 'emp'
   Table emp is ENABLED
   emp
   ```

```
COLUMN FAMILIES DESCRIPTION
{NAME => 'personal details', DATA_BLOCK_ENCODING => 'NONE',
BLOOMFILTER => 'ROW', REPLICATION_SCOPE => '0', VERSIONS => '1',
COMPRESSION => 'NONE'
, MIN_VERSIONS => '0', TTL => 'FOREVER', KEEP_DELETED_CELLS =>
'FALSE', BLOCKSIZE => '65536', IN_MEMORY => 'false', BLOCKCACHE =>
'true'}
{NAME => 'professional details', DATA_BLOCK_ENCODING => 'NONE',
BLOOMFILTER => 'ROW', REPLICATION_SCOPE => '0', VERSIONS => '1',
COMPRESSION => 'N
ONE', MIN_VERSIONS => '0', TTL => 'FOREVER', KEEP_DELETED_CELLS =>
'FALSE', BLOCKSIZE => '65536', IN_MEMORY => 'false', BLOCKCACHE =>
'true'}
2 row(s) in 0.0170 seconds
```

7. Inserting data into the table

   We can insert data into the tables using the `put` command, as shown here:

   ```
   hbase(main):018:0> put 'emp','1','personal details:name','Ram'
   0 row(s) in 0.0820 seconds

   hbase(main):019:0> put 'emp','1','personal
   details:location','Pune'
   0 row(s) in 0.0100 seconds

   hbase(main):020:0>
   hbase(main):021:0* put 'emp','1','professional
   details:designation','Software Engineer'
   0 row(s) in 0.0090 seconds

   hbase(main):022:0> put 'emp','1','professional
   details:salary','10000'
   0 row(s) in 0.0060 seconds
   ```

8. Viewing records:

   We can see the inserted data by using the `scan` command, as shown here:

   ```
   hbase(main):023:0> scan 'emp'
   ROW                            COLUMN+CELL
    1                             column=personal
   details:location, timestamp=1448777442105, value=Pune

    1                             column=personal
   details:name, timestamp=1448777442076, value=Ram
   ```

```
  1                                          column=professional
details:designation, timestamp=1448777442149, value=Software
Engineer
  1                                          column=professional
details:salary, timestamp=1448777442169, value=10000

1 row(s) in 0.0280 seconds
```

9. Updating the record:

   To update the record, we need to use the `put` command, as shown in the following code snippet. Here, we will be updating the salary to `12000`:

   ```
   hbase(main):024:0> put 'emp','1','professional
   details:salary','12000'
   0 row(s) in 0.0070 seconds


   hbase(main):025:0> scan 'emp'
   ROW                            COLUMN+CELL
    1                                          column=personal
   details:location, timestamp=1448777442105, value=Pune
    1                                          column=personal
   details:name, timestamp=1448777442076, value=Ram
    1                                          column=professional
   details:designation, timestamp=1448777442149, value=Software
   Engineer
    1                                          column=professional
   details:salary, timestamp=1448777689830, value=12000

   1 row(s) in 0.0110 seconds
   ```

10. Getting the record

    To get the record from Hbase, we can use the `get` command:

    ```
    hbase(main):026:0> get 'emp', '1'
    COLUMN                              CELL

     personal details:location           timestamp=1448777442105, val
    ue=Pune
     personal details:name               timestamp=1448777442076, val
    ue=Ram
     professional details:designation    timestamp=1448777442149,
    value=Software Engineer
     professional details:salary         timestamp=1448777689830,
    value=12000
    4 row(s) in 0.0240 seconds
    ```

11. Getting a specific column from the record:

    ```
    hbase(main):002:0> get 'emp', '1', { COLUMN => 'personal
    details:name'}
    COLUMN                              CELL
     personal details:name                 timestamp=1448777442076,
    value=Ram
    1 row(s) in 0.2270 seconds
    ```

12. Deleting a specific column:

    We can delete a specific column in Hbase by executing the `delete` commanding in the following manner

    ```
    hbase(main):004:0> delete 'emp', '1', 'personal details:location',
    1448777442076
    0 row(s) in 0.0430 seconds
    ```

13. Deleting a complete row:

    We can delete a complete row by using the `delete all` command.

    ```
    hbase(main):006:0> deleteall 'emp','1'
    0 row(s) in 0.0070 seconds

    hbase(main):007:0> scan 'emp'
    ROW                              COLUMN+CELL
    0 row(s) in 0.0060 seconds
    ```

14. Counting the number of rows:

    We can use the `count` command to count the number of rows in a specific table.

    ```
    hbase(main):014:0> count 'emp'
    1 row(s) in 0.0090 seconds
    => 1
    ```

15. Dropping a table.

    We can drop a table by first disabling it and then executing the dropped table:

    ```
    hbase(main):016:0> disable 'emp'
    0 row(s) in 1.2120 seconds

    hbase(main):017:0> drop 'emp'
    0 row(s) in 0.1670 seconds
    ```

How it works...

Hbase is a NoSQL database, which runs on top of HDFS. We know that HDFS is used for the batch access of data, but it cannot be used to randomly access data, whereas Hbase is used to randomly access data. It is a columnar database where we can have thousands of columns for a particular row. The following is the table structure in which we can save data:

Row Id	Personal Details		Professional Details	
EMP ID	Name	Location	Designation	Salary
1	Ram	Pune	Software Engineer	12000
2	Ramesh	Mumbai	Manager	15000
3	Radha	Delhi	QA	8000
4	Rahul	Mumbai	Test Manager	10000

In the preceding table, we have a table called `emp`, and we have two column families, personal details and professional details. Each row is identified by the row ID, which is unique for each record. Hbase consists of master and slave architecture. It has one master and multiple slaves called region servers. Each region server manages multiple regions. A table is partitioned into multiple regions across the region servers. Actual data is saved to HFile. This is a block indexed file format where data is stored into a sequence of blocks, and a separate index is maintained at the end of file. Hbase maintains the in-memory log file called HLog. This file contains the updates happening in tables. This cache is flushed periodically.

Performing Hbase operations in Java

Hbase provides a Java client with which we can perform operations similar to those performed through the command line.

Getting ready

To perform this recipe, you should have a running Hadoop cluster as well as the latest version of Hbase installed on it.

How to do it

To get started, we first need to create a maven project and add the Hbase client dependency:

```xml
<dependency>
    <groupId>org.apache.hbase</groupId>
    <artifactId>hbase-client</artifactId>
    <version>1.0.1.1</version>
</dependency>
```

Now, we write a Java class, which uses APIs from the Hbase client to perform various operations:

```
package com.demo.hbase.hbase.client;

import java.io.IOException;

import org.apache.hadoop.conf.Configuration;
import org.apache.hadoop.hbase.HBaseConfiguration;
import org.apache.hadoop.hbase.HColumnDescriptor;
import org.apache.hadoop.hbase.HTableDescriptor;
import org.apache.hadoop.hbase.TableName;
import org.apache.hadoop.hbase.client.Admin;
import org.apache.hadoop.hbase.client.Connection;
import org.apache.hadoop.hbase.client.ConnectionFactory;
import org.apache.hadoop.hbase.client.Get;
import org.apache.hadoop.hbase.client.HTable;
import org.apache.hadoop.hbase.client.Put;
import org.apache.hadoop.hbase.client.Result;
import org.apache.hadoop.hbase.util.Bytes;

public class JavaHbase {

    public static void main(String args[]) throws IOException {

        // Create connection and admin client
        Configuration config = HBaseConfiguration.create();
        Connection connection = ConnectionFactory.
createConnection(config);
        Admin admin = connection.getAdmin();

        // Provide table description
        HTableDescriptor descriptor = new HTableDescriptor(TableName.
valueOf("emp"));
        descriptor.addFamily(new HColumnDescriptor("personal
details"));
        descriptor.addFamily(new HColumnDescriptor("professional
details"));
        // create table
        admin.createTable(descriptor);
        System.out.println("Table Created");

        // Insert data
        Put name = new Put(Bytes.toBytes("1"));
```

```
        name.addColumn(Bytes.toBytes("personal details"), Bytes.
toBytes("name"), Bytes.toBytes("Ram"));

        HTable table = new HTable(config, "emp");
        table.put(name);

        System.out.println("Added data into Table");

        // Get data
        Get g = new Get(Bytes.toBytes("1"));
        Result r = table.get(g);
        byte[] value = r.getValue(Bytes.toBytes("personal details"),
Bytes.toBytes("name"));
        System.out.println("Fetched Data:" + value.toString());

    }
}
```

Now, we create a runnable jar, and execute it in the following manner:

```
java -cp hbase-client-1.0-jar-with-dependencies.jar com.demo.hbase.
hbase.client.JavaHbase
```

How it works...

Hbase provides clients in various languages such as Java, Scala, and C/C++. You can choose a language of your choice to handle data in Hbase remotely. You don't need anything special to use those APIs.

Executing the MapReduce programming with an Hbase Table

In this recipe, we are going to see how to use Hbase data as input to the MapReduce program.

Getting ready

To perform this recipe, you should have a running Hadoop cluster as well as the latest version of Hbase installed on it. You will also need an IDE such as Eclipse.

How to do it

To get started, we first need to create a maven project, and add the following dependencies to it:

```
<dependency>
    <groupId>org.apache.hbase</groupId>
    <artifactId>hbase-client</artifactId>
    <version>1.0.1.1</version>
</dependency>
<dependency>
    <groupId>org.apache.hadoop</groupId>
    <artifactId>hadoop-mapreduce-client-core</artifactId>
    <version>2.7.1</version>
</dependency>
<dependency>
    <groupId>org.apache.hadoop</groupId>
    <artifactId>hadoop-common</artifactId>
    <version>2.7.1</version>
</dependency>
<dependency>
    <groupId>org.apache.hbase</groupId>
    <artifactId>hbase-server</artifactId>
    <version>1.0.1.1</version>
</dependency>
```

Next, we write a driver class, which uses `TableMapReduceUtils`. In this example, we will be reading data from one Hbase table and write it to another Hbase table:

```
public class HbaseExample {
    public static void main(String[] args) throws Exception {
        Configuration config = HBaseConfiguration.create();
        Job job = Job.getInstance(config, "Hbase Example");
        job.setJarByClass(HbaseExample.class);

        Scan scan = new Scan();
        scan.setCaching(500);
        scan.setCacheBlocks(false);

        TableMapReduceUtil.initTableMapperJob("emp", scan, MyMapper.
class, Text.class, IntWritable.class, job);
        TableMapReduceUtil.initTableReducerJob("new_emp",
MyTableReducer.class, job);
        job.setNumReduceTasks(1);
```

```
        boolean b = job.waitForCompletion(true);
        if (!b) {
            throw new IOException("error with job!");
        }
    }
}
```

We write a `Mapper` class, which reads data from the Hbase table:

```
public static class MyMapper extends TableMapper<Text, IntWritable> {

        private final IntWritable ONE = new IntWritable(1);
        private Text text = new Text();

        public void map(ImmutableBytesWritable row, Result value,
Context context)
                throws IOException, InterruptedException {
            String val = new String(value.getValue(Bytes.
toBytes("peronsonal details"), Bytes.toBytes("name")));
            text.set(val);

            context.write(text, ONE);
        }
    }
```

Now, it's time to read the `Reducer` class, which writes each record to the new table:

```
public static class MyTableReducer extends TableReducer<Text,
IntWritable, ImmutableBytesWritable> {

        public void reduce(Text key, Iterable<IntWritable> values,
Context context)
                throws IOException, InterruptedException {
            int i = 0;
            for (IntWritable val : values) {
                i += val.get();
            }
            Put put = new Put(Bytes.toBytes(key.toString()));
            put.add(Bytes.toBytes("details"), Bytes.toBytes("count"),
Bytes.toBytes(i));

            context.write(null, put);
        }
    }
```

We build a jar out of these classes and execute them on Hadoop using the following command:

```
hadoop jar hbase-mr-1.0-jar-with-dependencies.jar com.demo.hbase.hbase.
client.HbaseExample
```

How it works

As Hbase also uses HDFS as its base to store data, it's quite easy to read that into a Map Reduce job using clients provided by Hbase. All other functionalities of Map Reduce remain the same.

5

Advanced Data Analysis Using Hive

- ▸ Processing JSON data in Hive using JSON `SerDe`
- ▸ Processing XML data in Hive using XML `SerDe`
- ▸ Processing Hive data in the Avro format
- ▸ Writing a user-defined function in Hive
- ▸ Performing table joins in Hive
- ▸ Executing map side joins in Hive
- ▸ Performing context Ngram in Hive
- ▸ Analyzing a call data record using Hive
- ▸ Performing sentiment analysis using Hive on Twitter data
- ▸ Implementing **Change Data Capture** (**CDC**) using Hive
- ▸ Inserting data in multiple tables data using Hive

Introduction

In the previous chapter, we discussed various tasks that can be performed using Hive, Pig, and Hbase. In this chapter, we are going to take a look at how to perform some advanced tasks using Hive. We will see how to analyze data in various formats such as JSON, XML, and AVRO. We will also explore how to write **User-Defined Functions** (**UDFs**) in Hive, deploy them, and use them in Hive queries. Now let's get started.

Processing JSON data in Hive using JSON SerDe

These days, JSON is a very common data structure that's used for data communication and storage. Its key value-based structure gives great flexibility in handling data. In this recipe, we are going to take a look at how to process data stored in the JSON format in Hive. Hive does not have any built-in support to handle JSON, so we will be using JSON SerDe. SerDe is a program that consists of a serializer and deserializer, which tell Hive how to read and write data.

Getting ready

To perform this recipe, you should have a running Hadoop cluster with the latest version of Hive installed on it. Here, I am using Hive 1.2.1. Apart from Hive, we also need JSON SerDe.

There are various JSON SerDe binaries available from various developers. The most popular, though, can be found at https://github.com/rcongiu/Hive-JSON-Serde.

This project contains code for JSON SerDe and is compatible with the latest version of Hive. You can either download the code and build your own JAR, or you can download the precompiled jars from https://github.com/sheetaldolas/Hive-JSON-Serde/tree/master/dist.

I am using https://github.com/sheetaldolas/Hive-JSON-Serde/blob/master/dist/json-serde-1.1.9.9-Hive1.2.jar.

Download the jar, and copy it to the node where you have Hive installed.

How to do it...

Now that we have set up our environment, let's consider a use situation where we have the JSON data with us and want to process this data using Hive. Let's say we have an e-commerce website where we have data coming in the JSON format for various products, as shown here:

```
{
    "name": "iPhone 6",
    "price": 600,
    "category": "phone",
    "color": "gold",
    "stock": 10,
    "tags": ["phone", "iphone", "cell"]
}
```

To do this, we first need to put this data in HDFS. Here is some sample data:

```
{"name":"iPhone 6", "price": 600, "category" :"phone", "color":
"gold", "stock": 10, "tags" : ["phone", "iphone", "cell"] }
{"name":"iPhone 6 plus", "price": 660, "category" :"phone", "color":
"silver", "stock": 20, "tags" : ["phone", "iphone", "cell"] }
{"name":"Samsung S6", "price": 600, "category" :"phone", "color":
"white", "stock": 10, "tags" : ["phone", "samsung", "cell"] }
{"name":"Macbook Pro", "price": 800, "category" :"computer", "color":
"silver", "stock": 8, "tags" : ["laptop", "apple"] }
{"name":"Samsung Refrigerator 13 Ltr", "price": 400, "category"
:"fridge", "color": "red", "stock": 10, "tags" : ["fridge", "samsung"]
}
```

hadoop fs -mkdir /data/products

hadoop fs -copyFromLocalproducts.json /data/products

Now let's start the Hive prompt and add the jar we downloaded earlier.

```
hive> ADD JAR json-serde-1.1.9.9-Hive1.2.jar;
Added [json-serde-1.1.9.9-Hive1.2.jar] to class path
Added resources: [json-serde-1.1.9.9-Hive1.2.jar]
```

Now, it's time to create a Hive table using JSON `SerDe`:

```
CREATE TABLE products_json (
name STRING,
price DOUBLE,
category STRING,
color STRING,
stock INT,
tags ARRAY<STRING>)
ROW FORMAT SERDE 'org.openx.data.jsonserde.JsonSerDe'
LOCATION '/data/products';
```

When using `SerDe`, we also have to use Row format `SerDe` and provide the main class for this JAR.

If everything is okay, you will get a confirmation that the Hive table has been created.

Now we can query and process this data like any other Hive query. To confirm that the data has been loaded properly, we can execute the `select` query:

```
hive> select * from products_json;
OK
iPhone 6  600.0  phone  gold   10     ["phone","iphone","cell"]
iPhone 6 plus    660.0  phone  silver 20     ["phone","iphone","cell"]
```

```
Samsung S6          600.0  phone  white  10      ["phone","samsung","cell"]
Macbook Pro         800.0  computer      silver 8       ["laptop","apple"]
Samsung Refrigerator 13 Ltr   400.0  fridge red     10
    ["fridge","samsung"]
Time taken: 0.763 seconds, Fetched: 5 row(s)
```

We can run a query to get product counts by their category, as shown here:

```
SELECT category, count(*) FROM products_json
GROUP BY category;
```

This will start a map reduce job, and on its completion, we will have results like this:

```
computer   1
fridge     1
phone      3
```

JSON SerDe supports nested JSON as well. Consider a situation where we have an attribute called a feature, as shown here:

```
{
    "name": "iPhone 6",
    "price": 600,
    "category": "phone",
    "color": "gold",
    "stock": 10,
    "tags": ["phone", "iphone", "cell"],
    "features": {
        "storage": "64GB",
        "battery": "15Hrs",
        "warranty": "1 Yr"
    }
}
```

To have this type of data, we need to update the create table statement:

```
CREATE TABLE products_json (
name STRING,
price DOUBLE,
category STRING,
color STRING,
stock INT,
tags ARRAY<STRING>,
features STRUCT<
storage:STRING,
battery:STRING,
```

```
warranty:STRING>)
ROW FORMAT SERDE 'org.openx.data.jsonserde.JsonSerDe'
LOCATION '/data/products';
```

How it works...

▸ While reading the input, Hive's execution engine first reads the records using the default `InputFormat`. `RecordReader` keeps sending one record at a time. Here, we don't provide `InputFormat`, so the default is text. The engine then invokes `Serde.deserialize()` to deserialize the record. The Hive engine also gets hold of an object inspector by invoking the `Serde.getObjectInspector()` method. The engine then passes the deserialized object and object inspector to the operators for their use. Each operator uses this deserialized object and object inspector to get data from the data structure.

> Hive also supports the writing of your own custom `SerDe`; the documentation for this can be found at—`https://cwiki.apache.org/confluence/display/Hive/DeveloperGuide#DeveloperGuide-HowtoWriteYourOwnSerDe`.

Processing XML data in Hive using XML SerDe

XML has been one of the most important data structures and has been used for quite a long time for data transfers and storage. Parsing XML data and then processing it is always a tricky task as parsing XML is one of the most costliest operations. Hive does not have any built-in support for XML data processing, but many organizations and individuals have made open source contributions to XML `SerDe`.

Getting ready

To perform this recipe, you should have a running Hadoop cluster as well as the latest version of Hive installed on it. Here, I am using Hive 1.2.1. Apart from Hive, we also need XML `SerDe`.

There are various XML `SerDe` that have been made available by open source developers. Out of these, XML `SerDe` at `https://github.com/dvasilen/Hive-XML-SerDe` is well developed and quite useful. So, we can download the jar from `http://search.maven.org/remotecontent?filepath=com/ibm/spss/hive/serde2/xml/hivexmlserde/1.0.5.3/hivexmlserde-1.0.5.3.jar`.

How to do it...

Now, let's assume that in our e-commerce project, we have data that is stored in the XML format, as follows:

```xml
<products>
    <product id="1">
        <name>iPhone 6</name>
        <category>phone</category>
        <price>600</price>
        <stock>14</stock>
        <features>
            <storage>64GB</storage>
            <battery>20Hrs</battery>
        </features>
    </product>
    <product id="2">
        <name>iPhone 6 Plus</name>
        <category>phone</category>
        <price>800</price>
        <stock>15</stock>
        <features>
            <storage>64GB</storage>
            <battery>10Hrs</battery>
        </features>
    </product>
    <product id="3">
        <name>Samsung S6</name>
        <category>phone</category>
        <price>650</price>
        <stock>12</stock>
        <features>
            <storage>16GB</storage>
            <battery>10Hrs</battery>
        </features>
    </product>
</products>
```

We will be using the XML SerDe to analyze this data. First of all, we need to start a Hive prompt and add the downloaded jar:

```
hive> ADD JAR hivexmlserde-1.0.5.3.jar;
Added [hivexmlserde-1.0.5.3.jar] to class path
Added resources: [hivexmlserde-1.0.5.3.jar]
```

Next, we'll write create a table statement, as shown here:

```
CREATE TABLE product_xml(
id STRING,
name STRING,
category STRING,
price DOUBLE,
stock BIGINT,
features map<string,string>)
ROW FORMAT SERDE 'com.ibm.spss.hive.serde2.xml.XmlSerDe'
WITH SERDEPROPERTIES (
"column.xpath.id"="/product/@id",
"column.xpath.name"="/product/name/text()",
"column.xpath.category"="/product/category/text()",
"column.xpath.price"="/product/price/text()",
"column.xpath.stock"="/product/stock/text()",
"column.xpath.features"="/product/features/*"
)
STORED AS
INPUTFORMAT 'com.ibm.spss.hive.serde2.xml.XmlInputFormat'
OUTPUTFORMAT 'org.apache.hadoop.hive.ql.io.IgnoreKeyTextOutputFormat'
TBLPROPERTIES (
"xmlinput.start"="<product id",
"xmlinput.end"="</product>"
);
```

Now that the table is created, we can load the data into this table and execute the `select` query to check whether the data is loaded properly:

```
LOAD DATA LOCAL INPATH 'products.xml' INTO TABLE product_xml;
hive> select * from product_xml;
OK
1   iPhone 6      phone   600.0  14      {"battery":"20Hrs","storage":"64G
B"}
2   iPhone 6 Plus phone   800.0  15      {"battery":"10Hrs","storage":"64G
B"}
3   Samsung S6    phone   650.0  12
      {"battery":"10Hrs","storage":"16GB"}
Time taken: 0.071 seconds, Fetched: 3 row(s)
```

We can execute various queries, such as other Hive queries, and the XML `SerDe` will automatically take care of serialization and deserialization:

```
hive> select * from product_xml
>where price > 620;
OK
```

```
2   iPhone 6 Plus phone  800.0  15    {"battery":"10Hrs","storage":"64G
B"}
3   Samsung S6    phone  650.0  12    {"battery":"10Hrs","storage":"16G
B"}
Time taken: 0.123 seconds, Fetched: 2 row(s)
```

How it works

All SerDe work in the manner that is explained in the *How it works* section of the previous recipe.

Processing Hive data in the Avro format

Avro is an evolvable schema-driven binary data format. It is hosted and maintained by the Apache Software Foundation (http://avro.apache.org/). It provides a rich data structure to store compact, fast binary data, and it relies on schemas. Avro files store data and schemas together; this helps faster reading of data as the files do not need to look for schema anywhere else. It can also be used in **Remote Procedure Calls** (**RPC**). There, the schema is transferred at the time of handshake between a client and server. In this recipe, we will take a look at how to process Avro files in Hive.

Getting ready

To perform this recipe, you should have a running Hadoop cluster as well as the latest version of Hive installed on it. Here, I am using Hive 1.2.1. Hive has built-in support for the Avro file format, so we don't need to import any third-party JARs.

How to do it...

Using Avro SerDe, we can either read data that is already in the Avro format or write new data in the Avro file. We cannot write the Avro file using an editor, so we will be using a sample file that's provided along with the Hive installation, that is, doctors.avro. This contains a list of doctors. To read the Avro data, we need to create a table in the following manner:

```
CREATE TABLE doctors(
number INT,
first_name STRING,
last_name STRING)
STORED AS AVRO;
```

Now, let's load data into this table, as shown here:

```
LOAD DATA LOCAL INPATH '/usr/local/hive/examples/files/doctors.avro'
INTO TABLE doctors;
```

We can execute the SELECT query to check whether we are able read the records:

```
hive> select * from doctors;
OK
    6  Colin  Baker
    3  Jon       Pertwee
    4  Tom       Baker
    5  Peter  Davison
    11 Matt    Smith
    1  William      Hartnell
    7  Sylvester    McCoy
    8  Paul    McGann
    2  Patrick      Troughton
    9  Christopher  Eccleston
    10 David   Tennant
    Time taken: 0.051 seconds, Fetched: 11 row(s)
```

We can execute any query just like other Hive queries in this table.

We can also write the output of a Hive query in the Avro format by creating another table, as shown here:

```
CREATE TABLE doctors_selected(
number INT,
first_name STRING,
last_name STRING)
STORED AS AVRO;
```

We import the selected data from the previous table, as shown here:

```
INSERT INTO TABLE doctors_selected
SELECT * FROM doctors where number > 5;
```

Once the map reduce execution is complete, we can take a look at the imported data:

```
hive> select * from doctors_selected;
OK
    6  Colin  Baker
    11 Matt    Smith
    7  Sylvester    McCoy
    8  Paul    McGann
    9  Christopher  Eccleston
    10 David   Tennant
    Time taken: 0.061 seconds, Fetched: 6 row(s)
```

We can also take a look at the generated file:

```
hadoop fs -ls /user/hive/warehouse/doctors_selected
    Found 1 items
    -rwxr-xr-x   1 admin1 supergroup         420 2015-12-06 12:44
    /user/hive/warehouse/doctors_selected/000000_0
```

Here the `000000_0` file is in the Avro file format.

How it works...

All `SerDe` work in a similar manner as explained in the *How it works* sections of the recipe—*Processing JSON data using Hive JSON SerDe*.

Writing a user-defined function in Hive

In the previous chapter, we talked about how to write user-defined functions in Pig; in this recipe, we are going to do the same for Hive. Hive supports the adding of temporary functions, which can be used to process data. We will be writing UDF in Java and will also create functions that can be used in data processing.

Getting ready

To perform this recipe, you should have a running Hadoop cluster as well as the latest version of Hive installed on it. Here, I am using Hive 1.2.1. We will also need the Eclipse IDE for development.

How to do it

There are various system functions that are supported by Hive, but sometimes, you will need to do something different that cannot be handled by system provided functions. To do this, we will need to write a custom function.

Take a situation where we have census data and a person's income, and we want to categorize them into three parts based on the person's income. The following is some sample data where we have the ID, name, and salary:

```
1|Tanmay|10000
2|Sneha|12000
3|Sakalya|14000
4|Ramesh|3000
5|Rahul|4000
```

```
6|Rajesh|18000
7|Ram|3000
```

Now, we will create a Hive table and load this data into the table:

```
CREATE TABLE census(
id INT,
name STRING,
salary INT)
ROW FORMAT DELIMITED
FIELDS TERMINATED BY '|'
STORED AS TEXTFILE;

LOAD DATA LOCAL INPATH 'census.txt' INTO TABLE census;
```

We can check the loaded data, as shown here:

```
hive> select * from census;
OK
    1   Tanmay 10000
    2   Sneha  12000
    3   Sakalya        14000
    4   Ramesh 3000
    5   Rahul  4000
    6   Rajesh 18000
    7   Ram    3000
    Time taken: 0.052 seconds, Fetched: 7 row(s)
```

Let's write a UDF to segregate people based on their income group. To do so, we will need to create a maven project, and add the following dependency in it:

```
<dependency>
        <groupId>org.apache.hive</groupId>
        <artifactId>hive-exec</artifactId>
        <version>1.2.1</version>
</dependency>
```

Here is the Java class that provides logic for the income group function. To write a UDF, we need to extend the UDF class from `hive-exec` jar:

```
packagecom.demo.hive.udfs;

importorg.apache.hadoop.hive.ql.exec.UDF;
importorg.apache.hadoop.io.IntWritable;
```

```
importorg.apache.hadoop.io.Text;

public class IncomeClassifier extends UDF {

    public Text evaluate(IntWritable income) {
        Text incomeGroup = new Text();
        if (income.get() <= 5000) {
            incomeGroup.set("lower");
        } else if (income.get() >= 5001 &&income.get() <= 15000) {
            incomeGroup.set("middle");
        } else if (income.get() >= 15001) {
            incomeGroup.set("upper");
        }
        returnincomeGroup;
    }
}
```

We compile this code and create a jar out of it. Now, we copy this jar to the place where Hive is installed, and do the following things to create a function:

```
LOAD DATA LOCAL INPATH 'census.txt' INTO TABLE census;
ADD JAR hive-udfs.jar
CREATE TEMPORARY FUNCTION income_group as 'com.demo.hive.udf.
IncomeClassifier';
```

Use this UDF in the following manner:

```
SELECT id, name, income_group(salary)
FROM census;
hive> SELECT id, name, income_group(salary)
> FROM census;
OK
    1   Tanmay middle
    2   Sneha  middle
    3   Sakalya        middle
    4   Ramesh lower
    5   Rahul  lower
    6   Rajesh upper
    7   Ram    lower
    Time taken: 0.058 seconds, Fetched: 7 row(s)
```

How it works...

Whenever UDF is referenced during execution, the respective class is invoked and the `evaluate` method is executed. Based on the logic provided, a value is returned. UDFs are effective till the time your session is alive. When the terminal is closed, the same UDF cannot be referenced again. If we want to do that, we need add the jar again.

Performing table joins in Hive

In the previous chapter, we talked about how to perform joins in Pig. In this recipe, we are going to take a look at how to perform joins in Hive. Hive supports various types of joins such as inner, outer, and so on.

Getting ready

To perform this recipe, you should have a running Hadoop cluster as well as the latest version of Hive installed on it. Here, I am using Hive 1.2.1.

How to do it...

To perform joins, we will need two types of datasets, which have something in common to join. Consider a situation where we have two employee tables and departments, and every employee table has a structure (ID, name, salary, and department ID) and every department table has an ID and a name. We will quickly create tables and load data into them:

```
CREATE TABLE emp(
id INT,
name STRING,
salary DOUBLE,
deptId INT)
ROW FORMAT DELIMITED
FIELDS TERMINATED BY '|'
STORED AS TEXTFILE;

LOAD DATA LOCAL INPATH 'emp.txt' INTO TABLE emp;

hive> select * from emp;
OK
1    Tanmay 3500.0 101
2    Sneha  5599.0 101
3    Avinash        6700.0 102
4    Manisha        6400.0 103
```

```
5  Sakalya       3200.0 102
6  Vinit  3200.0 105
Time taken: 0.064 seconds, Fetched: 6 row(s)
CREATE TABLE dept(
id INT,
name STRING)
ROW FORMAT DELIMITED
FIELDS TERMINATED BY '|'
STORED AS TEXTFILE;
LOAD DATA LOCAL INPATH 'dept.txt' INTO TABLE dept;

hive> select * from dept;
OK
101        Engineering
102        HR
103        Finance
104        Facilities
Time taken: 0.061 seconds, Fetched: 4 row(s)
```

Now, let's start performing various joins.

For the inner join, here is the code:

```
SELECT e.name, d.name FROM
emp e JOIN dept d
ON (e.deptId = d.id);
```

The result will look similar to the following code. The inner join only returns matching records from both tables:

```
Tanmay Engineering
Sneha  Engineering
Avinash        HR
Manisha        Finance
Sakalya        HR
```

Left outer join

The Left outer join gives all records from the left-hand side of a table and only matches records with the other table:

```
SELECT e.name, d.name FROM
emp e LEFT OUTER JOIN dept d
ON (e.deptId = d.id);
```

The results of this are as follows:

```
Tanmay      Engineering
Sneha       Engineering
Avinash     HR
Manisha     Finance
Sakalya     HR
Vinit       NULL
```

Right outer join

The right outer join gives all the records from the right-hand side of a table and only matches records from the other table:

```
SELECT e.name, d.name FROM
emp e RIGHT OUTER JOIN dept d
ON (e.deptId = d.id);
```

The results of this are as follows:

```
Tanmay      Engineering
Sneha       Engineering
Avinash     HR
Sakalya     HR
Manisha     Finance
NULL        Facilities
```

Full outer join

The full outer join gives a complete set of matching and non-matching records from both tables:

```
SELECT e.name, d.name FROM
emp e FULL OUTER JOIN dept d
ON (e.deptId = d.id);
```

The results of this are as follows:

```
Sneha       Engineering
Tanmay      Engineering
Sakalya     HR
Avinash     HR
Manisha     Finance
NULL        Facilities
Vinit       NULL
```

Left semi join

The left semi join can be used when you want columns from only one table. When compared to the inner join, it gives a similar output except that it does not return columns from the right-hand side of the table:

```
SELECT e.name, e. salary FROM
emp e LEFT SEMI JOIN dept d
ON (e.deptId = d.id);
```

The results of this are as follows:

```
Tanmay    3500.0
Sneha     5599.0
Avinash   6700.0
Manisha   6400.0
Sakalya   3200.0
```

How it works...

In every join operation, Hive will execute a Map Reduce job. In *Chapter 3*, *Mastering Map Reduce Programs*, we took a look at the code that gets implemented for various join operations. Refer to those recipes for more details.

Executing map side joins in Hive

Map side joins are special types of optimizations; Hive executes these automatically based on table sizes. In this recipe, we are going to explore map side joins in further detail.

Getting ready

To perform this recipe, you should have a running Hadoop cluster as well as the latest version of Hive installed on it. Here, I am using Hive 1.2.1.

How to do it...

To perform map joins, we need two types of datasets that have something in common to join. One dataset also has to be big, and the other has to be small in comparison. Consider a situation where we have two tables for employees and departments; the employee table has a structure (ID, name, salary, and department ID) and the department table has an ID and a name.

We will quickly create tables and load data into them:

```
CREATE TABLE emp(
id INT,
name STRING,
salary DOUBLE,
deptId INT)
ROW FORMAT DELIMITED
FIELDS TERMINATED BY '|'
STORED AS TEXTFILE;

LOAD DATA LOCAL INPATH 'emp.txt' INTO TABLE emp;

hive> select * from emp;
OK
1    Tanmay 3500.0 101
2    Sneha  5599.0 101
3    Avinash      6700.0 102
4    Manisha      6400.0 103
5    Sakalya      3200.0 102
6    Vinit 3200.0 105
Time taken: 0.064 seconds, Fetched: 6 row(s)

CREATE TABLE dept(
id INT,
name STRING)
ROW FORMAT DELIMITED
FIELDS TERMINATED BY '|'
STORED AS TEXTFILE;

LOAD DATA LOCAL INPATH 'dept.txt' INTO TABLE dept;

hive> select * from dept;
OK
101 Engineering
102 HR
103 Finance
104 Facilities
Time taken: 0.061 seconds, Fetched: 4 row(s)
```

To execute map side joins, we don't need to do anything special; Hive automatically decides when to execute the map side join and convert it into a map side join:

```
> SELECT * FROM
>emp e  JOIN dept d
> ON (e.deptId = d.id);
Query ID = admin1_20151213081130_ad7a6c17-0c98-4e82-bd51-b9a6a9d687b7
Total jobs = 1
15/12/13 08:11:32 WARN util.NativeCodeLoader: Unable to load native-
hadoop library for your platform... using builtin-java classes where
applicable
Execution log at: /tmp/admin1/admin1_20151213081130_ad7a6c17-0c98-
4e82-bd51-b9a6a9d687b7.log
2015-12-13 08:11:33     Starting to launch local task to process map
join;    maximum memory = 477364224
2015-12-13 08:11:35     Dump the side-table for tag: 1 with group
count: 4 into file: file:/tmp/admin1/4406a7b1-64cf-44e3-968f-
857c4bd17bb7/hive_2015-12-13_08-11-30_543_7059067307272955469-1/-
local-10003/HashTable-Stage-3/MapJoin-mapfile51--.hashtable
2015-12-13 08:11:35     Uploaded 1 File to: file:/tmp/
admin1/4406a7b1-64cf-44e3-968f-857c4bd17bb7/hive_2015-12-13_08-11-
30_543_7059067307272955469-1/-local-10003/HashTable-Stage-3/MapJoin-
mapfile51--.hashtable (370 bytes)
2015-12-13 08:11:35     End of local task; Time Taken: 1.255 sec.
Execution completed successfully
MapredLocal task succeeded
Launching Job 1 out of 1
Number of reduce tasks is set to 0 since there's no reduce operator
Starting Job = job_1449972302581_0007, Tracking URL = http://
admin1:8088/proxy/application_1449972302581_0007/
Kill Command = /usr/local/hadoop/bin/hadoopjob  -kill
job_1449972302581_0007
Hadoop job information for Stage-3: number of mappers: 1; number of
reducers: 0
2015-12-13 08:11:40,923 Stage-3 map = 0%,  reduce = 0%
2015-12-13 08:11:46,201 Stage-3 map = 100%,  reduce = 0%, Cumulative
CPU 1.7 sec
MapReduce Total cumulative CPU time: 1 seconds 700 msec
Ended Job = job_1449972302581_0007
MapReduce Jobs Launched:
Stage-Stage-3: Map: 1  Cumulative CPU: 1.7 sec  HDFS Read: 6787 HDFS
Write: 160 SUCCESS
```

```
Total MapReduce CPU Time Spent: 1 seconds 700 msec
OK
1    Tanmay 3500.0 101     101     Engineering
2    Sneha  5599.0 101     101     Engineering
3    Avinash       6700.0 102     102     HR
4    Manisha       6400.0 103     103     Finance
5    Sakalya       3200.0 102     102     HR
Time taken: 17.748 seconds, Fetched: 5 row(s)
```

The preceding execution shows that Hive informs you when it has converted this join into a map side join.

How it works...

Map side joins are performed when we have one small table and a very big table join. While executing, Hive reads the small table completely into memory and writes this table to a hash table. This hash table is referenced by each mapper to join the bigger table. By getting one table in its memory, Hive has fewer disk I/O operations, and this means less time to get records. There are limits that are set in the Hive configurations that decide whether the table is small or not. The `hive.auto.convert.join.noconditionaltask` and `hive.auto. convert.join.noconditionaltask.size` configurations decide the auto conversion of joins and the size of the table that can fit into the memory.

> You can read more about map side joins at `https://www.facebook. com/notes/facebook-engineering/join-optimization-in- apache-hive/470667928919`.

Performing context Ngram in Hive

Ngrams are sequences that are collected from specific sets of words and are based on their occurrence in a given text. N-grams are generally used to find the occurrence of certain words in a sequence, which helps in the calculation of sentiment analysis. Hive provides built-in support for Ngram calculations by providing a function. In this recipe, we will take a look at how to use this function in order to analyze text data.

Getting ready

To perform this recipe, you should have a running Hadoop cluster as well as the latest version of Hive installed on it. Here, I am using Hive 1.2.1.

How to do it...

N-gram can be used to find the most frequently used word after a sequence of words in a give text dataset. To do this, let's first create a Hive table and load data into it.

Take a situation where we have data from Twitter where people are writing about their sentiments about chocolate. Let's assume that we have text data, as follows:

```
Chocolate is good
Chocolate is bad
Chocolate is harmful
Chocolate is sweet
Chocolate is good
Chocolate is bad
Chocolate is good
Chocolate is bad
Chocolate is good
Chocolate is bad
Chocolate is harmful
Chocolate is sweet Chocolate is harmful
Chocolate is sweet Chocolate is harmful
Chocolate is sweet Chocolate is harmful
Chocolate is sweet
Chocolate is good
Chocolate is bad
```

Let's load this data into the Hive table:

```
CREATE TABLE textData(
data STRING)
ROW FORMAT DELIMITED;

LOAD DATA LOCAL INPATH 'twitter.txt' INTO TABLE textData;
```

Now, we will write a Hive query to find out what the most frequent word after `Chocolate is` is:

```
SELECT context_ngrams(sentences(data),
array("Chocolate","is",null),10) FROM
textData;
```

On complete execution, we will get the following output:

```
[{
    "ngram": ["bad"],
    "estfrequency": 5.0
}, {
    "ngram": ["good"],
    "estfrequency": 5.0
}, {
    "ngram": ["harmful"],
    "estfrequency": 5.0
}, {
    "ngram": ["sweet"],
    "estfrequency": 5.0
}]
```

This way, we can easily find out frequent words after a set of strings. This also helps in performing natural language processing on unstructured text data.

How it works...

Context Ngrams looks for a specific sequence of words and keep counting them using the map reduce program. On complete execution, they sort out the output by the given frequency of words in order to know the top word/s being used after a set of strings.

> To know more about Ngrams, you can visit
> https://en.wikipedia.org/wiki/N-gram.

Call Data Record Analytics using Hive

Call Data Records (**CDR**) are special types of records that are used in the telecom domain to keep track of calls made by individuals. We can use Hive to analyze these records in order to give special offers to customers.

> You can read more about CDR at
> https://en.wikipedia.org/wiki/Call_detail_record.

Getting ready

To perform this recipe, you should have a running Hadoop cluster as well as the latest version of Hive installed on it. Here, I am using Hive 1.2.1.

How to do it...

First of all, let's consider a situation where we have the following type of dataset with us. To analyze it, we first need to create a Hive table and load data into it:

```
CALLER_PHONE_NO|RECEIVER_PHONE_NUMBER|START_TIME|END_TIME|CALL_TYPE
11111|22222|2015-01-12 01:20:00|2015-01-12 01:30:00|VOICE
11111|22222|2015-02-12 01:35:00|2015-02-12 01:35:30|VOICE
11111|22222|2015-02-12 02:20:00|2015-02-12 02:20:00|SMS
33333|44444|2015-01-12 01:20:00|2015-01-12 01:30:00|VOICE
11111|33333|2015-05-12 04:02:00|2015-05-12 05:12:00|VOICE
22222|44444|2015-07-12 06:12:00|2015-07-12 06:12:00|SMS
22222|33333|2015-08-12 08:45:00|2015-08-12 08:50:00|VOICE
```

Let's create this Hive table and load data into it:

```
CREATE TABLE CDR(
caller_phone_no string,
receiver_phone_no string,
start_time timestamp,
end_time timestamp,
call_type string)
ROW FORMAT DELIMITED
FIELDS TERMINATED BY '|'
STORED AS TEXTFILE;

LOAD DATA LOCAL INPATH 'cdr.txt' INTO TABLE CDR;
```

Now that the data is loaded, we can execute the query to find out the duration of voice calls made by each subscriber in the given data:

```
SELECT caller_phone_no,
SUM(UNIX_TIMESTAMP(end_time) - UNIX_TIMESTAMP(start_time))
FROM cdr
WHERE call_type = 'VOICE'
GROUP BY caller_phone_no;
```

This will use the caller phone number and calculate the number of seconds it made calls for:

```
11111     4830
22222     300
33333     600
```

Next, we can execute queries to find out what the most frequently used medium of communication is. To know this, we will execute the following query:

```
SELECT call_type, count(*) as call_count FROM
CDR
GROUP BY call_type
ORDER  BYcall_count DESC;
```

On execution, we will get the following results:

```
VOICE     5
SMS       2
```

How it works...

The preceding section explains regular Hive queries, and we already know how they work.

Twitter sentiment analysis using Hive

Twitter is one of the most important data sources that helps you to know the sentiments behind various things. In this recipe, we will take a look at how to perform sentiment analysis using Hive on Twitter data.

Getting ready

To perform this recipe, you should have a running Hadoop cluster as well as the latest version of Hive installed on it. Here, I am using Hive 1.2.1.

How to do it...

First of all, we need a dataset to perform this recipe. We will be using a dataset that can be found at http://s3.amazonaws.com/hw-sandbox/tutorial13/SentimentFiles.zip.

Next, we will unzip this data and upload it on HDFS. The zip contains three folders: the first for raw Twitter data, the second for a dictionary, and the third for a time zone:

```
hadoop fs -mkdir /data
hadoop fs -put tweets_raw /data
hadoop fs -put time_zone_map /data
hadoop fs -put dictionary /data
```

We use Hive's JSON SerDe jar to read the tweeter data, as shown here:

```
ADD JAR json-serde-1.1.9.9-Hive1.2-jar-with-dependencies.jar;
CREATE EXTERNAL TABLE tweets_raw (
id BIGINT,
created_at STRING,
source STRING,
favorited BOOLEAN,
retweet_count INT,
retweeted_status STRUCT<
text:STRING,
user_rt:STRUCT<screen_name:STRING,name:STRING>>,
entities STRUCT<
urls:ARRAY<STRUCT<expanded_url:STRING>>,
user_mentions:ARRAY<STRUCT<screen_name:STRING,name:STRING>>,
hashtags:ARRAY<STRUCT<text:STRING>>>,
text STRING,
user_struct STRUCT<
screen_name:STRING,
name:STRING,
friends_count:INT,
followers_count:INT,
statuses_count:INT,
verified:BOOLEAN,
utc_offset:STRING,
time_zone:STRING>,
in_reply_to_screen_name STRING
)
ROW FORMAT SERDE 'org.openx.data.jsonserde.JsonSerDe'
WITH SERDEPROPERTIES ( "mapping.user_rt" = "user", "mapping.user_
struct" = "user" )
LOCATION '/data/tweets_raw';
```

This will create a Hive table and link data to it. Hive 1.2.1 puts certain constraints on reserve keywords such as user. So, we have to explicitly map these words to some other words.

Next, we load the dictionary and time zone tables. The dictionary will be used to determine whether a word is positive or negative:

```
CREATE EXTERNAL TABLE dictionary (
type string,
lengthint,
word string,
pos string,
stemmed string,
```

```
polarity string
)
ROW FORMAT DELIMITED FIELDS TERMINATED BY '\t'
STORED AS TEXTFILE
LOCATION '/data/dictionary';

CREATE EXTERNAL TABLE time_zone_map (
time_zone string,
country string,
notes string
)
ROW FORMAT DELIMITED FIELDS TERMINATED BY '\t'
STORED AS TEXTFILE
LOCATION '/data/time_zone_map';
```

We only select text column from the tweets_raw table and then clean it up:

```
CREATE VIEW tweets_simple AS
SELECT
id,
  cast ( from_unixtime( unix_timestamp(concat( '2013 ',
substring(created_at,5,15)), 'yyyy MMM ddhh:mm:ss')) as timestamp) ts,
text,
user_struct.time_zone
FROM tweets_raw;

CREATE VIEW tweets_clean AS
SELECT
id,
ts,
text,
m.country
  FROM tweets_simple t LEFT OUTER JOIN time_zone_map m ON t.time_zone =
m.time_zone;
```

We execute some queries in order to add the tweet ID and calculated sentiment:

```
create view l1 as select id, words from tweets_raw lateral view
explode(sentences(lower(text))) dummy as words;

create view l2 as select id, word from l1 lateral view explode( words
) dummy as word ;

create view l3 as select
id,
    l2.word,
```

```
cased.polarity
when  'negative' then -1
when 'positive' then 1
else 0 end as polarity
from l2 left outer join dictionary d on l2.word = d.word;


 -- give rights to hive user on tmpdir
 !hadoop fs -chmod -R 777 /tmp;



create table tweets_sentiment stored as RCFILE as select
id,
case
when sum( polarity ) > 0 then 'positive'
when sum( polarity ) < 0 then 'negative'
else 'neutral' end as sentiment
from l3 group by id;



CREATE TABLE tweets_senti
STORED AS RCFILE
AS
SELECT
t.*,
cases.sentiment
when 'positive' then 2
when 'neutral' then 1
when 'negative' then 0
end as sentiment
FROM tweets_clean t LEFT OUTER JOIN tweets_sentiment s on t.id = s.id;
```

As a result, you have now reached the tweet and its sentiment.

How it works

To perform the sentiment analysis, we first get only the text column from the raw table. Next, we explode each word in the text using the lateral view. Then, we join these words with the dictionary to know how they're polarized. Now that we know how each word's polarized, we perform 'group by' on the tweet ID to sum up the polarization. Once we have the final polarization, we check whether it is positive, negative, or neutral and save it against each tweet.

Implementing Change Data Capture using Hive

Change Data Capture or CDC is one the most painful areas in Data Warehousing. CDC captures the changes that occur in a table. A change could be in the form of new records getting added, updated, or getting deleted. In this recipe, we are going to take a look at how to perform CDC in Hive.

Getting ready

To perform this recipe, you should have a running Hadoop cluster as well as the latest version of Hive installed on it. Here, I am using Hive 1.2.1.

How to do it

First of all, we need a data sample. Consider a simple employee table that has columns, such as the employee ID, name, and salary. Let's say we import this table from a source table in week 1, and after a week, we want to know about the changes that have taken place in the same table. Let's say we have a table, employee1, which was imported in week 1, and we have another table, which was imported in week 2. Week 2 being the latest week, we want to know the changes that have taken place. Here is some sample data:

Table – employee1

```
1,A,1000
2,B,2000
3,C,3000
4,D,2000
5,E,1000
6,F,3000
7,G,1000
8,H,3000
9,I,1000
10,J,2000
11,K,1000
12,L,1000
13,M,1000
14,N,3000
15,O,3000
```

```
16,P,1000
17,Q,1000
18,R,1000
19,S,2000
20,T,3000
```

Table – employee2

```
1,A,1000
2,B,2000
3,C,5000
4,D,2000
5,EE,1000
6,F,3000
7,G,1000
8,H,3000
10,J,2000
11,K,1000
12,L,1000
13,MM,1000
14,N,3000
15,O,3000
16,PQ,1000
17,Q,1000
19,S,2000
20,T,3000
21,S,2000
22,T,3000
23,S,2000
24,T,3000
```

Now, we want to know which row is updated, which row is deleted, and which rows are newly added. In order to do know this, we can execute the following query:

Create the employee1 table and load data into it:

```
CREATE TABLE employee1 (
id INT,
name STRING,
```

```
salary BIGINT
)
ROW FORMAT DELIMITED
FIELDS TERMINATED BY ','
STORED AS TEXTFILE;
```

Create the employee2 table and load into data:

```
LOAD DATA LOCAL INPATH 'emp1.txt' INTO TABLE employee1;


CREATE TABLE employee2 (
id INT,
name STRING,
salary BIGINT
)
ROW FORMAT DELIMITED
FIELDS TERMINATED BY ','
STORED AS TEXTFILE;


LOAD DATA LOCAL INPATH 'emp2.txt' INTO TABLE employee2;
```

Now, we write a query in order to know the CDC:

```
select
case when b1.cdc_codes = 'Updates' then b1.employee1s
 when b1.cdc_codes = 'NoChange' then b1.employee2s
 when b1.cdc_codes = 'New' then b1.employee2s
 when b1.cdc_codes = 'Deletes' then b1.employee1s
else 'Error' end as fin_cols
from (select case when e1.id = e2.id and concat(e1.name,e1.salary) =
concat(e2.name,e2.salary)     then  'NoChange'
when e1.id = e2.id and  concat(e1.name,e1.salary) <> concat(e2.name,e2.
salary) then  'Updates'
when e1.id is null then 'New'
when e2.id is null then 'Deletes'
else 'Error' end as cdc_codes,
concat(e1.id,',',e1.name,',',e1.salary) as employee1s,
concat(e2.id,',',e2.name,',',e2.salary) as employee2s
from employee1 as e1 full outer join employee2 as e2
on e1.id = e2.id) as b1
```

Once we execute the preceding query, we get the following data, which is the updated data:

```
1,A,1000
2,B,2000
3,C,3000
4,D,2000
5,E,1000
6,F,3000
7,G,1000
8,H,3000
9,I,1000
10,J,2000
11,K,1000
12,L,1000
13,M,1000
14,N,3000
15,O,3000
16,P,1000
17,Q,1000
18,R,1000
19,S,2000
20,T,3000
21,S,2000
22,T,3000
23,S,2000
24,T,3000
```

How it works

In order to find the changed data, we perform a full outer join of two tables. This will include the entries from both tables that match with their IDs. Next, we check the data that is present and then decide whether the record is new, updated, or deleted. This way, we can easily capture the changes that have taken place. This technique is very useful in cases where you have built your data warehouse using Hive.

Multiple table inserting using Hive

Hive allows you to write data to multiple tables or directories at a time. This is an optimized solution as a source table needs to be read only once, which helps reduce the time. In this recipe, we are going to take a look at how write data to multiple tables/directories in a single query.

Getting ready

To perform this recipe, you should have a running Hadoop cluster as well as the latest version of Hive installed on it. Here, I am using Hive 1.2.1.

How to do it

Let's say we have an employee table with columns such as ID, name, and salary:

Table – employee

```
1,A,1000
2,B,2000
3,C,3000
4,D,2000
5,E,1000
6,F,3000
7,G,1000
8,H,3000
9,I,1000
10,J,2000
11,K,1000
12,L,1000
13,M,1000
14,N,3000
15,O,3000
16,P,1000
17,Q,1000
18,R,1000
19,S,2000
20,T,3000
```

Let's create the table and load the data into it:

```
CREATE TABLE employee (
id INT,
name STRING,
salary BIGINT
)
ROW FORMAT DELIMITED
FIELDS TERMINATED BY ','
STORED AS TEXTFILE;

LOAD DATA LOCAL INPATH 'emp.txt' INTO TABLE employee;
```

First, we need to create tables, and data from the employee table is inserted into these table:

```
CREATE TABLE emp1 LIKE employee;
CREATE TABLE emp2 LIKE employee;
```

Now, in order to insert data into two tables at a time, we can execute the following query:

```
FROM employee
INSERT INTO TABLE emp1
SELECT * WHERE id <= 10
INSERT INTO TABLE emp2
SELECT * WHERE id > 10 ;
```

As a result, you should see something like this:

```
hive> select * from emp1;
OK
1       A       1000
2       B       2000
3       C       3000
4       D       2000
5       E       1000
6       F       3000
7       G       1000
8       H       3000
9       I       1000
10      J       2000
```

```
Time taken: 0.161 seconds, Fetched: 10 row(s)
hive> select * from emp2;
OK
11      K       1000
12      L       1000
13      M       1000
14      N       3000
15      O       3000
16      P       1000
17      Q       1000
18      R       1000
19      S       2000
20      T       3000
```

We can also write data to the HDFS directory and table at a time, as shown here:

```
FROM employee1
INSERT INTO TABLE emp1
SELECT * WHERE id <= 10
INSERT OVERWRITE DIRECTORY '/data/emp1'
SELECT * WHERE id > 10 ;
```

This will write data to both the table and directory at one go.

How it works

The preceding queries read the data from the source table only once and write it in multiple places using multiple jobs. The benefit of doing it in this way is that you only read the data once, which optimizes the data read time.

6

Data Import/Export Using Sqoop and Flume

The chapter covers the following topics:

- ▶ Importing data from RDMBS to HDFS using Sqoop
- ▶ Exporting data from HDFS to RDBMS
- ▶ Using query operator in Sqoop import
- ▶ Importing data using Sqoop in compressed format
- ▶ Performing Atomic export using Sqoop
- ▶ Importing data into Hive tables using Sqoop
- ▶ Importing data into HDFS from Mainframes
- ▶ Incremental import using Sqoop
- ▶ Creating and executing Sqoop job
- ▶ Importing data from RDBMS to Hbase using Sqoop
- ▶ Importing Twitter data into HDFS using Flume
- ▶ Importing data from Kafka into HDFS using Flume
- ▶ Importing web logs data into HDFS using Flume

Introduction

In the previous chapter, we talked about advanced analytics options using Apache Hive. In this chapter, we are going to talk about two very important tools, Sqoop and Flume, which do not directly help us do analytics but help us get the data in and out of Hadoop. So, let's try to understand more about these technologies.

Importing data from RDMBS to HDFS using Sqoop

Most organizations use RDBMS databases as their primary storage for their data. To analyze the data, we need to first import that data on HDFS. Sqoop is a tool that helps us achieve this with ease, and with just a single command, we can import data into HDFS as required. In this recipe, we are going to see how to import data from MySQL to Hadoop using Sqoop.

Getting ready

To perform this recipe, you should have a Hadoop cluster running with you as well as the latest version of Sqoop installed on it. Here I am using Sqoop 1.4.6. We would also need MySQL database to be present in the network. Installing Sqoop is easy by downloading Sqoop tar ball and setting it in the system path. As we are going to import data from MySQL, we would also need to download MySQL connector from `https://dev.mysql.com/downloads/connector/`. Based on your MySQL version, download the right connector jar and copy it into the `lib` directory of Sqoop installation.

How to do it...

Perform the following steps:

1. First we will log into MySQL and create a database called company and create a table in it called `employee`.

   The schema for the same is as follows:

   ```
   mysql> desc employee;
   +--------+-------------+------+-----+---------+-------+
   | Field  | Type        | Null | Key | Default | Extra |
   +--------+-------------+------+-----+---------+-------+
   | id     | int(11)     | YES  |     | NULL    |       |
   | name   | varchar(20) | YES  |     | NULL    |       |
   +--------+-------------+------+-----+---------+-------+
   2 rows in set (0.00 sec)
   ```

2. Next we will add some records into it, so the MySQL employee table would look like as shown in the following:

   ```
   mysql> select * from employee;
   +------+--------+
   | id   | name   |
   ```

```
+------+--------+
|   16 | john   |
|   17 | robert |
|   18 | andrew |
|   19 | katty  |
|   21 | tom    |
|   22 | tim    |
|   23 | james  |
|   24 | paul   |
|   27 | edward |
|   29 | alan   |
|   31 | kerry  |
|   34 | terri  |
+------+--------+
12 rows in set (0.00 sec)
```

3. Now we are going to execute Sqoop command to import this data into the HDFS directory called /data/employee.

```
$sqoop import --connect jdbc:mysql://localhost:3306/company
--username root --password password --table employee --target-dir
/data/employee -m 1
```

Once you execute the preceding command, a Map Reduce job will start and import the records and write them to HDFS. Here we need to provide the host on which MySQL is running, its credentials, which table to import, and in which directory on HDFS you wish to store the data. I have also given m = 1, which means using a single mapper to do sequential import. This is a mandatory setting if your table does not have a primary ID. The console output would look like the following:

```
16/02/28 09:29:24 INFO impl.YarnClientImpl: Submitted application
application_1456628547885_0004
16/02/28 09:29:24 INFO mapreduce.Job: The url to track the job:
http://admin1:8088/proxy/application_1456628547885_0004/
16/02/28 09:29:24 INFO mapreduce.Job: Running job:
job_1456628547885_0004
16/02/28 09:29:37 INFO mapreduce.Job: Job job_1456628547885_0004
running in uber mode : false
16/02/28 09:29:37 INFO mapreduce.Job:  map 0% reduce 0%
16/02/28 09:29:49 INFO mapreduce.Job:  map 100% reduce 0%
16/02/28 09:29:49 INFO mapreduce.Job: Job job_1456628547885_0004
completed successfully
16/02/28 09:29:49 INFO mapreduce.Job: Counters: 30
```

```
File System Counters
        FILE: Number of bytes read=0
        FILE: Number of bytes written=132328
        FILE: Number of read operations=0
        FILE: Number of large read operations=0
        FILE: Number of write operations=0
        HDFS: Number of bytes read=87
        HDFS: Number of bytes written=104
        HDFS: Number of read operations=4
        HDFS: Number of large read operations=0
        HDFS: Number of write operations=2
Job Counters
        Launched map tasks=1
        Other local map tasks=1
        Total time spent by all maps in occupied slots (ms)=8607
        Total time spent by all reduces in occupied slots (ms)=0
        Total time spent by all map tasks (ms)=8607
        Total vcore-seconds taken by all map tasks=8607
        Total megabyte-seconds taken by all map tasks=8813568
Map-Reduce Framework
        Map input records=12
        Map output records=12
        Input split bytes=87
        Spilled Records=0
        Failed Shuffles=0
        Merged Map outputs=0
        GC time elapsed (ms)=57
        CPU time spent (ms)=1960
        Physical memory (bytes) snapshot=142516224
        Virtual memory (bytes) snapshot=407183360
        Total committed heap usage (bytes)=85983232
File Input Format Counters
        Bytes Read=0
File Output Format Counters
        Bytes Written=104
16/02/28 09:29:49 INFO mapreduce.ImportJobBase: Transferred 104
bytes in 29.694 seconds (3.5024 bytes/sec)
16/02/28 09:29:49 INFO mapreduce.ImportJobBase: Retrieved 12
records.
```

4. Now we can look at the HDFS directory to see the records getting imported:

```
hadoop fs -cat /data/employee/part-m-00000
    16,john
    17,robert
```

```
18,andrew

19,katty

21,tom

22,tim

23,james

24,paul

27,edward

29,alan

31,kerry

34,terri
```

By default, Sqoop uses a comma (,) as a column delimiter. We can also specify our own delimited data, as shown in the following:

```
sqoop import --connect jdbc:mysql://localhost:3306/company
--username root --password password --table employee --target-dir
/data/employee_pipe --fields-terminated-by '|' -m 1
```

```
$ hadoop fs -cat /data/employee_pipe/part-m-00000

16|john

17|robert

18|andrew

19|katty

21|tom

22|tim

23|james

24|paul

27|edward

29|alan

31|kerry

34|terri
```

In case you feel that providing a password in plain text is not safe, you may also provide that interactively:

```
sqoop import --connect jdbc:mysql://localhost:3306/company --username
root --table employee --target-dir /data/employee_pipe_1 --fields-
terminated-by '|' -m 1 -P
```

It will ask you to enter your password.

You can also get the password from the password file. For that, first you need to upload that file to HDFS and then point that in the sqoop command:

```
echo "password" > mysql.password
hadoop fs -put mysql.password /user/admin
hadoop fs -chown 400 /user/admin1/mysql.password
```

Now we can use this file in password:

```
sqoop import --connect jdbc:mysql://localhost:3306/company --username
root --table employee --target-dir /data/employee_pipe_3 --fields-
terminated-by '|' -m 1 --password-file /user/admin1/mysql.password
```

How it works...

When sqoop command is executed, it generates a Map Reduce job, rather a map only job, to import the data from the given RDBMS. By default, it uses four mappers to import the data from a given table. If the table has a primary key, then each mapper takes care of importing an equal number of records based on their primary ID. If the table does not have a primary ID, we need to use only a single mapper that will import the data sequentially. Based on the delimiter provided, the columns would be separated by the given characters.

Exporting data from HDFS to RDBMS

In the previous recipe, we spoke about how to import data from MySQL to HDFS. Now it is time to see how to export data from HDFS to RDBMS using Sqoop. Generally, this is required when you want to keep processed data in RDBMS to be used by some reporting tools.

Getting ready

To perform this recipe, you should have a Hadoop cluster running with you as well as the latest version of Sqoop installed on it. Here I am using Sqoop 1.4.6. We would also need the MySQL database to be present in the network. Installing Sqoop is easy; by downloading Sqoop tar ball and setting it in system path. As we are going to import data from MySQL, we would also need to download MySQL connector. Based on your MySQL version, download the right connector jar and copy it into the lib directory of Sqoop installation.

How to do it...

In the previous recipe, we imported data from MySQL into HDFS. Now we are going to export this data back to some different MySQL table.

1. To do this, first we need to create the table in MySQL:

    ```
    mysql> create table employee_export like employee;
    Query OK, 0 rows affected (0.02 sec)
    ```

2. Now we will execute the `sqoop export` command to fetch the data from the `/data/employee` directory and put it into the `employee_export` table we just created in the previous step:

    ```
    sqoop export --connect jdbc:mysql://localhost/company --username
    root --password password --table employee_export --export-dir /
    data/employee
    ```

    The console output for this will look like the following:

    ```
    16/02/28 09:34:23 INFO mapreduce.Job: Running job:
    job_1456628547885_0005
    16/02/28 09:34:36 INFO mapreduce.Job: Job job_1456628547885_0005
    running in uber mode : false
    16/02/28 09:34:36 INFO mapreduce.Job:  map 0% reduce 0%
    16/02/28 09:35:04 INFO mapreduce.Job:  map 100% reduce 0%
    16/02/28 09:35:09 INFO mapreduce.Job: Job job_1456628547885_0005
    completed successfully
    16/02/28 09:35:10 INFO mapreduce.Job: Counters: 30
        File System Counters
            FILE: Number of bytes read=0
            FILE: Number of bytes written=528692
            FILE: Number of read operations=0
            FILE: Number of large read operations=0
            FILE: Number of write operations=0
            HDFS: Number of bytes read=788
            HDFS: Number of bytes written=0
            HDFS: Number of read operations=16
            HDFS: Number of large read operations=0
            HDFS: Number of write operations=0
        Job Counters
            Launched map tasks=4
            Data-local map tasks=4
            Total time spent by all maps in occupied slots (ms)=109699
            Total time spent by all reduces in occupied slots (ms)=0
            Total time spent by all map tasks (ms)=109699
            Total vcore-seconds taken by all map tasks=109699
    ```

```
            Total megabyte-seconds taken by all map tasks=112331776
      Map-Reduce Framework
            Map input records=12
            Map output records=12
            Input split bytes=516
            Spilled Records=0
            Failed Shuffles=0
            Merged Map outputs=0
            GC time elapsed (ms)=838
            CPU time spent (ms)=8110
            Physical memory (bytes) snapshot=507035648
            Virtual memory (bytes) snapshot=1635950592
            Total committed heap usage (bytes)=317456384
      File Input Format Counters
            Bytes Read=0
      File Output Format Counters
            Bytes Written=0
16/02/28 09:35:10 INFO mapreduce.ExportJobBase: Transferred 788
bytes in 51.1218 seconds (15.4142 bytes/sec)
16/02/28 09:35:10 INFO mapreduce.ExportJobBase: Exported 12
records.
```

3. Once the command execution is completed, you can go to `mysql` prompt and check if the data import is proper:

```
mysql> select * from employee_export;
+------+---------+
| id   | name    |
+------+---------+
|   24 | paul    |
|   27 | edward  |
|   29 | alan    |
|   19 | katty   |
|   21 | tom     |
|   22 | tim     |
|   23 | james   |
|   31 | kerry   |
|   34 | terri   |
|   16 | john    |
|   17 | robert  |
|   18 | andrew  |
+------+---------+
12 rows in set (0.01 sec)
```

If, in your HDFS files, the column delimiter is other than a comma (,) then we have to specify the delimiter as shown in the following:

```
sqoop export --connect jdbc:mysql://localhost/company --username
root --password password --table employee_export --export-dir /
data/employee  --fields-terminated-by '|'
```

This will read the | delimited data from the given HDFS directory and save it into the `employee_export` table.

Here you can protect the plain text password being mentioned in the command directly by using the following options.

First, we can choose the – + *P* option, which would ask for the password in interactive mode:

```
sqoop export --connect jdbc:mysql://localhost/company --username
root --table employee_export --export-dir /data/employee -P
```

Second, you can also create a password file as explained in the previous recipe:

```
sqoop export --connect jdbc:mysql://localhost/company --username
root --table employee_export --export-dir /data/employee
--password-file /user/admin1/mysql.password
```

How it works...

`sqoop export` also creates a Map Reduce job for exporting data to RDBMS. It uses the provided credentials to insert records into a given table. Here it is important to match the data type in files with the data type in table. We should also make sure that the destination table exists before starting the `sqoop export` job, otherwise it would fail. In case the column delimiter is other than comma, then make sure you mention that in the `sqoop export` command to avoid wrong entries.

Using query operator in Sqoop import

In previous examples, we saw how we import/export complete table. Sometimes you may want to only use selective data, so to achieve this, Sqoop provides a query operation in which we can write SQL query as we need to import data into HDFS.

Getting ready

To perform this recipe, you should have a Hadoop cluster running with you as well as the latest version of Sqoop installed on it. Here I am using Sqoop 1.4.6. We would also need a MySQL database to be present in the network. Installing Sqoop is easy by downloading Sqoop tar ball and setting it in system path. As we are going to import data from MySQL, we would also need to download MySQL connector. Based on your MySQL version, download the right connector jar and copy it into the `lib` directory of the Sqoop installation.

How to do it...

1. Now we, again, log in to MySQL and take a look at the employee table. Let's say we want to import only those employees whose IDs are greater than 20. Then we can either use query or use `where` condition as shown in the following:

```
sqoop import --connect jdbc:mysql://localhost:3306/company
--username root --password password --target-dir /data/employee_
query_1 --query 'SELECT * FROM employee WHERE $CONDITIONS AND id>
20' -m 1
```

2. On successful execution, you should see only those records on HDFS whose IDs are greater than 20:

```
$hadoop fs -cat /data/employee_query_1/part-m-00000
    21,tom
    22,tim
    23,james
    24,paul
    27,edward
    29,alan
    31,kerry
    34,terri
```

You can also use query options to import data from multiple tables together. You can also import joined records using query options:

```
sqoop import --connect jdbc:mysql://localhost:3306/company --username
root --password password --target-dir /data/a_b_join --query SELECT
a.*, b.* FROM a JOIN b on (a.id == b.id) WHERE $CONDITIONS' -m 1
```

The preceding `sqoop` job would join two tables a and b on column ID and would be imported into the `/data/a_b_join` folder.

How it works...

With query option, `Sqoop import` works exactly the same the way it works for other cases. The only difference is that we can write a free-form query with it.

Importing data using Sqoop in compressed format

In this recipe, we are going to talk about a very important feature of Sqoop that allows us to compress the imported data. We can also choose the compression algorithm.

Getting ready

To perform this recipe, you should have a Hadoop cluster running with you as well as the latest version of Sqoop installed on it. Here I am using Sqoop 1.4.6. We would also need a MySQL database to be present in the network. Installing Sqoop is easy; by downloading Sqoop tar ball and setting it in the system path. As we are going to import data from MySQL, we would also need to download MySQL connector. Based on your MySQL version, download the right connector jar and copy it into the `lib` directory of the Sqoop installation.

How to do it...

1. Sqoop import allows us to import the data in a compressed format. We don't need to install anything else apart from default installation. The following query will import the employee data into a compressed format and will store in a given directory:

```
sqoop import \
--connect jdbc:mysql://localhost/company \
--username root \
--password password \
--table employee \
--compress \
--target-dir /data/employee_compressed \
--m 1
```

2. Once the job execution is complete, we can take a look at the HDFS directory:

```
hadoop fs -ls /data/employee_compressed
    Found 2 items
    -rw-r--r--   1 admin1 supergroup          0 2015-12-29
    14:41 /data/employee_compressed/_SUCCESS
    -rw-r--r--   1 admin1 supergroup        106 2015-12-29
    14:41 /data/employee_compressed/part-m-00000.gz
```

By default, the data is compressed in gun `zip` format. In case you want any other compression format, then you can specify the same as shown in the following:

```
sqoop import \
--connect jdbc:mysql://localhost/company \
```

```
--username root \
--password password \
--table employee \
--compress \
--target-dir /data/employee_compressed_bz2 \
--m 1 \
--compression-codec org.apache.hadoop.io.compress.BZip2Codec
```

3. On completion, you can take a look at the target directory:

```
hadoop fs -ls /data/employee_compressed_bz2

    Found 2 items
    -rw-r--r--   1 admin1 supergroup        0 2015-12-29
    14:45 /data/employee_compressed_bz2/_SUCCESS
    -rw-r--r--   1 admin1 supergroup      113 2015-12-29
    14:45 /data/employee_compressed_bz2/part-m-00000.bz2
```

Similarly, you can choose which compression algorithm you need and specify it in the `sqoop import` command.

How it works...

As Sqoop has come from the Hadoop family, it inherits support for various compression algorithms. It's very handy to import compressed data and save it on HDFS for efficient space utilization. We have to be very careful while choosing the compression algorithm as some algorithms do not allow splitting files. LZOP is one algorithm that allows file splitting; you can think about using it.

Performing Atomic export using Sqoop

We have learned in basic database concepts about atomicity, which means doing a complete job or doing nothing. Similarly, if you are exporting data using Sqoop to a table that is very important from the application's point of view and you want make sure that Sqoop should export all data present in HDFS or do nothing, this recipe will help. In this recipe, we are going to see how to ensure atomicity of data export.

Getting ready

To perform this recipe, you should have a Hadoop cluster running with you as well as the latest version of Sqoop installed on it. Here I am using Sqoop 1.4.6. We would also need a MySQL database to be present in the network. Installing Sqoop is easy; by downloading Sqoop tar ball and setting it in the system path. As we are going to import data from MySQL, we would also need to download MySQL connector. Based on your MySQL version, download the right connector jar and copy it into the `lib` directory of the Sqoop installation.

How to do it...

1. To perform the atomic export, first we need to create a table that can be used as a staging table:

```
mysql> create table staging_employee like employee;

Query OK, 0 rows affected (0.01 sec)
```

2. Then you can execute the `sqoop export` command specifying the destination table as well as the staging table:

```
sqoop export \
--connect jdbc:mysql://localhost/company \
--username root \
--password password \
--table atomic_employee \
--export-dir /data/employee \
--staging-table staging_employee
```

3. Last couple of lines of the job log will inform you that Sqoop is migrating data from the staging table to the destination table:

```
15/12/29 15:11:04 INFO mapreduce.ExportJobBase: Transferred 788
bytes in 21.6322 seconds (36.4272 bytes/sec)
15/12/29 15:11:04 INFO mapreduce.ExportJobBase: Exported 12
records.
15/12/29 15:11:04 INFO mapreduce.ExportJobBase: Starting to
migrate data from staging table to destination.
15/12/29 15:11:04 INFO manager.SqlManager: Migrated 12 records
from `staging_employee` to `atomic_employee`
```

Sqoop makes sure that if any parallel executing jobs fail, it will not copy anything to the destination table.

How it works...

During atomic export, Sqoop first writes data to the staging table. If any of the parallel executing jobs fail, Sqoop will not copy data to the destination table. This way we make sure that no half writes would go to the destination table. The only disadvantage of using the staging table is we would need to have that much space available for us in our database. Generally, it is recommended to use the staging table while exporting data to production tables.

Importing data into Hive tables using Sqoop

Till now we have seen how to import data into HDFS folders. Now it's time to understand how to import data directly into Hive table.

Getting ready

To perform this recipe, you should have a Hadoop cluster running with you as well as the latest version of Sqoop installed on it. Here I am using Sqoop 1.4.6. We would also need a MySQL database to be present in the network. Installing Sqoop is easy; by downloading Sqoop tar ball and setting it in the system path. As we are going to import data from MySQL, we would also need to download MySQL connector. Based on your MySQL version, download the right connector jar and copy it into the `lib` directory of Sqoop installation.

How to do it...

Sqoop provides us the facility to directly import data into Hive table. This saves our time in creating Hive tables, specifying matching schema, loading data into HDFS, and then creating external Hive table. We can do this in a couple of commands:

1. The following first command creates a table in Hive as per the schema of the source table, and the second command imports the actual data from the source RDBMS table and stores it into Hive table:

    ```
    sqoop create-hive-table --connect jdbc:mysql://localhost/company \
    --table employee --hive-table employee_sqoop \
    --username root \
    --password password \
    ```

2. The following creates a table in Hive as per the schema of the source table; we can go to Hive and check if the table is created:

    ```
    hive> desc employee_sqoop;
    OK
    id                      int
    name                    string
    Time taken: 0.114 seconds, Fetched: 2 row(s)
    ```

3. Next, we execute the following command to import the data into the newly created Hive table:

    ```
    sqoop import --hive-import --connect jdbc:mysql://localhost/
    company \
    --table employee --hive-table employee_sqoop \
    ```

```
--username root \
--password password \
--m 1
```

4. We can then go to the Hive prompt and see if the data is present:

```
hive> select * from employee_sqoop;
    OK
    16 john
    17 robert
    18 andrew
    19 katty
    21 tom
    22 tim
    23 james
    24 paul
    27 edward
    29 alan
    31 kerry
    34 terri
    Time taken: 1.297 seconds, Fetched: 12 row(s)
```

How it works...

Sqoop Hive import works similar to regular import; the only extra thing it does is copying data under the Hive warehouse directory. The `create-hive-table` command reads the source table schema first and then creates Hive table accordingly.

Importing data into HDFS from Mainframes

Mainframes is one of the most used datasets in financial domain for quite a long time. Sqoop supports importing datasets from Mainframes into HDFS. This is an important recipe for those who are looking to migrate from Mainframes to Hadoop base systems.

Getting ready

To perform this recipe, you should have a Hadoop cluster running with you as well as the latest version of Sqoop installed on it. Here I am using Sqoop 1.4.6. We would also need a MySQL database to be present in the network. Installing Sqoop is easy by downloading Sqoop tar ball and setting it in the system path.

How to do it...

Sqoop provides a tool called `import-mainframe`, using which, we can connect to a certain mainframe host and select the dataset to be imported. The following command connects to a mainframe host with the provided credentials and then imports the mentioned dataset into the HDFS target directory:

```
sqoop import-mainframe --connnect <mainframes-host> \
--dataset <dataset-to-be-imported> \
--target-dir /dest \
 --username foo\
 --password bar
```

You can also choose in which format you wish to import the data, if it needs to be compressed and if you wish to have different field delimiter than the default.

How it works...

Sqoop mainframes imports sequential data into a partitioned dataset. It has certain limitations like records in a dataset should be character data only. Once imported data will be saved as a single text record, and it would still be in its early stages. It would get more mature as time passes.

Incremental import using Sqoop

In an enterprise world, the data gets increased every single day, hour, minute, and second. It's important to import data in an incremental way to do our analysis on up-to-date data. In this recipe, we are going to learn how to import data incrementally.

Getting ready

To perform this recipe, you should have a Hadoop cluster running with you as well as the latest version of Sqoop installed on it. Here I am using Sqoop 1.4.6. We would also need a MySQL database to be present in the network. Installing Sqoop is easy by downloading Sqoop tar ball and setting it in the system path. As we are going to import data from MySQL, we would also need to download MySQL connector. Based on your MySQL version, download the right connector jar and copy it into the `lib` directory of the Sqoop installation.

How to do it...

1. To learn about incremental `import`, we will create a new table in MySQL called `newemployee` and add some records in it:

```
create table newemployee(id INT NOT NULL AUTO_INCREMENT,
 name varchar(20) ,
 salary float,
 PRIMARY KEY ( id ) );
insert into newemployee (name, salary) values ("Tanmay", 2000.00);
insert into newemployee (name, salary) values ("Sneha", 5000.00);
insert into newemployee (name, salary) values ("Avinash",
8000.00);
insert into newemployee (name, salary) values ("Sakalya",
6000.00);
insert into newemployee (name, salary) values ("Manisha",
4000.00);
```

So, the table would like the following:

```
mysql> select * from newemployee;

+----+---------+--------+
| id | name    | salary |
+----+---------+--------+
|  1 | Tanmay  |   2000 |
|  2 | Sneha   |   5000 |
|  3 | Avinash |   8000 |
|  4 | Sakalya |   6000 |
|  5 | Manisha |   4000 |
+----+---------+--------+
5 rows in set (0.00 sec)
```

2. First, we import data in a regular manner:

```
sqoop import \
--connect jdbc:mysql://localhost/company \
--username root \
--password password \
--table newemployee \
--target-dir /data/newemployee \
--m 1
```

Now let's assume that a few more rows got added into our `newemployee` table:

```
insert into newemployee (name, salary) values
("Kapila",4400.00);
insert into newemployee (name, salary) values ("Vinit",
6500.00);
```

mysql> select * from newemployee;

```
+----+---------+--------+
| id | name    | salary |
+----+---------+--------+
|  1 | Tanmay  |   2000 |
|  2 | Sneha   |   5000 |
|  3 | Avinash |   8000 |
|  4 | Sakalya |   6000 |
|  5 | Manisha |   4000 |
|  6 | Kapila  |   4400 |
|  7 | Vinit   |   6500 |
+----+---------+--------+
7 rows in set (0.00 sec)
```

3. Now to import only new rows, we can use the incremental option in `sqoop import`. Following is the command we need to use:

```
sqoop import \
--connect jdbc:mysql://localhost/company \
--username root \
--password password \
--table newemployee \
--target-dir /data/newemployee \
--incremental append \
--check-column id \
--last-value 5 \
--m 1
```

4. Here we need to specify which column Sqoop should look at and what its last value is. Append mode is helpful when you have incremental IDs and you wish to import only those rows.

    Once you execute the job, you will see that only two new rows get imported into HDFS.

5. In case you wish to import updated rows using Sqoop, you can use `--incremental lastmodified`. To use this, first we need to have a column where we can save the last modified date and make sure that on every update, you update the last modified data column as well. Then you can execute the following command to get only updated records:

```
sqoop import \
--connect jdbc:mysql://localhost/company \
--username root \
--password password \
--table newemployee \
--target-dir /data/newemployee \
--incremental lastmodified \
--check-column lastmod \
--last-value 01-01-1970 \
--m 1
```

Here `lastmod` is my column in MySQL table where I am storing the `lastmodified` date.

How it works...

Sqoop incremental import modifies the underlying Map Reduce job based on the conditions given in the command. It filters out values for the columns specified in the command. This is a very useful tool where the database gets updated periodically.

Creating and executing Sqoop job

Sqoop provides you the facility to store certain jobs that can be used easily. In this recipe, we are going to see how to create a job and execute the same.

Getting ready

To perform this recipe, you should have a Hadoop cluster running with you as well as the latest version of Sqoop installed on it. Here I am using Sqoop 1.4.6. We would also need a MySQL database to be present in the network. Installing Sqoop is easy by downloading Sqoop tar ball and setting it in system path. As we are going to import data from MySQL, we would also need to download MySQL connector. Based on your MySQL version, download the right connector jar and copy it into the `lib` directory of Sqoop installation.

How to do it...

1. We will create a `sqoop job` for incremental import that we performed in the last recipe. Following is the command to create a `sqoop` job:

```
sqoop job \
--create incremental_import_job \
-- import \
--connect jdbc:mysql://localhost/company \
--username root \
--password password \
--table newemployee \
--target-dir /data/newemployee \
--incremental append \
--check-column id \
--last-value 7 \
--m 1
```

2. We can see the list of jobs as shown in the following:

```
$ sqoop job --list
15/12/30 12:00:38 INFO sqoop.Sqoop: Running Sqoop version: 1.4.6
Available jobs:
   incremental_import_job
```

We can also view details of a particular job:

```
$ sqoop job --show incremental_import_job
15/12/30 12:05:51 INFO sqoop.Sqoop: Running Sqoop version: 1.4.6
Job: incremental_import_job
Tool: import
Options:
----------------------------
verbose = false
incremental.last.value = 7
db.connect.string = jdbc:mysql://localhost/company
codegen.output.delimiters.escape = 0
codegen.output.delimiters.enclose.required = false
codegen.input.delimiters.field = 0
hbase.create.table = false
db.require.password = true
hdfs.append.dir = true
db.table = newemployee
codegen.input.delimiters.escape = 0
import.fetch.size = null
accumulo.create.table = false
```

```
codegen.input.delimiters.enclose.required = false
db.username = root
reset.onemapper = false
codegen.output.delimiters.record = 10
import.max.inline.lob.size = 16777216
hbase.bulk.load.enabled = false
hcatalog.create.table = false
db.clear.staging.table = false
incremental.col = id
codegen.input.delimiters.record = 0
enable.compression = false
hive.overwrite.table = false
hive.import = false
codegen.input.delimiters.enclose = 0
accumulo.batch.size = 10240000
hive.drop.delims = false
codegen.output.delimiters.enclose = 0
hdfs.delete-target.dir = false
codegen.output.dir = .
codegen.auto.compile.dir = true
relaxed.isolation = false
mapreduce.num.mappers = 1
accumulo.max.latency = 5000
import.direct.split.size = 0
codegen.output.delimiters.field = 44
export.new.update = UpdateOnly
incremental.mode = AppendRows
hdfs.file.format = TextFile
codegen.compile.dir = /tmp/sqoop-admin1/compile/
b125ff516f7a0143479b9582373230e7
direct.import = false
hdfs.target.dir = /data/newemployee
hive.fail.table.exists = false
db.batch = false
```

3. Next, we can execute the job using the following command:

```
sqoop job --exec incremental_import_job
```

This will execute the job we had specified. Now you can add more records into the MySQL table and execute this job. It will automatically keep on updating the lastvalue parameter.

How it works...

Sqoop saves the configuration provided in the job, and the next time you execute, it will remember the parameters you provided. It will also make sure to update the last-value attribute in case of incremental imports. It's a very handy tool for taking care of daily imports with ease.

Importing data from RDBMS to Hbase using Sqoop

These days, lots of people want to make use of the power of NoSQL databases. In order to do so, they need to migrate their existing application from RDBMS to NoSQL databases like Hbase. In this recipe, we are going to learn how to import data from MySQL to Hbase.

Getting ready

To perform this recipe, you should have a Hadoop cluster running with you as well as the latest version of Sqoop installed on it. Here I am using Sqoop 1.4.6. We would also need a MySQL database to be present in the network. Installing Sqoop is easy; by downloading Sqoop tar ball and setting it in the system path. As we are going to import data from MySQL, we would also need to download MySQL connector. Based on your MySQL version, download the right connector jar and copy it into the `lib` directory of the Sqoop installation.

How to do it...

First of we need to create a table in MySQL and insert some records in it:

```
mysql> desc employee;
+--------+-------------+------+-----+---------+-------+
| Field  | Type        | Null | Key | Default | Extra |
+--------+-------------+------+-----+---------+-------+
| id     | int(11)     | YES  |     | NULL    |       |
| name   | varchar(20) | YES  |     | NULL    |       |
+--------+-------------+------+-----+---------+-------+
2 rows in set (0.00 sec)
mysql> select * from employee;
+------+--------+
| id   | name   |
+------+--------+
```

```
|   16 | john   |
|   17 | robert |
|   18 | andrew |
|   19 | katty  |
|   21 | tom    |
|   22 | tim    |
|   23 | james  |
|   24 | paul   |
|   27 | edward |
|   29 | alan   |
|   31 | kerry  |
|   34 | terri  |
+------+--------+
12 rows in set (0.02 sec)
```

Next we need to create a table in Hbase:

```
hbase>create 'emp', 'personal data', 'professional data'
```

Now we can write a Sqoop job in order to fetch data from this MySQL table as shown in the following:

```
sqoop import \
    --connect jdbc:mysql://localhost:3306/company \
    --username root -P \
    --table employee \
    --columns "id,name" \
    --hbase-table emp \
    --column-family 'personal data' \
    --hbase-row-key id -m 1
```

In the preceding command, we are specifying the source table, destination table, columns to be imported, and which column should be used as the key.

Executing the preceding command will start a Map Reduce job and you will see records getting imported into Hbase:

```
16/02/28 08:44:53 INFO mapreduce.Job: The url to track the job: http://
admin1:8088/proxy/application_1456628547885_0002/

16/02/28 08:44:53 INFO mapreduce.Job: Running job: job_1456628547885_0002

16/02/28 08:45:08 INFO mapreduce.Job: Job job_1456628547885_0002 running
in uber mode : false

16/02/28 08:45:08 INFO mapreduce.Job:  map 0% reduce 0%
```

```
16/02/28 08:45:23 INFO mapreduce.Job:  map 100% reduce 0%

16/02/28 08:45:24 INFO mapreduce.Job: Job job_1456628547885_0002
completed successfully

16/02/28 08:45:24 INFO mapreduce.Job: Counters: 30
    File System Counters
        FILE: Number of bytes read=0
        FILE: Number of bytes written=159042
        FILE: Number of read operations=0
        FILE: Number of large read operations=0
        FILE: Number of write operations=0
        HDFS: Number of bytes read=87
        HDFS: Number of bytes written=0
        HDFS: Number of read operations=1
        HDFS: Number of large read operations=0
        HDFS: Number of write operations=0
    ob Counters
        Launched map tasks=1
        Other local map tasks=1
        Total time spent by all maps in occupied slots (ms)=11945
        Total time spent by all reduces in occupied slots (ms)=0
        Total time spent by all map tasks (ms)=11945
        Total vcore-seconds taken by all map tasks=11945
        Total megabyte-seconds taken by all map tasks=12231680
    Map-Reduce Framework
        Map input records=12
        Map output records=12
        Input split bytes=87
        Spilled Records=0
        Failed Shuffles=0
        Merged Map outputs=0
        GC time elapsed (ms)=194
        CPU time spent (ms)=4060
        Physical memory (bytes) snapshot=160456704
        Virtual memory (bytes) snapshot=418877440
        Total committed heap usage (bytes)=81002496
    File Input Format Counters
```

```
        Bytes Read=0

   File Output Format Counters

        Bytes Written=0
```

16/02/28 08:45:24 INFO mapreduce.ImportJobBase: Transferred 0 bytes in 38.7996 seconds (0 bytes/sec)

16/02/28 08:45:24 INFO mapreduce.ImportJobBase: Retrieved 12 records.

Now we can check in the Hbase table as shown in the following:

```
hbase(main):006:0> scan 'emp'
ROW                    COLUMN+CELL
 16                    column=personal data:name, timestamp=1456629321444,
value=
                       John
 17                    column=personal data:name, timestamp=1456629321444,
value=
                       Robert
 18                    column=personal data:name, timestamp=1456629321444,
value=
                       Andrew
 19                    column=personal data:name, timestamp=1456629321444,
value=
                       Katty
 21                    column=personal data:name, timestamp=1456629321444,
value=
                       Tom
 22                    column=personal data:name, timestamp=1456629321444,
value=
                       Tim
 23                    column=personal data:name, timestamp=1456629321444,
value=
                       James
 24                    column=personal data:name, timestamp=1456629321444,
value=
                       Paul
 27                    column=personal data:name, timestamp=1456629321444,
value=
                       Edward
 29                    column=personal data:name, timestamp=1456629321444,
value=
                       Alan
 31                    column=personal data:name, timestamp=1456629321444,
value=
                       Kerry
 34                    column=personal data:name, timestamp=1456629321444,
value=
                       Terri
12 row(s) in 0.2990 seconds
```

How it works...

Sqoop reads the command provided and makes a JDBC connection to MySQL. It verifies the existence of source and destination tables and then starts the import. Hbase being a columnar store database, means it writes row data and a column definition in each record.

Importing Twitter data into HDFS using Flume

Flume is another tool that helps us import data from various other sources into HDFS. In this recipe, we are going to see how to import Twitter data using Flume. Twitter data is a great source of information provided by individuals. This data can be used to do sentiment analytics of certain products, persons, companies, and so on.

Getting ready

To perform this recipe, you should have a Hadoop cluster running with you as well as the latest version of Flume installed on it. Here I am using Flume 1.6.

How to do it...

To import data using Flume, first of all we need to have a Twitter account and we need to generate credentials. These credentials would be used by Flume agent to import the data. Flume by default supports sources to import data from Twitter, so there is no need to do anything else other than having an account and generating credentials.

Following is the step-by-step process to generate Twitter authorization tokens:

1. Log in to `https://apps.twitter.com/`.

2. Click on **Create New Application**. Fill in the required form as shown in the following screenshot:

Application Details

Name *

HadoopTutorialsFlume

Your application name. This is used to attribute the source of a tweet and in user-facing authorization screens. 32 characters max.

Description *

Handle to import Twitter data using Flume

Your application description, which will be shown in user-facing authorization screens. Between 10 and 200 characters max.

Website *

http://hadooptutorials.co.in

Your application's publicly accessible home page, where users can go to download, make use of, or find out more information about your application. This fully-qualified URL is used in the source attribution for tweets created by your application and will be shown in user-facing authorization screens.

(If you don't have a URL yet, just put a placeholder here but remember to change it later.)

Callback URL

Where should we return after successfully authenticating? OAuth 1.0a applications should explicitly specify their oauth_callback URL on the request token step, regardless of the value given here. To restrict your application from using callbacks, leave this field blank.

3. Read and accept the **Developer Agreement** if you think it's good for you:

Developer Agreement

Effective: May 18, 2015.

This Twitter Developer Agreement ("**Agreement**") is made between you (either an individual or an entity, referred to herein as "**you**") and Twitter, Inc. and Twitter International Company (collectively, "**Twitter**") and governs your access to and use of the Licensed Material (as defined below).

PLEASE READ THE TERMS AND CONDITIONS OF THIS AGREEMENT CAREFULLY, INCLUDING WITHOUT LIMITATION ANY LINKED TERMS AND CONDITIONS APPEARING OR REFERENCED BELOW, WHICH ARE HEREBY MADE PART OF THIS LICENSE AGREEMENT. BY USING THE LICENSED MATERIAL, YOU ARE AGREEING THAT YOU HAVE READ, AND THAT YOU AGREE TO COMPLY WITH AND TO BE BOUND BY THE TERMS AND CONDITIONS OF THIS AGREEMENT AND ALL APPLICABLE LAWS AND REGULATIONS IN THEIR ENTIRETY WITHOUT LIMITATION OR QUALIFICATION. IF YOU DO NOT AGREE TO BE BOUND BY THIS AGREEMENT, THEN YOU MAY NOT ACCESS OR OTHERWISE USE THE LICENSED MATERIAL. THIS AGREEMENT IS EFFECTIVE AS OF THE FIRST DATE THAT YOU USE THE LICENSED MATERIAL ("**EFFECTIVE DATE**").

IF YOU ARE AN INDIVIDUAL REPRESENTING AN ENTITY, YOU ACKNOWLEDGE THAT YOU HAVE THE APPROPRIATE AUTHORITY TO ACCEPT THIS AGREEMENT ON BEHALF OF SUCH ENTITY. YOU MAY NOT USE THE LICENSED MATERIAL AND MAY NOT

Yes, I agree

Create your Twitter application

4. Click on **Create your Twitter application** to save your application. Now we can use this handle to import data from Twitter:

Your application has been created. Please take a moment to review and adjust your application's settings.

HadoopTutorialsFlume

Test OAuth

Details   Settings   Keys and Access Tokens   Permissions

Handle to import Twitter data using Flume

http://hadooptutorials.co.in

Organization

Information about the organization or company associated with your application. This information is optional.

Organization	None
Organization website	None

Application Settings

Your application's Consumer Key and Secret are used to authenticate requests to the Twitter Platform.

Access level	Read and write (modify app permissions)

5. Click on **Keys and Access Tokens**; there you will find the application specific **Consumer Key** and **Consumer Secret** Key. Keep a copy of it as we will need it in the next steps.

HadoopTutorialsFlume

Test OAuth

Details   Settings   Keys and Access Tokens   Permissions

Application Settings

Keep the "Consumer Secret" a secret. This key should never be human-readable in your application.

Consumer Key (API Key)	GWYT5k3uL1gqn2UKWGiC96BdN
Consumer Secret (API Secret)	I9WLpXL6pQHVZ2pNky97x3XpUkW5kfRUo2pzGu1OSemhsYchkC
Access Level	Read and write (modify app permissions)
Owner	HadoopTutorials
Owner ID	2825680861

Application Actions

Regenerate Consumer Key and Secret   Change App Permissions

6. On scrolling down, you will also see an option to generate an access token, so do that and keep a copy of it for future use.

7. Now edit `$FLUME_HOME/conf/flume.conf` to copy the exact values of the access key, secret key, access token, and access token secret. Save the changes made to the file.

The following is how your `flume.conf` should look like:

```
#### TwitterAgent for collecting Twitter data to Hadoop HDFS #####

TwitterAgent.sources = Twitter
TwitterAgent.channels = FileChannel
TwitterAgent.sinks = HDFS

TwitterAgent.sources.Twitter.type = org.apache.flume.source.
twitter.TwitterSource
TwitterAgent.sources.Twitter.channels = FileChannel
TwitterAgent.sources.Twitter.consumerKey = <consumer-key>
TwitterAgent.sources.Twitter.consumerSecret = <consume-secret>
TwitterAgent.sources.Twitter.accessToken = <access-token>
TwitterAgent.sources.Twitter.accessTokenSecret = <access-token-
secret>
TwitterAgent.sources.Twitter.maxBatchSize = 50000
TwitterAgent.sources.Twitter.maxBatchDurationMillis = 100000

#TwitterAgent.sources.Twitter.keywords = Apache, Hadoop,
Mapreduce, hadooptutorial, Hive, Hbase, MySql

TwitterAgent.sinks.HDFS.channel = FileChannel
TwitterAgent.sinks.HDFS.type = hdfs
TwitterAgent.sinks.HDFS.hdfs.path = hdfs://localhost:9000/user/
flume/tweets/
TwitterAgent.sinks.HDFS.hdfs.fileType = DataStream
TwitterAgent.sinks.HDFS.hdfs.writeFormat = Text
TwitterAgent.sinks.HDFS.hdfs.batchSize = 200000
TwitterAgent.sinks.HDFS.hdfs.rollSize = 0
TwitterAgent.sinks.HDFS.hdfs.rollCount = 2000000

TwitterAgent.channels.FileChannel.type = file
TwitterAgent.channels.FileChannel.checkpointDir = /var/log/flume/
checkpoint/
TwitterAgent.channels.FileChannel.dataDirs = /var/log/flume/data/
```

8. Now it's time to execute Flume agent to start fetching data from Twitter and save it on HDFS:

```
/usr/local/flume/bin/flume-ng agent -n TwitterAgent -c /usr/local/
flume/conf -f /usr/local/flume/conf/flume.conf
```

Execute the preceding command to fetch data from Twitter and save it on HDFS.

9. Now you can take a look at the HDFS path `/user/flume/tweets` to see the actual Twitter data.

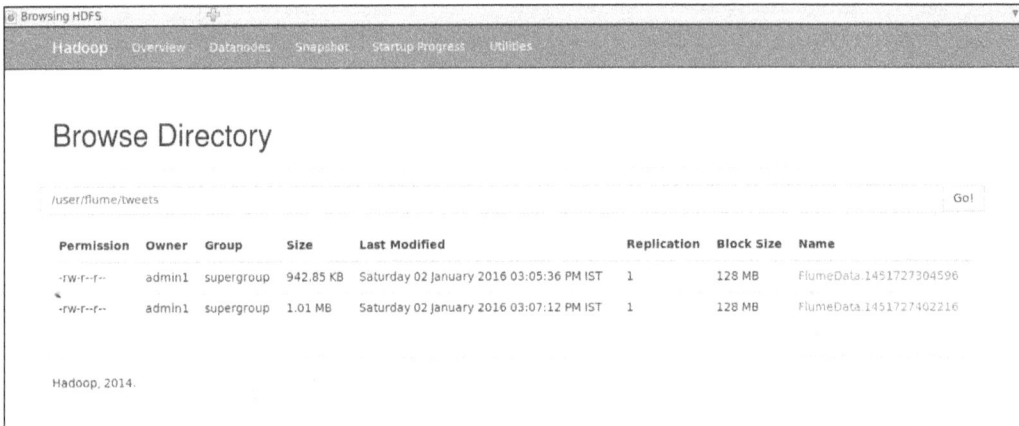

How it works

Flume has built-in support for the Twitter source. It uses Twitter exposed APIs to download the data and store it on HDFS. It internally browses through the tweets available for your user and downloads them. It keeps on creating a new file based on time. You can also download only those tweets with certain keywords by uncommenting the following line from `flume.conf` and rerunning the Flume agent:

```
TwitterAgent.sources.Twitter.keywords = Apache, Hadoop, Mapreduce,
hadooptutorial, Hive, Hbase, MySql
```

> Please make a note that the application you have created has all of the same rights as a user. So don't share the keys with anyone else.

Importing data from Kafka into HDFS using Flume

Kafka is one the most popular message queue systems being used these days. We can listen to Kafka topics and put the message data directly into HDFS using Flume. The latest Flume version supports importing data from Kafka easily. In this recipe, we are going to learn how to import Kafka messages to HDFS.

Getting ready

To perform this recipe, you should have a Hadoop cluster running with you as well as the latest version of Flume installed on it. Here I am using Flume 1.6. We also need Kafka installed and running on one of the machines. I am using kafka_2.10-0.9.0.0.

How to do it...

1. To import the data from Kafka, first you need to have Kafka running on your machine. The following command starts Kafka and Zookeeper:

   ```
   bin/zookeeper-server-start.sh config/zookeeper.properties
   bin/kafka-server-start.sh config/server.properties
   ```

2. Next I create a topic called `weblogs` which we will be listening to:

   ```
   bin/kafka-topics.sh --create --zookeeper localhost:2181
   --replication-factor 1 --partitions 1 --topic weblogs
   ```

3. Next we will start a producer which we will write to weblogs topic:

   ```
   bin/kafka-console-producer.sh --broker-list localhost:9092 --topic
   weblogs
   ```

4. Now that all Kafka-related infra is set up, we need to also create Flume configuration, which will be listening to the weblogs topic and writing it to HDFS:

   ```
   # Flume config to listen to Kakfa topic and write to HDFS.
   flume1.sources  = kafka-source-1
   flume1.channels = hdfs-channel-1
   flume1.sinks    = hdfs-sink-1

   # For each source, channel, and sink, set
   # standard properties.
   flume1.sources.kafka-source-1.type = org.apache.flume.source.
   kafka.KafkaSource
   flume1.sources.kafka-source-1.zookeeperConnect = localhost:2181
   flume1.sources.kafka-source-1.topic = weblogs
   flume1.sources.kafka-source-1.batchSize = 100
   ```

```
flume1.sources.kafka-source-1.channels = hdfs-channel-1

flume1.channels.hdfs-channel-1.type    = memory
flume1.sinks.hdfs-sink-1.channel = hdfs-channel-1
flume1.sinks.hdfs-sink-1.type = hdfs
flume1.sinks.hdfs-sink-1.hdfs.writeFormat = Text
flume1.sinks.hdfs-sink-1.hdfs.fileType = DataStream
flume1.sinks.hdfs-sink-1.hdfs.filePrefix = test-events
flume1.sinks.hdfs-sink-1.hdfs.useLocalTimeStamp = true
flume1.sinks.hdfs-sink-1.hdfs.path = /tmp/kafka/%{topic}/%y-%m-%d
flume1.sinks.hdfs-sink-1.hdfs.rollCount=100
flume1.sinks.hdfs-sink-1.hdfs.rollSize=0

# Other properties are specific to each type of
# source, channel, or sink. In this case, we
# specify the capacity of the memory channel.
flume1.channels.hdfs-channel-1.capacity = 10000
```

5. I am saving this configuration as `kafka.conf`. Now to execute this Flume agent, we use the following command:

```
/usr/local/flume/bin/flume-ng agent -n flume1 -c /usr/local/
flume/conf -f /usr/local/flume/conf/kafka.conf -Dflume.root.
logger=INFO,console
```

This will start a process that will be listening to the weblogs topic in Kafka. Now to test this setup, go to the screen where we are running the Kafka producers and send some messages to the weblogs topic. As soon as you send a message to the topic, you will see logs on Flume agent conveying that it is writing to HDFS.

You can now check out the HDFS path to see if the messages are being written there:

```
hadoop fs -cat /tmp/kafka/weblogs/16-01-02/test-events.1451730937398
Hello World
```

Browsing HDFS

Hadoop   Overview   Datanodes   Snapshot   Startup Progress   Utilities

Browse Directory

/tmp/kafka/weblogs/16-01-02   Go!

Permission	Owner	Group	Size	Last Modified	Replication	Block Size	Name
-rw-r--r--	admin1	supergroup	18 B	Saturday 02 January 2016 03:51:41 PM IST	1	128 MB	test-events.1451730081684
-rw-r--r--	admin1	supergroup	12 B	Saturday 02 January 2016 04:06:09 PM IST	1	128 MB	test-events.1451730937398

Hadoop, 2014.

How it works

Flume agent listens to a given topic. As soon as the message is received, it uses the defined HDFS sinks to write the data to the HDFS path. First it creates a `.tmp file`, and after a certain message is received, it renames it to a regular file. Flume, by default, uses the group ID as Flume to avoid any message loss from the actual application. We can also run multiple Flume agents to distribute the load.

Importing web logs data into HDFS using Flume

One of the most important use cases of Flume is importing logs data into HDFS as and when it is produced. In this recipe, we will be executing a Flume agent which will be listening to the logs file.

Getting ready

To perform this recipe, you should have a Hadoop cluster running with you as well as the latest version of Flume installed on it.

How to do it...

1. To import data into HDFS from web servers, we have to install Flume agent on each web server instance.Following is the configuration we have to use for Flume agent configuration:

```
flume1.sources  = weblogs-source-1
flume1.channels = hdfs-channel-1
flume1.sinks    = hdfs-sink-1

# For each source, channel, and sink, set
# standard properties.
flume1.sources.weblogs-source-1.type = exec
flume1.sources.weblogs-source-1.command = tail -f /path/to/log/
file.log
flume1.sources.weblogs-source-1.batchSize = 100
flume1.sources.weblogs-source-1.channels = hdfs-channel-1

flume1.channels.hdfs-channel-1.type   = memory
flume1.sinks.hdfs-sink-1.channel = hdfs-channel-1
flume1.sinks.hdfs-sink-1.type = hdfs
flume1.sinks.hdfs-sink-1.hdfs.writeFormat = Text
```

```
flume1.sinks.hdfs-sink-1.hdfs.fileType = DataStream
flume1.sinks.hdfs-sink-1.hdfs.filePrefix = test-events
flume1.sinks.hdfs-sink-1.hdfs.useLocalTimeStamp = true
flume1.sinks.hdfs-sink-1.hdfs.path = /logs/web/%y-%m-%d
flume1.sinks.hdfs-sink-1.hdfs.rollCount=100
flume1.sinks.hdfs-sink-1.hdfs.rollSize=0

# Other properties are specific to each type of
# source, channel, or sink. In this case, we
# specify the capacity of the memory channel.
flume1.channels.hdfs-channel-1.capacity = 10000
```

2. This will be listening to the given log file path. Here we are using `exec` source, which executes given command after a certain time interval.

   Here the source is an output of the `exec` command we have provided. The channel transfers the data to Sink, which writes it to HDFS.

3. To execute the preceding configuration, we have to run the following command:

```
/usr/local/flume/bin/flume-ng agent -n flume1 -c /usr/local/
flume/conf -f /usr/local/flume/conf/weblogs.conf -Dflume.root.
logger=INFO,console
```

Now, as and when the log file is updated, the data will be written to HDFS as well:

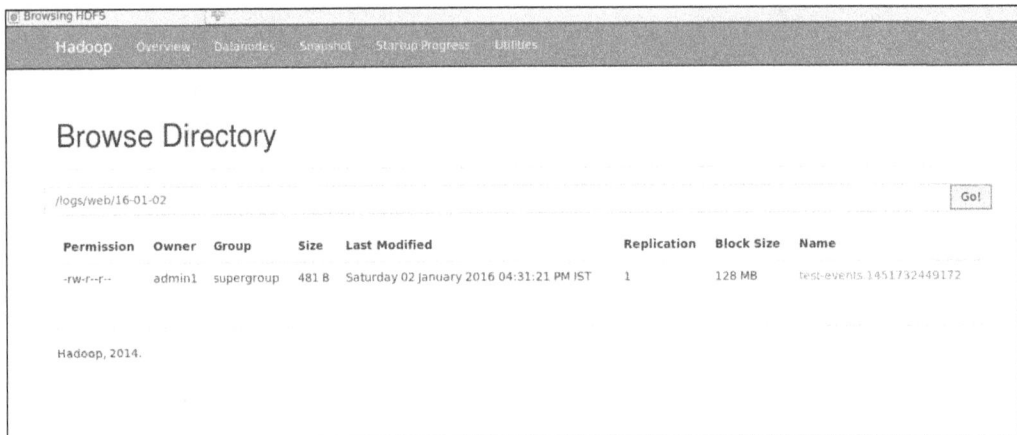

How it works...

`Exec` source executes the command on a given instance and redirects the output to a channel. The Channel then makes sure that it is given to the sink. Here we are using HDFS sink, which writes the data to HDFS in the given format.

7

Automation of Hadoop Tasks Using Oozie

In this chapter, we'll take a look at the following recipes:

- Implementing a Sqoop action job using Oozie
- Implementing a Map Reduce action job using Oozie
- Implementing a Java action job using Oozie
- Implementing a Hive action job using Oozie
- Implementing a Pig action job using Oozie
- Implementing an e-mail action job using Oozie
- Executing parallel jobs using Oozie (fork)
- Scheduling a job in Oozie

Introduction

In the previous chapter, we talked about two very important tools, Sqoop and Flume, which help us seamlessly import and export data in and out of Hadoop. Now that we have talked about most of the Hadoop ecosystem tools and their advanced usage, it's time to understand how to automate these tasks using another interesting tool called Oozie. Oozie is a job scheduler, which helps us execute a series of Hadoop tasks in a workflow.

Implementing a Sqoop action job using Oozie

In the previous chapter, we took a look at how to use Sqoop to import and export data from RDBMS to HDFS. In this recipe, you are going to learn how to automate this Sqoop import and export using Oozie.

Getting ready

To perform this recipe, you should have a running Hadoop cluster as well as the latest version of Sqoop and Oozie installed on it.

How to do it...

Any Oozie job execution consists of two important things, a `workflow.xml` and a properties file. The `workflow.xml` file is where we need to specify the flow of an execution. The following is an example of `workflow.xml`, which uses the Sqoop action:

```
<workflow-app xmlns="uri:oozie:workflow:0.2" name="sqoop-wf">
<start to="sqoop-node"/>

<action name="sqoop-node">
<sqoop xmlns="uri:oozie:sqoop-action:0.2">
<job-tracker>${jobTracker}</job-tracker>
<name-node>${nameNode}</name-node>

<configuration>
<property>
<name>mapred.job.queue.name</name>
<value>${queueName}</value>
</property>
</configuration>
<command>import --connect jdbc:mysql://localhost:3306/company
--username root --password password --table employee --target-dir /
data/employee-oozie -m 1</command>
</sqoop>
<ok to="end"/>
<error to="fail"/>
</action>
```

```
<kill name="fail">
<message>Sqoop failed, error message[${wf:errorMessage(wf:lastErrorNo
de())}]</message>
</kill>
<end name="end"/>
</workflow-app>
```

This is the command section where we need to provide the actual command that is to be executed from Sqoop.

Now, we have to upload `workflow.xml` to HDFS. After this, we need to create a `job.properties` file, which would invoke this workflow. Here is a sample code snippet for this purpose:

```
nameNode=hdfs://localhost:9000
jobTracker=localhost:8032
queueName=default
examplesRoot=examples
oozie.libpath=${nameNode}/user/admin1/share/lib
oozie.use.system.libpath=true

oozie.wf.application.path=${nameNode}/user/admin1/share/examples/apps/
sqoop
```

We have a property called `jobTracker` for which we have to give `ResourceManager` a host and a port.

Now, we have to submit this job using the following command:

```
oozie job -oozie http://localhost:11000/oozie -config job.properties
-run
```

This will start the workflow which will fetch data from MySQL and store it in the given HDFS directory. From Oozie's UI, you can track the progress of this job.

How it works

Oozie internally calls Sqoop libraries in order to import and export data as given in the command section. You can also use the `<prepare>` statements in order to make sure that directory where you export the data has been cleared before executing the job.

Implementing a Map Reduce action job using Oozie

In the previous recipe, we talked about how to use a Sqoop action to import data to HDFS. In this recipe, we are going to take a look at how to execute Map Reduce jobs using Oozie.

Getting ready

To perform this recipe, you should have a running Hadoop cluster as well as the latest version of Oozie installed on it.

How to do it...

Any Oozie job execution consists of two important things, `workflow.xml` and a properties file. The `Workflow.xml` file is where we need to specify the flow of execution. The following is an example of `workflow.xml`, which uses the MR action. Here, we also need to provide the jar file that contains the the map reduce code:

```
<workflow-app xmlns="uri:oozie:workflow:0.2" name="map-reduce-wf">
<start to="mr-node"/>
<action name="mr-node">
<map-reduce>
<job-tracker>${jobTracker}</job-tracker>
<name-node>${nameNode}</name-node>
<prepare>
<delete path="${nameNode}/user/${wf:user()}/${examplesRoot}/output-
data/${outputDir}"/>
</prepare>
<configuration>
<property>
<name>mapred.job.queue.name</name>
<value>${queueName}</value>
</property>
<property>
<name>mapred.mapper.class</name>
<value>com.demo.WordMapper</value>
</property>
<property>
<name>mapred.reducer.class</name>
<value>com.demo.SumReducer</value>
</property>
<property>
```

```
<name>mapred.input.dir</name>
<value>/in</value>
</property>
<property>
<name>mapred.output.dir</name>
<value>${outputDir}</value>
</property>
</configuration>
</map-reduce>
<ok to="end"/>
<error to="fail"/>
</action>
<kill name="fail">
<message>Map/Reduce failed, error message[${wf:errorMessage(wf:lastErr
orNode())}]</message>
</kill>
<end name="end"/>
</workflow-app>
```

In the preceding `workflow.xml`, it is important to provide the mapper and reducer classes, respectively.

Now, we have to upload `workflow.xml` and the jar file to HDFS. After this, we need to create the `job.properties` file, which will invoke this workflow. Here is a sample code snippet for this purpose:

```
nameNode=hdfs://localhost:9000
jobTracker=localhost:8032
queueName=default

oozie.wf.application.path=${nameNode}/user/admin1/share/examples/apps/
map-reduce/workflow.xml
outputDir=/newout
```

For the property called `jobTracker`, we can pass the `ResourceManager` host and port number.

We have to submit this job using the following command:

```
oozie job -oozie http://localhost:11000/oozie -config job.properties
-run
```

This will start the workflow, which will start reading data from the `/in` directory, calculate the word count, and write the output to the `/newout` directory.

How it works...

Oozie internally submits the map reduce job to the Resource Managers and works similar to our regular map reduce jobs. You can also use the `<prepare>` statements in order to make sure that the directory where you export the data has been cleared before executing the job.

Implementing a Java action job using Oozie

In the previous recipe, we talked about how to use Oozie to execute the Map Reduce job. In this recipe, we are going to take a look at how to execute any Java class using Oozie.

Getting ready

To perform this recipe, you should have a running Hadoop cluster as well as the latest version of Oozie installed on it.

How to do it

Any Oozie job execution consists of two important things, `workflow.xml` and a properties file. The `workflow.xml` is where we need to specify the flow of execution. The following is an example of `workflow.xml`, which uses a Java action. Here, we need to provide the jar file in which the code is present:

```xml
<workflow-app xmlns="uri:oozie:workflow:0.2" name="java-main-wf">
<start to="java-node"/>
<action name="java-node">
<java>
<job-tracker>${jobTracker}</job-tracker>
<name-node>${nameNode}</name-node>
<configuration>
<property>
<name>mapred.job.queue.name</name>
<value>${queueName}</value>
</property>
</configuration>
<main-class>com.demo.JavaMain</main-class>
<arg>Hello</arg>
<arg>Oozie!</arg>
</java>
<ok to="end"/>
<error to="fail"/>
</action>
```

```
<kill name="fail">
<message>Java failed, error message[${wf:errorMessage(wf:lastErrorNo
de())}]</message>
</kill>
<end name="end"/>
</workflow-app>
```

In the preceding e `workflow.xml`, we need to provide the main class that should be the entry point of our Java program. We can also provide arguments that can be passed to the Java class.

Now, we have to upload `workflow.xml` and the jar file to HDFS. After this, we need to create the `job.properties` file, which will invoke this workflow. Here is a sample code snippet for this purpose:

```
nameNode=hdfs://localhost:8020
jobTracker=localhost:8032
queueName=default
examplesRoot=examples

oozie.wf.application.path=${nameNode}/user/admin1/${examplesRoot}/
apps/java-main
```

Here, we have a property called `jobTracker` for which we have to provide `ResourceManager` a host and a port.

Now, we have to submit this job using the following command:

```
oozie job -oozie http://localhost:11000/oozie -config job.properties
-run
```

This will start the workflow, which will execute the code given in the `Main` class using the arguments that are passed.

How it works

Oozie executes the `Main` class provided along with the arguments in `workflow.xml`. It is important to note that while using Oozie, if you are trying to access any resources, make sure that a user has access to them.

Implementing a Hive action job using Oozie

In this recipe, we are going to take a look at how to use a Hive action in order to automate Hive query executions.

Getting ready

To perform this recipe, you should have a running Hadoop cluster as well as the latest version of Oozie and Hive installed on it.

How to do it...

Any Oozie job execution consists of two important things, workflow.xml and a properties file. The workflow.xml file is where we need to specify the flow of execution. The following is an example of workflow.xml, which uses the Hive action:

```
<workflow-app xmlns="uri:oozie:workflow:0.2" name="hive-wf">
<start to="hive-node"/>

<action name="hive-node">
<hive xmlns="uri:oozie:hive-action:0.2">
<job-tracker>${jobTracker}</job-tracker>
<name-node>${nameNode}</name-node>
<configuration>
<property>
<name>mapred.job.queue.name</name>
<value>${queueName}</value>
</property>
</configuration>
<script>script.q</script>
</hive>
<ok to="end"/>
<error to="fail"/>
</action>

<kill name="fail">
<message>Hive failed, error message[${wf:errorMessage(wf:lastErrorNo
de())}]</message>
</kill>
<end name="end"/>
</workflow-app>
```

Here, we can provide the Hive commands that are to be executed in the `script.q` file. The following is an example of the contents of `script.q`:

```
CREATE EXTERNAL TABLE test (a INT) STORED AS TEXTFILE LOCATION '/data/
input/test';
CREATE TABLE test_new (a INT) STORED AS TEXTFILE;
INSERT OVERWRITE TABLE test_new SELECT * FROM test;
```

In this script, you can write as many Hive queries as you wish to execute using Oozie.

Now, we have to upload `workflow.xml` and `script.q` to HDFS. After this, we need to create the `job.properties` file, which will invoke this workflow. Here is a sample code snippet for this purpose:

```
nameNode=hdfs://localhost:9000
jobTracker=localhost:8032
queueName=default
examplesRoot=examples

oozie.use.system.libpath=true

oozie.wf.application.path=${nameNode}/user/admin1/share/examples/apps/
hive
```

Here, we have a property called `jobTracker` for which we have to give `ResourceManager` a host and a port.

Now, we have to submit this job using the following command:

```
oozie job -oozie http://localhost:11000/oozie -config job.properties
-run
```

This will start the workflow, which will execute the given Hive queries.

How it works...

Oozie internally calls Hive to execute the given Hive query. It is important to provide fully qualified paths for input directories and not relative directories so there are no errors because of invalid paths. Each and everytime this can be performed from the Hive action as well.

Implementing a Pig action job using Oozie

In this recipe, we are going to take a look at how to use a Pig action in order to automate the `Pigscripts` executions.

Getting ready

To perform this recipe, you should have a running Hadoop cluster as well as the latest version of Oozie and Pig installed on it.

How to do it...

A Oozie job execution consists of two important things, `workflow.xml` and a properties file. The `workflow.xml` file is where we need to specify the flow of execution. The following is an example of `workflow.xml`, which uses the Pig action:

```
<workflow-app xmlns="uri:oozie:workflow:0.2" name="pig-wf">
<start to="pig-node"/>
<action name="pig-node">
<pig>
<job-tracker>${jobTracker}</job-tracker>
<name-node>${nameNode}</name-node>
<prepare>
<delete path="${nameNode}/user/${wf:user()}/${examplesRoot}/output-
data/pig"/>
</prepare>
<configuration>
<property>
<name>mapred.job.queue.name</name>
<value>${queueName}</value>
</property>
</configuration>
<script>script.pig</script>
<param>INPUT=/user/${wf:user()}/${examplesRoot}/input-data/text</
param>
<param>OUTPUT=/user/${wf:user()}/${examplesRoot}/output-data/pig</
param>
</pig>
<ok to="end"/>
<error to="fail"/>
</action>
<kill name="fail">
```

```
<message>Pig failed, error message[${wf:errorMessage(wf:lastErrorNo
de())}]</message>
</kill>
<end name="end"/>
</workflow-app>
```

Here, we can provide the Pig commands to be executed in the `script.pig` file. The following is an example of the contents of `script.pig`:

```
A = load '$INPUT' using PigStorage(':');
B = foreach A generate $0 as id;
store B into '$OUTPUT' USING PigStorage();
```

In this script, you can write any Pig command that you wish to execute using Oozie.

Now, we have to upload `workflow.xml` and `script.pig` to HDFS. After this, we need to create the `job.properties` file, which will invoke this workflow. Here is a sample code snippet for this purpose:

```
nameNode=hdfs://localhost:9000
jobTracker=localhost:8032
queueName=default
examplesRoot=examples

oozie.use.system.libpath=true

oozie.wf.application.path=${nameNode}/user/admin1/share/examples/apps/
pig
```

Here, we have a property, called `jobTracker`, for which we have to give `ResourceManager` a host and a port.

Now, we have to submit this job using the following command:

```
oozie job -oozie http://localhost:11000/oozie -config job.properties
-run
```

This will start the workflow, which will execute the given `Pigcommands`.

How it works

Oozie internally calls Pig to execute the given Pig script. It is important to provide fully qualified paths for input directories and not relative directories. Each and everytime, this can be performed from the Pig action as well.

Implementing an e-mail action job using Oozie

In this recipe, we are going to take a look at how to use an e-mail action in order to notify users about job executions in Oozie.

Getting ready

To perform this recipe, you should have a running Hadoop cluster as well as the latest version of Oozie installed on it.

How to do it...

An Oozie job execution consists of two important things, `workflow.xml` and a properties file. The `workflow.xml` file is where we need to specify the flow of execution. The following is an example of `workflow.xml`, which uses the e-mail action:

```
<workflow-app xmlns="uri:oozie:workflow:0.2" name="pig-wf">
<start to="notify"/>
<action name="notify">
<email xmlns="uri:oozie:email-action:0.1">
<to>a@.b.com</to>
<cc>b@b.com</cc>
<subject>Email notifications for ${wf:id()}</subject>
<body>The wf ${wf:id()} successfully completed.</body>
</email>
<error to="fail"/>
</action>
<kill name="fail">
<message>Email, error message[${wf:errorMessage(wf:lastErrorNo
de())}]</message>
</kill>
<end name="end"/>
</workflow-app>
```

To use the e-mail action, we first need to configure SMTP settings in `oozie-site.xml`, and the following properties need to be set:

▶ `oozie.email.smtp.host`: The host where the e-mail action may find the SMTP server (the localhost by default)

▶ `oozie.email.smtp.port`: The port to connect to for the SMTP server (25 by default)

- ▶ `oozie.email.from.address`: The `from` address to be used for the purpose of mailing all e-mails (`oozie@localhost` by default)

- ▶ `oozie.email.smtp.auth`: The Boolean property that toggles when an authentication is to be done or not (false by default)

- ▶ `oozie.email.smtp.username`: If an authentication is enabled, this shows the username to login as (empty by default)

- ▶ `oozie.email.smtp.password`: If the authentication is enabled, this shows the username's password (empty by default)

Now, we have to upload `workflow.xml` to HDFS. After this, we need to create the `job.properties` file, which will invoke this workflow. Here is a sample code snippet for this purpose:

```
nameNode=hdfs://localhost:9000
jobTracker=localhost:8032
queueName=default
examplesRoot=examples

oozie.use.system.libpath=true

oozie.wf.application.path=${nameNode}/user/admin1/share/examples/apps/
email
```

Here, we have a property, called `jobTracker`, for which we have to give `ResourceManager` a host and a port.

Now, we have to submit this job using the following command:

```
oozie job -oozie http://localhost:11000/oozie -config job.properties
-run
```

This will start the workflow, which will send the e-mail with given the details.

How it works...

The e-mail action is very important as it helps us notify users about the progress. My recommendation is that you should use this action at the start of the workflow, in case of any errors, and on successful completion.

Executing parallel jobs using Oozie (fork)

In this recipe, we are going to take a look at how to execute parallel jobs using the Oozie fork node. Here, we will be executing one Hive and one Pig job in parallel.

Getting ready

To perform this recipe, you should have a running Hadoop cluster as well as the latest version of Oozie, Hive, and Pig installed on it.

How to do it...

For parallel execution, we need to use the fork node given by Oozie. The following is a sample workflow that executes Hive and Pig jobs in parallel:

```
<workflow-app xmlns="uri:oozie:workflow:0.2" name="demo-wf">

<start to="fork-node"/>


<fork name="fork-node">
<path start="pig-node"/>
<path start="hive-node"/>
</fork>

<action name="pig-node">
<pig>
<job-tracker>${jobTracker}</job-tracker>
<name-node>${nameNode}</name-node>
<prepare>
<delete path="${nameNode}/user/${wf:user()}/${examplesRoot}/output-
data/pig"/>
</prepare>
<configuration>
<property>
<name>mapred.job.queue.name</name>
<value>${queueName}</value>
</property>
</configuration>
<script>script.pig</script>
<param>INPUT=/user/${wf:user()}/${examplesRoot}/input-data/text</
param>
```

```
<param>OUTPUT=/user/${wf:user()}/${examplesRoot}/output-data/pig</
param>
</pig>
<ok to="join-node"/>
<error to="fail"/>
</action>


<action name="hive-node">
<hive xmlns="uri:oozie:hive-action:0.2">
<job-tracker>${jobTracker}</job-tracker>
<name-node>${nameNode}</name-node>
<configuration>
<property>
<name>mapred.job.queue.name</name>
<value>${queueName}</value>
</property>
</configuration>
<script>script.q</script>
</hive>
<ok to="join-node"/>
<error to="fail"/>
</action>



<join name="join-node" to="end"/>

<kill name="fail">
<message>Demo workflow failed, error message[${wf:errorMessage(wf:last
ErrorNode())}]</message>
</kill>

<end name="end"/>

</workflow-app>
```

We can provide any number of jobs in the fork node to execute it in parallel. Each forked node should be joined back in a join node.

Now, we have to submit this job using the following command:

```
oozie job -oozie http://localhost:11000/oozie -config job.properties
-run
```

This will start the workflow that will execute Hive and Pig scripts in parallel.

How it works...

The fork node is helpful when we have two more processes which are independent of each other. This helps reduce the time for execution by consuming available resources.

Scheduling a job in Oozie

In this recipe, we are going to take a look at a schedule that has recurring jobs using the Oozie coordinator.

Getting ready

To perform this recipe, you should have a running Hadoop cluster as well as the latest version of Oozie installed on it.

How to do it...

Oozie provides one more type of job called a coordinator job. This type of job is used to schedule application jobs. With the help of a coordinator job, we can execute an application job. The following is an example of a coordinator job that runs daily:

```
<coordinator-app name="sample-coordinator"
  frequency="${coord:days(1)}"
  start="2016-01-01T18:56Z" end="2017-01-01T18:56Z" timezone="UTC"
  xmlns="uri:oozie:coordinator:0.2">

<controls>

<concurrency>1</concurrency>
<execution>FIFO</execution>
<throttle>5</throttle>
</controls>


<action>
<workflow>
<app-path>${applicationPath}</app-path>
<configuration>
        . . .
</configuration>
</workflow>
</action>
</coordinator-app>
```

Coordinator jobs contain one important attribute called frequency, which decides the frequency of job executions within a given start and end time.

Here is sample `job.properties` to execute the preceding workflow:

```
nameNode=hdfs://localhost:9000
jobTracker=localhost:8032
queueName=default
examplesRoot=examples

oozie.use.system.libpath=true

oozie.coord.application.path=${nameNode}/user/admin1/share/examples/
apps/coordinator
```

Now, we have to submit this job using the following command:

```
oozie job -oozie http://localhost:11000/oozie -config job.properties
-run
```

This will start the coordinator workflow, which will keep on running as per the schedule.

How it works...

Coordinator jobs work like `crontab`, where you set the frequency of certain task executions. Internally, it then invokes the application workflow provided in the coordinator workflow.

8
Machine Learning and Predictive Analytics Using Mahout and R

In this chapter, we'll cover the following recipes:

- ▸ Setting up the Mahout development environment
- ▸ Creating an item-based recommendation engine using Mahout
- ▸ Creating a user-based recommendation engine using Mahout
- ▸ Using predictive analytics for the marketing data of a bank
- ▸ Clustering text data using K-Means
- ▸ Performing population data analytics using R
- ▸ Performing Twitter Sentiment Analytics using R
- ▸ Performing Predictive Analytics using R

Introduction

In the previous chapter, we talked about how to automate Hadoop and its ecosystem tasks using Oozie. In this chapter, we will go deeper into the concepts of machine learning using Mahout and R. Mahout is a machine learning library, which allows us to solve machine learning problems with ease, whereas R is a statistical tool, which helps us build models. So, let's get started.

Setting up the Mahout development environment

In this recipe, we are going to take a look at how to set up the Mahout development environment.

Getting ready

To perform this recipe, you should have a running Hadoop cluster.

How to do it...

Setting up the Mahout environment is very easy:

1. To start with, we first need to download the latest version of Mahout from `http://www.apache.org/dyn/closer.cgi/mahout/`.

2. I am going to use version 0.11.1 ,which can be found at `http://www.eu.apache.org/dist/mahout/0.11.1/apache-mahout-distribution-0.11.1.tar.gz`.

3. Next, unzip the tar and rename the folder as Mahout for simplicity's sake:

   ```
   sudo tar  -xzf  apache-mahout-distribution-0.11.1.tar.gz
   sudo mv apache-mahout-distribution-0.11.1 mahout
   ```

4. To use the Mahout commands from everywhere, we add the distribution path to PATH. Edit `~/.bashrc` and add the following commands to it:

   ```
   export MAHOUT_HOME=/usr/local/mahout
   export PATH=$PATH:$MAHOUT_HOME/bin
   ```

5. Execute the following command to take a look at whether the changes are effective:

   ```
   source ~/.bashrc
   ```

6. Now you are all set to use Mahout:

   ```
   $ mahout
   Running on hadoop, using /usr/local/hadoop/bin/hadoop and HADOOP_
   CONF_DIR=
   MAHOUT-JOB: /usr/local/mahout/mahout-examples-0.11.1-job.jar
   An example program must be given as the first argument.
   Valid program names are:
     arff.vector: : Generate Vectors from an ARFF file or directory
     baumwelch: : Baum-Welch algorithm for unsupervised HMM training
     canopy: : Canopy clustering
     cat: : Print a file or resource as the logistic regression
   models would see it
   ```

cleansvd: : Cleanup and verification of SVD output

clusterdump: : Dump cluster output to text

clusterpp: : Groups Clustering Output In Clusters

cmdump: : Dump confusion matrix in HTML or text formats

cvb: : LDA via Collapsed Variation Bayes (0th deriv. approx)

cvb0_local: : LDA via Collapsed Variation Bayes, in memory locally.

describe: : Describe the fields and target variable in a data set

evaluateFactorization: : compute RMSE and MAE of a rating matrix factorization against probes

fkmeans: : Fuzzy K-means clustering

hmmpredict: : Generate random sequence of observations by given HMM

itemsimilarity: : Compute the item-item-similarities for item-based collaborative filtering

kmeans: : K-means clustering

lucene.vector: : Generate Vectors from a Lucene index

matrixdump: : Dump matrix in CSV format

matrixmult: : Take the product of two matrices

parallelALS: : ALS-WR factorization of a rating matrix

qualcluster: : Runs clustering experiments and summarizes results in a CSV

recommendfactorized: : Compute recommendations using the factorization of a rating matrix

recommenditembased: : Compute recommendations using item-based collaborative filtering

regexconverter: : Convert text files on a per line basis based on regular expressions

resplit: : Splits a set of SequenceFiles into a number of equal splits

rowid: : Map SequenceFile<Text,VectorWritable> to {SequenceFile< IntWritable,VectorWritable>, SequenceFile<IntWritable,Text>}

rowsimilarity: : Compute the pairwise similarities of the rows of a matrix

runAdaptiveLogistic: : Score new production data using a probably trained and validated AdaptivelogisticRegression model

runlogistic: : Run a logistic regression model against CSV data

seq2encoded: : Encoded Sparse Vector generation from Text sequence files

seq2sparse: : Sparse Vector generation from Text sequence files

seqdirectory: : Generate sequence files (of Text) from a directory

seqdumper: : Generic Sequence File dumper

seqmailarchives: : Creates SequenceFile from a directory containing gzipped mail archives

```
    seqwiki: : Wikipedia xml dump to sequence file
    spectralkmeans: : Spectral k-means clustering
    split: : Split Input data into test and train sets
    splitDataset: : split a rating dataset into training and probe
parts
    ssvd: : Stochastic SVD
    streamingkmeans: : Streaming k-means clustering
    svd: : Lanczos Singular Value Decomposition
    testnb: : Test the Vector-based Bayes classifier
    trainAdaptiveLogistic: : Train an AdaptivelogisticRegression
model
    trainlogistic: : Train a logistic regression using stochastic
gradient descent
    trainnb: : Train the Vector-based Bayes classifier
    transpose: : Take the transpose of a matrix
    validateAdaptiveLogistic: : Validate an
AdaptivelogisticRegression model against hold-out data set
    vecdist: : Compute the distances between a set of Vectors (or
Cluster or Canopy, they must fit in memory) and a list of Vectors
    vectordump: : Dump vectors from a sequence file to text
viterbi: : Viterbi decoding of hidden states from given output
states sequence
```

How it works...

We have just set the Mahout home, and it shows all the algorithms that are supported along with their purpose. Not all Mahout algorithms are able to use Hadoop/Map Reduce in order to understand that in a better manner.

> I suggest that you take a look at https://mahout.apache.org/users/basics/algorithms.html.

Creating an item-based recommendation engine using Mahout

In this recipe, we are going to take a look at how to use Mahout to generate item-based recommendations. Recommendation engine is one of the most seen use cases. A recommendation engine generates recommendations based on the input data provided to it. In this recipe, we are going to take a look at how to generate recommendations based on user preferences for certain items.

Getting ready

To perform this recipe, you should have a running Hadoop cluster as well as the latest version of Mahout installed on it.

How to do it...

Mahout provides built-in support for item-based recommendations. In order to execute a program using Mahout, we first need to prepare the input data and store it in a certain folder. The input data needs to be in a specified format (`userId`, `itemId`, and preference). Here, `userId` is the unique user identifier, `itemId`, is the unique item identifier, while the preference can be a rating given by a user to a specific item, number of items that are ordered, and so on.

First, we capture and prepare our data and store it in HDFS:

```
hadoop fs -mkdir /recommender-in
hadoop fs -put user-item.txt /recommender-in
```

Here is some sample input:

```
1,10,1.0
1,11,2.0
1,12,5.0
1,13,5.0
1,14,5.0
1,15,4.0
1,16,5.0
1,17,1.0
1,18,5.0
2,10,1.0
2,11,2.0
2,15,5.0
2,16,4.5
2,17,1.0
2,18,5.0
3,11,2.5
3,12,4.5
3,13,4.0
3,14,3.0
3,15,3.5
```

```
3,16,4.5
3,17,4.0
3,18,5.0
4,10,5.0
4,11,5.0
4,12,5.0
4,13,0.0
4,14,2.0
4,15,3.0
4,16,1.0
4,17,4.0
4,18,1.0
```

To start the job, we have to execute the following command:

```
mahout recommenditembased -s SIMILARITY_LOGLIKELIHOOD -i /recommender-in
-o /recommender-out --numRecommendations 5
```

The preceding command starts a series of Map Reduce programs, which run over the input data. `SIMILARITY_LOGLIKELIHOOD` is the name of a class that determines the similarity between items. You can either use this default, or you can choose from a variety of similar algorithms that are available.

Once the execution is complete, the output that's generated is as follows:

```
$ hadoop fs -ls /recommender-out
    Found 2 items
    -rw-r--r--   1 admin1 supergroup          0 2016-01-28 11:46
    /recommender-out/_SUCCESS
    -rw-r--r--   1 admin1 supergroup         28 2016-01-28 11:46
    /recommender-out/part-r-00000
$ hadoop fs -cat /recommender-out/part-r-00000
    3   [10:3.8597424]
    4   [13:4.0]
```

This output indicates that the recommender has generated two recommendations. For user 3, it recommends item 10, and for user 4, it recommends item 13.

This way, you can keep on putting your data in HDFS and keep running the recommendation jobs every time that the data is updated. You can write custom code to use this output and integrate it into your application.

How it works...

Mahout uses various algorithms to generate the recommendations. It first puts the data that's been given as the input in the form of model data. It uses a similarity calculation algorithm given by the user in order to do this. These two things are used as input in order to calculate the similarity between the items. Once this is calculated, based on the items that are not used by users, it recommends them.

This implementation can used as is without any modifications if it can get your data in the given format. You can use this recommendation engine to generate recommendations on e-commerce websites for production recommendations, or it can also be used to track web user activity and recommend web pages accordingly.

Creating a user-based recommendation engine using Mahout

In this recipe, we are going to take a look at how to use Mahout to generate user-based recommendations. The user-based recommendation engine is not available directly to be used as a Map Reduce job. We have to run it in a sequential manner, as described in the next section.

Getting ready

To perform this recipe, you should have a running Hadoop cluster as well as the latest version of Mahout installed on it. We will also need an Eclipse-like IDE or any other IDE of your choice for code development.

How to do it...

User-based recommendations work on the simple principle of user similarities and their likelihood toward the same set of items. To implement them, we first need to create a Maven project, and add the following dependency to it:

```
<dependency>
    <groupId>org.apache.mahout</groupId>
    <artifactId>mahout-mr</artifactId>
    <version>0.10.0</version>
</dependency>
```

Next, we create a Java class, as shown here:

```java
package com.demo.recommender;

import java.io.File;
import java.io.IOException;
import java.util.List;

import org.apache.mahout.cf.taste.common.TasteException;
import org.apache.mahout.cf.taste.impl.model.file.FileDataModel;
import org.apache.mahout.cf.taste.impl.neighborhood.
ThresholdUserNeighborhood;
import org.apache.mahout.cf.taste.impl.recommender.
GenericUserBasedRecommender;
import org.apache.mahout.cf.taste.impl.similarity.
PearsonCorrelationSimilarity;
import org.apache.mahout.cf.taste.model.DataModel;
import org.apache.mahout.cf.taste.neighborhood.UserNeighborhood;
import org.apache.mahout.cf.taste.recommender.RecommendedItem;
import org.apache.mahout.cf.taste.recommender.UserBasedRecommender;
import org.apache.mahout.cf.taste.similarity.UserSimilarity;

public class MyUserBasedRecommender
{
    public static void main( String[] args ) throws IOException,
TasteException
    {
    ClassLoader classLoader = MyUserBasedRecommender.class.
getClassLoader();
    DataModel model = new FileDataModel(new File(classLoader.
getResource("dataset.csv").getFile()));
    UserSimilarity similarity = new PearsonCorrelationSimilarity(mod
el);
    UserNeighborhood neighborhood = new ThresholdUserNeighborhood(0.1,
similarity, model);
        UserBasedRecommender recommender = new GenericUserBasedRecomme
nder(model, neighborhood, similarity);
    List<RecommendedItem> recommendations = recommender.recommend(2,
3);
    for (RecommendedItem recommendation : recommendations) {
      System.out.println(recommendation);
    }
    }
}
```

In the preceding code, we first need data from a resource folder. We have copied the `dataset.csv` file into the `src/main/resources` folder. The following code shows you the contents of this folder. You should read the data in the file in the specified format such as `UserId`, `ItemId`, and preference:

```
1,10,1.0
1,11,2.0
1,12,5.0
1,13,5.0
1,14,5.0
1,15,4.0
1,16,5.0
1,17,1.0
1,18,5.0
2,10,1.0
2,11,2.0
2,15,5.0
2,16,4.5
2,17,1.0
2,18,5.0
3,11,2.5
3,12,4.5
3,13,4.0
3,14,3.0
3,15,3.5
3,16,4.5
3,17,4.0
3,18,5.0
4,10,5.0
4,11,5.0
4,12,5.0
4,13,0.0
4,14,2.0
4,15,3.0
4,16,1.0
4,17,4.0
4,18,1.0
```

In order to create a user-based recommendation, we need to first calculate the similarity between these users. Here, we choose the Pearson Similarity Algorithm to calculate the similarity. Next, we pass the similarity, model, and the threshold to decide the neighborhood. Then, we create a user-based recommender by providing the preceding calculated values.

In the preceding code, on execution, we want the top three item recommendations for user 2.

On the execution of the code, we will get the following output. This is the list of items that are to be recommended along with the recommendation score:

```
RecommendedItem[item:12, value:4.8328104]
RecommendedItem[item:13, value:4.6656213]
RecommendedItem[item:14, value:4.331242]
```

How it works...

Mahout's user-based recommendation first tries to calculate the similarity between the users, and then it recommends other similar users from their kitty. There are various similarity calculations available, and you can choose any one of them; the preceding example uses the Pearson Similarity Algorithm. More on this can be found at https://en.wikipedia.org/wiki/Pearson_product-moment_correlation_coefficient.

Make a note that this recommendation can only be run in a sequential manner, so there is no Map Reduce implementation for this.

Predictive analytics on Bank Data using Mahout

In this recipe, we are going to take a look at how to use Mahout to generate a predictive model and validate how good this model is against some sample data. Here, we will be using the sample data collected by a bank during their marketing operations.

Getting ready

To perform this recipe, you should have a running Hadoop cluster as well as the latest version of Mahout installed on it.

How to do it...

In this recipe, we are going to use Logistic Regression in order to predict the occurrence of an event. It uses predictors from the given data in order to calculate the probability. The Mahout implementation uses the **Stochastic Gradient Descent** (**SGD**) algorithm for logistic regression. You can learn more about SGD for logistic regression at http://blog.trifork.com/2014/02/04/an-introduction-to-mahouts-logistic-regression-sgd-classifier/.

SGD is, by default, a sequential algorithm so we cannot run any parallel activities on it. Even though it is sequential, it runs blazing fast on large datasets for which we don't need to worry about the size of data that we are handling.

Now, we are going to take a look at how to execute this algorithm in our data. The following is sample data from a bank's marketing team, which has the last column labelled as 'out'. This is the output that is shown when a customer who's given their details has said yes to the term deposit or not:

```
age,job,marital,education,out
30,unemployed,married,primary,no
33,services,married,secondary,yes
35,management,single,tertiary,no
30,management,married,tertiary,no
59,blue-collar,married,secondary,no
35,management,single,tertiary,no,
36,self-employed,married,tertiary,yes
39,technician,married,secondary,no
41,entrepreneur,married,tertiary,no
43,services,married,primary,no
39,services,married,secondary,no
43,admin.,married,secondary,no
36,technician,married,tertiary,yes
20,student,single,secondary,no
31,blue-collar,married,secondary,yes
```

We save this data in a file called `bank.csv`. Now, let's execute the Mahout program to train a model for this data using this command:

```
mahout  trainlogistic --input bank.csv --output ./model --target out
--categories 2  --predictors age job marital education --types word
--features 4
```

Here is the `input` file in the CSV format, which is used to train the model. We want the output to be created in a file called model. We expect a type of output called `categories` (yes/no), `predictors` called columns are used to generate the mode, and `types` can be words/numerical. And no. of `features` to be used for generating model.

On execution, you will get the following output:

```
Running on hadoop, using /usr/local/hadoop/bin/hadoop and HADOOP_CONF_
DIR=
MAHOUT-JOB: /usr/local/mahout/mahout-examples-0.11.1-job.jar
4
out ~
-0.003*Intercept Term + -0.007*age=20 + -0.006*age=30 +
-0.005*age=31 + -0.002*age=33 + -0.005*age=35 + -0.006*age=36 +
-0.005*age=39 + -0.006*age=41 + -0.006*age=43 + -0.004*age=59
+ -0.007*education=primary + -0.002*education=secondary +
-0.004*education=tertiary + -0.002*job=admin. + -0.005*job=blue-
collar + -0.005*job=entrepreneur + -0.004*job=management +
-0.007*job=self-employed + -0.006*job=services + -0.005*job=student +
-0.006*job=technician + -0.006*job=unemployed + -0.006*marital=married
+ -0.007*marital=single
```

```
      Intercept Term -0.00298
             age=20 -0.00696
             age=30 -0.00645
             age=31 -0.00457
             age=33 -0.00159
             age=35 -0.00545
             age=36 -0.00645
             age=39 -0.00545
             age=41 -0.00557
             age=43 -0.00645
             age=59 -0.00398
   education=primary -0.00696
 education=secondary -0.00159
  education=tertiary -0.00406
          job=admin. -0.00159
     job=blue-collar -0.00457
     job=entrepreneur -0.00457
      job=management -0.00398
   job=self-employed -0.00696
        job=services -0.00557
         job=student -0.00457
       job=technician -0.00557
      job=unemployed -0.00645
     marital=married -0.00645
      marital=single -0.00696
   -0.003981019     -0.002976461     -0.001590416     -0.002469779
16/01/28 12:44:01 INFO MahoutDriver: Program took 644 ms (Minutes:
0.010733333333333333)
```

Now that we have generated the model to predict the outcome, we can validate it against the data shown here:

```
mahout runlogistic --input "bank.csv" --model ./model --auc -confusion
Running on hadoop, using /usr/local/hadoop/bin/hadoop and HADOOP_CONF_
DIR=
MAHOUT-JOB: /usr/local/mahout/mahout-examples-0.11.1-job.jar
AUC = 0.73
confusion: [[11.0, 4.0], [0.0, 0.0]]
entropy: [[-0.7, -0.4], [-0.7, -0.4]]
```

This will run the logistic regression on `bank.csv` using the model generated in the previous step in order to calculate AUC and a confusion matrix.

AUC stands for the Area Under a Curve. You can read more about AUC at http://www.mathwords.com/a/area_under_a_curve.htm.

The AUC should lie between 0.5 and 1.0 in scenarios where you're using a good model, while 1.0 indicates a perfect model.

A Confusion Matrix is a matrix that shows the performance of an algorithm by comparing its actual results with its predicted results. You can read more about the confusion matrix at `https://en.wikipedia.org/wiki/Confusion_matrix`.

How it works...

Mahout's implementation of SGD calculates the probability of the occurrence of a certain event based on the values considered as predictors. When creating a model, it considers the values of given predictors and these are used for predictions as well. In order to understand Logistic Regression and how it works internally.

> I would suggest that you read `http://blog.trifork.com/2014/02/04/an-introduction-to-mahouts-logistic-regression-sgd-classifier/`.

Text data clustering using K-Means using Mahout

In this recipe, we are going to take a look at how to use Mahout to cluster text data using Mahout's implementation of the K-Means algorithm. K-Means is very popular clustering algorithm; you can read more about it at `https://en.wikipedia.org/wiki/K-means_clustering`.

Getting ready

To perform this recipe, you should have a running Hadoop cluster as well as the latest version of Mahout installed on it.

How to do it...

In this recipe, we are going to use Mahout's K Means algorithm to cluster the text data that is available. To do this, we first need to get some text data and copy it to HDFS:

```
hadoop fs -mkdir /kmeans
hadoop fs -put mydata.txt /kmeans/input
```

In order to execute the K-Means job on the given data, we first need to convert it into sequential files and from these sequential files to TF-IDF vectors. Mahout provides built-in utilities to perform these actions. The following are the commands to do this.

To convert text data into a sequential file, here is the code:

```
mahout seqdirectory -i /kmeans/input/ -o /kmeans/sequencefiles
```

To convert a sequential file to a vector, here is the code:

```
mahout seq2sparse -i /kmeans/sequencefiles -o /kmeans/sparse
```

This command will take some time to work as it will run a series of Map Reduce programs to transform the data.

Next, we can run a clustering job on vectors that have been generated in the previous steps:

```
mahout kmeans -i hdfs://localhost:9000/kmeans/sparse/tfidf-vectors/ -c
hdfs://localhost:9000/kmeans/cl/ -o hdfs://localhost:9000/kmeans/out -dm
org.apache.mahout.common.distance.CosineDistanceMeasure -x 10 -clustering
```

This will start a Map Reduce program that performs the actual clustering.

The output of the clustering will be available in the `/kmeans/out` folder. We can also use the `clusterdump` command to view the output:

```
mahout clusterdump -dt sequencefile -d /kmeans/sparse/dictionary. file-0
-i /kmeans/out/clusters-1-final
```

In this way, we can use Mahout to perform the clustering of text data.

How it works...

The K-Means algorithm plots a graph of points. It then calculates the distance between nodes in order to classify them. In order to optimize the clustering, iterations are performed, and in each new iteration, the centroid of each cluster becomes the mean of the next set of calculations.

Apart from K-Means, Mahout supports various other clustering algorithms such as Canopy, Fuzzy K-means, Streaming K-Means, and so on.

Population Data Analytics using R

So far, we talked about how to use Mahout to solve various machine learning problems. Now, we are going to explain another tool/language called R, which has built-in support for various mathematical and statistical operations.

Getting ready

To perform this recipe, you should have R installed on your machine. You can download the installer from `https://cran.r-project.org/bin/windows/base/`.

How to do it...

In this recipe, we are going to learn some basic operations that one can perform using R. To start with, we will have one dataset that has information about Australia's population in various states. This is what the dataset looks like:

```
Year NSW Vic. Qld SA WA Tas. NT ACT Aust.
1917 1904 1409 683 440 306 193 5 3 4941
1927 2402 1727 873 565 392 211 4 8 6182
1937 2693 1853 993 589 457 233 6 11 6836
1947 2985 2055 1106 646 502 257 11 17 7579
1957 3625 2656 1413 873 688 326 21 38 9640
1967 4295 3274 1700 1110 879 375 62 103 11799
1977 5002 3837 2130 1286 1204 415 104 214 14192
1987 5617 4210 2675 1393 1496 449 158 265 16264
1997 6274 4605 3401 1480 1798 474 187 310 18532
```

I am saving this data in a file called `auspop.txt`. Now, we start R and load this file in an R object by executing the following command:

```
>austpop <- read.table("H:/workspace/austpop.txt", header=TRUE)
```

We can check whether the data is loaded properly by printing it:

```
>print(austpop)
    Year  NSW Vic.  Qld   SA   WA Tas.  NT ACT Aust.
1  1917 1904 1409  683  440  306  193   5   3  4941
2  1927 2402 1727  873  565  392  211   4   8  6182
3  1937 2693 1853  993  589  457  233   6  11  6836
4  1947 2985 2055 1106  646  502  257  11  17  7579
5  1957 3625 2656 1413  873  688  326  21  38  9640
6  1967 4295 3274 1700 1110  879  375  62 103 11799
7  1977 5002 3837 2130 1286 1204  415 104 214 14192
8  1987 5617 4210 2675 1393 1496  449 158 265 16264
9  1997 6274 4605 3401 1480 1798  474 187 310 18532
```

We can print the column names using the following command:

```
> names(austpop)
 [1] "Year"   "NSW"    "Vic."   "Qld"    "SA"     "WA"     "Tas."   "NT"
 "ACT"    "Aust."
```

Next, we can plot a graph. Let's plot a graph of the population in the state of NSW for the past few years. In order to do so, we have to execute the following command. The input to this will appear in the form of the x axis, y axis, and the size of the graph:

```
>plot(NSW ~ Year, data=austpop, pch=16)
```

The graph will look like this:

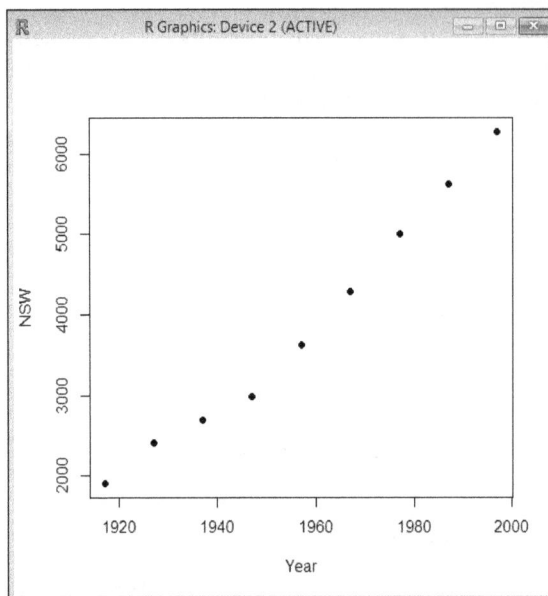

There are various options that are available for different types of graphs. This is how you can plot a bar graph for the total population of this state over the last few years:

```
> barplot(austpop$Aust.)
```

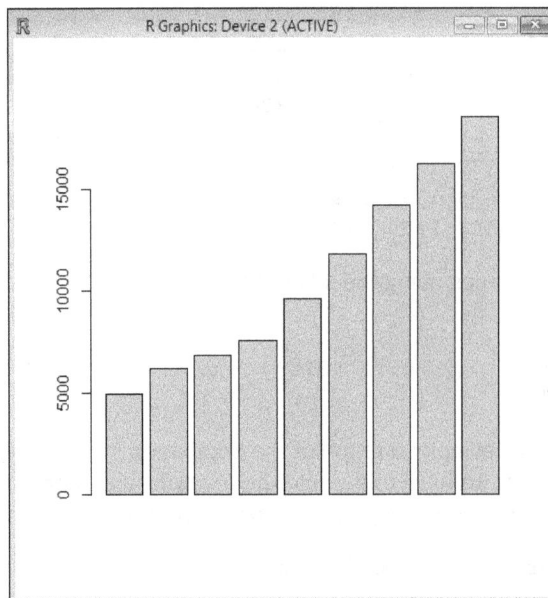

You can also easily get the summary of the values for each state by executing the following command:

```
> summary(austpop)
      Year                NSW                Vic.               Qld                SA
 WA
 Min.    :1917    Min.    :1904    Min.     :1409    Min.    : 683    Min.    :
 440.0   Min.    : 306
 1st Qu.:1937    1st Qu.:2693    1st Qu.:1853    1st Qu.: 993    1st Qu.:
 589.0   1st Qu.: 457
 Median :1957    Median :3625    Median :2656    Median :1413    Median :
 873.0   Median : 688
 Mean    :1957    Mean    :3866    Mean     :2847    Mean    :1664    Mean    :
 931.3   Mean    : 858
 3rd Qu.:1977    3rd Qu.:5002    3rd Qu.:3837    3rd Qu.:2130    3rd
 Qu.:1286.0    3rd Qu.:1204
 Max.    :1997    Max.     :6274    Max.     :4605    Max.    :3401    Max.
 :1480.0    Max.    :1798
      Tas.               NT               ACT               Aust.
 Min.    :193.0    Min.    : 4    Min.    : 3.0    Min.    : 4941
 1st Qu.:233.0    1st Qu.: 6    1st Qu.: 11.0    1st Qu.: 6836
 Median :326.0    Median : 21    Median : 38.0    Median : 9640
 Mean    :325.9    Mean    : 62    Mean    :107.7    Mean    :10663
 3rd Qu.:415.0    3rd Qu.:104    3rd Qu.:214.0    3rd Qu.:14192
 Max.    :474.0    Max.    :187    Max.    :310.0    Max.    :18532
```

In case you want the summary of only one column, you can get it by executing the following command:

```
> summary(austpop$Aust.)
   Min. 1st Qu.  Median    Mean 3rd Qu.    Max.
   4941    6836    9640   10660   14190   18530
```

You can also perform operations such as sorting the given data, as shown here:

```
> sort_pop <- sort(austpop$ACT)
> sort_pop
[1]    3    8   11   17   38 103 214 265 310
```

How it works...

As mentioned earlier, R has been built keeping statisticians in mind, so whatever they require on a daily basis is provided by R. There are various packages also available in case you wish to do something different. The working of the preceding commands is self-explanatory.

Twitter Sentiment Analytics using R

In an earlier chapter, we saw how to perform Twitter sentiment analytics using Hive and Hadoop. In this recipe, we are going to take a look at how to do this using R.

Getting ready

To perform this recipe, you should have R installed on your machine. You should also have a Twitter account and an application that has an API key, API secret, Access Token, and an Access Secret with you so that you can receive tweets in real time.

How to do it...

To get started, first of all, we need to install certain R packages, which will be required in this recipe. The following are the commands:

```
>install.packages("twitteR")
>install.packages("plyr")
>install.packages("stringr")
>install.packages(c("devtools", "rjson", "bit64", "httr"))
```

Once the installation is complete, load the following packages:

```
>library(devtools)
>library(twitteR)
```

Next, we need to provide the keys provided that are by Twitter on its application page, as follows:

```
>api_key <-  "XXXXXX"
>api_secret <- "XXXXXX"
>access_token <- "XXXXXX"
>access_secret <- "XXXXXXX"
>ssetup_twitter_oauth(api_key, api_secret, access_token, access_
secret)
```

Here, instead of XXXX, add your own keys.

If the keys that are provided by you are correct, you will not see any errors. If there are any missing keys, you will see an appropriate error message.

Next, we need some dictionary words, which are segregated as positive or negative, in order to determine the sentiment of each tweet. So, we download a list of words from http://www. cs.uic.edu/~liub/FBS/opinion-lexicon-English.rar and store them in a certain place. Download, extract, and save these files.

Then, we load these lists of words into objects, as shown here:

```
>pos.from.file = scan('H:/opinion-lexicon-English/positive-words.
txt',what='character', comment.char=';')
>neg.from.file = scan('H:/opinion-lexicon-English/negative-words.
txt',what='character', comment.char=';')
```

We also remove the comments that are labelled as headers in the text files.

We can also add some more words if they are not already part of the given files, as shown here:

```
>pos.words = c(pos.from.file,'upgrade', 'love','achievement','impress
ed')
>neg.words = c( neg.from.file, 'wtf', 'wait', 'waiting','hate', 'die')
```

Now, we are going to download the tweets using the `searchTwitter` method of the `TwitterR` package:

```
hadoop.tweets = searchTwitter('#hadoop', n=1000)
```

The preceding command will download 1,000 tweets with the `hadoop` hash tag and save it as the `hadoop.tweets` object.

You can check whether the data is imported properly:

```
> hadoop.tweets
[[1]]
[1] "bviallet: RT @IBMAnalytics: See how the video game industry is
using analytics to create happy customers: https://t.co/LcyTEFqUrT
#Hadoop https://t.c…"

[[2]]
[1] "sheltonmkagande: RT @SAS_Cares: Learn five ways #SAS gets to data
in #hadoop https://t.co/yMsXTVw7Dd #SASusers"

[[3]]
[1] "thinkittraining: Secondary Indexing for MapR-DB using
Elasticsearch @https://www.mapr.com/blog #Hadoop #Mapr #training"

[[4]]
[1] "BigDataTweetBot: RT @andnegr: https://t.co/Yd87vicD1z @SASitaly
#BigData #Hadoop @ClouderaITA"

[[5]]
[1] "BigDataTweetBot: RT @techjunkiejh: Is Apache #Hadoop the only
option to implement #BigData ? https://t.co/b4z7ZSHTiJ https://t.co/
mGRFXqS6Dx"
```

```
[[6]]
[1] "shakamunyi: RT @andnegr: https://t.co/Yd87vicDlz @SASitaly
#BigData #Hadoop @ClouderaITA"

[[7]]
[1] "shakamunyi: RT @techjunkiejh: Is Apache #Hadoop the only option
to implement #BigData ? https://t.co/b4z7ZSHTiJ https://t.co/
mGRFXqS6Dx"

[[8]]
[1] "andnegr: https://t.co/Yd87vicDlz @SASitaly #BigData #Hadoop @
ClouderaITA"

[[9]]
[1] "techjunkiejh: Is Apache #Hadoop the only option to implement
#BigData ? https://t.co/b4z7ZSHTiJ https://t.co/mGRFXqS6Dx"

[[10]]
[1] "gitsacademy: #fact of the day\n#Hadoop was created by Doug
Cutting (while at #Yahoo) and named it after his son's elephant
https://t.co/RUnDJzSpml"
```

Now, we want only the tweet text from the preceding data, so we execute the following command:

```
>hadoop.text = laply(hadoop.tweets, function(t) t$getText() )
```

We will be writing one algorithm that takes each tweet and then computes how many positive and negative words it has. It will give a score based on the sentiment of the overall tweet:

```
score.sentiment = function(sentences, pos.words, neg.words,
.progress='none')
{
require(plyr)
require(stringr)

#Get vectors from the list
scores = laply(sentences, function(sentence, pos.words, neg.words) {

# clean up sentences, remove punctuations etc.
sentence = gsub('[[:punct:]]', '', sentence)
sentence = gsub('[[:cntrl:]]', '', sentence)
sentence = gsub('\\d+', '', sentence)
# and convert to lower case:
sentence = tolower(sentence)

# split into words.
```

```
word.list = str_split(sentence, '\\s+')
words = unlist(word.list)

# compare our words to the dictionaries of positive & negative terms
pos.matches = match(words, pos.words)
neg.matches = match(words, neg.words)

# match() returns the position of the matched term or NA
# we just want a TRUE/FALSE so we remove all NA
pos.matches = !is.na(pos.matches)
neg.matches = !is.na(neg.matches)

# and conveniently enough, TRUE/FALSE will be treated as 1/0 by sum():
score = sum(pos.matches) - sum(neg.matches)

return(score)
}, pos.words, neg.words, .progress=.progress )

scores.df = data.frame(score=scores, text=sentences)
return(scores.df)
}
```

We can test this algorithm by using some sample text, as shown here:

```
> sample = c("You're awesome and I love you",
"I hate and hate and hate. So angry. Die!",
"Impressed and amazed: you are peerless in your
achievement of unparalleled mediocrity.")

> result = score.sentiment(sample, pos.words, neg.words)
```

Now, we can see the results:

```
> result
  score                                                         text
1     2
You're awesome and I love you
2    -5                                            I hate and hate
and hate. So angry. Die!
3     3 Impressed and amazed: you are peerless in your\nachievement of
unparalleled mediocrity.
```

This means that our algorithm works, so we will test on real Twitter data now:

```
>hadoop.scores = score.sentiment(hadoop.text, pos.words, neg.words,
.progress='text')
```

Here are the results:

```
> hadoop.scores
    score
text
1       1 RT @IBMAnalytics: See how the video game industry is using
analytics to create happy customers: https://t.co/LcyTEFqUrT #Hadoop
https://t.c…
2       0                                      RT @SAS_Cares:
Learn five ways #SAS gets to data in #hadoop https://t.co/yMsXTVw7Dd
#SASusers
3       0                            Secondary Indexing for
MapR-DB using Elasticsearch @https://www.mapr.com/blog #Hadoop #Mapr
#training
4       0
RT @andnegr: https://t.co/Yd87vicDlz @SASitaly #BigData #Hadoop @
ClouderaITA
5       0                  RT @techjunkiejh: Is Apache #Hadoop the only
option to implement #BigData ? https://t.co/b4z7ZSHTiJ https://t.co/
mGRFXqS6Dx
6       0
RT @andnegr: https://t.co/Yd87vicDlz @SASitaly #BigData #Hadoop @
ClouderaITA
7       0                  RT @techjunkiejh: Is Apache #Hadoop the only
option to implement #BigData ? https://t.co/b4z7ZSHTiJ https://t.co/
mGRFXqS6Dx
8       0
https://t.co/Yd87vicDlz @SASitaly #BigData #Hadoop @ClouderaITA
9       0                            Is Apache #Hadoop the only
option to implement #BigData ? https://t.co/b4z7ZSHTiJ https://t.co/
mGRFXqS6Dx
10      0          #fact of the day\n#Hadoop was created by Doug Cutting
(while at #Yahoo) and named it after his son's elephant https://t.co/
RUnDJzSpml
```

This way, you can perform sentiment analytics for any kind of Twitter data.

How it works...

Our sentiment analysis algorithm is very simple. We first get the sentence, break it into words, remove any punctuation, and so on. Later, we compare each word with a predefined list of positive and negative words. Next, we subtract the number of negative words from the number of positive words and get the score. If the score is a positive number, then it means that the sentiment of the tweet is positive, and if the score is negative, it means that the tweet is negative. If the score is zero, this means that it is a neutral tweet.

This algorithm can be extended further to understand sarcasm.

Performing Predictive Analytics using R

In the previous recipe, we talked about how to perform sentiment analytics using R. In this recipe, we are going to take a look at how to perform predictive analytics using R. Here, we will be using the IRIS flower classification data in order to predict its species based on the features. You can learn more about this at `https://en.wikipedia.org/wiki/Iris_flower_data_set`.

Getting ready

To perform this recipe, you should have R installed on your machine.

How to do it...

To get started, we need to install an R package called `e1071`:

```
>install.packages("e1071")
```

This package contains the IRIS flower dataset. So, we load the library and then load the data into it:

```
>library(e1071)
>data(iris)
```

You can check whether the data is loaded properly or not by executing the following command:

```
>iris
```

In this example, we are going to use the Naive Bayes algorithm to classify the data into specifies. So, now we have to train the model using Naive Bayes, as shown here:

```
>model<- naiveBayes(Species~., data=iris)
```

You can print the model in order to take a look at how it has calculated probabilities:

```
>model

    Naive Bayes Classifier for Discrete Predictors

    Call:
    naiveBayes.default(x = X, y = Y, laplace = laplace)

    A-priori probabilities:
    Y
        setosa versicolor  virginica
      0.3333333  0.3333333  0.3333333
```

```
Conditional probabilities:
          Sepal.Length
Y                [,1]       [,2]
  setosa        5.006 0.3524897
  versicolor 5.936 0.5161711
  virginica  6.588 0.6358796

          Sepal.Width
Y                [,1]       [,2]
  setosa        3.428 0.3790644
  versicolor 2.770 0.3137983
  virginica  2.974 0.3224966

          Petal.Length
Y                [,1]       [,2]
  setosa        1.462 0.1736640
  versicolor 4.260 0.4699110
  virginica  5.552 0.5518947

          Petal.Width
Y                [,1]       [,2]
  setosa        0.246 0.1053856
  versicolor 1.326 0.1977527
  virginica  2.026 0.2746501

> summary(model)
          Length Class  Mode
apriori 3         table  numeric
tables  4         -none- list
levels  3         -none- character
call    4         -none- call
```

Now, we test this model against actual data:

```
>predictions <- predict(model, iris[,1:4])
```

This will give us the model and data to be used for predictions. On execution, the predictions object will have these predicted values:

```
> predictions

    [1] setosa     setosa     setosa     setosa     setosa     setosa
setosa
    [8] setosa     setosa     setosa     setosa     setosa     setosa
setosa
   [15] setosa     setosa     setosa     setosa     setosa     setosa
setosa
```

```
     [22] setosa      setosa      setosa      setosa      setosa      setosa
setosa
     [29] setosa      setosa      setosa      setosa      setosa      setosa
setosa
     [36] setosa      setosa      setosa      setosa      setosa      setosa
setosa
     [43] setosa      setosa      setosa      setosa      setosa      setosa
setosa
     [50] setosa      versicolor versicolor virginica   versicolor
versicolor versicolor
     [57] versicolor versicolor versicolor versicolor versicolor
versicolor versicolor
     [64] versicolor versicolor versicolor versicolor versicolor
versicolor versicolor
     [71] virginica   versicolor versicolor versicolor versicolor
versicolor versicolor
     [78] virginica   versicolor versicolor versicolor versicolor
versicolor versicolor
     [85] versicolor versicolor versicolor versicolor versicolor
versicolor versicolor
     [92] versicolor versicolor versicolor versicolor versicolor
versicolor versicolor
     [99] versicolor versicolor virginica   virginica   virginica   virginica
virginica
    [106] virginica   versicolor virginica   virginica   virginica   virginica
virginica
    [113] virginica   virginica   virginica   virginica   virginica   virginica
virginica
    [120] versicolor virginica   virginica   virginica   virginica   virginica
virginica
    [127] virginica   virginica   virginica   virginica   virginica   virginica
virginica
    [134] versicolor virginica   virginica   virginica   virginica   virginica
virginica
    [141] virginica   virginica   virginica   virginica   virginica   virginica
virginica
    [148] virginica   virginica   virginica
Levels: setosa versicolor virginica
```

Next, we can build the confusion matrix in order to show how good our model is:

```
> table(predictions, iris$Species)

predictions  setosa versicolor virginica
  setosa         50          0         0
  versicolor      0         47         3
  virginica       0          3        47
```

This way, you can build a model using various algorithms and validate them.

How it works...

R is a platform that allows us to perform various operations. The package we installed contains implementations of various well-know algorithms; here, we are just making use of those that are useful for real-world problem solving.

> You can do read more about the Naive Bayes algorithm at
> `https://en.wikipedia.org/wiki/Naive_Bayes_classifier`.

9
Integration with Apache Spark

In this chapter, we'll take a look at the following recipes:

- ▶ Running Spark standalone
- ▶ Running Spark on YARN
- ▶ Performing Olympics Athletes analytics using the Spark Shell
- ▶ Creating Twitter trending topics using Spark Streaming
- ▶ Analyzing Parquet files using Spark
- ▶ Analyzing JSON data using Spark
- ▶ Processing graphs using Graph X
- ▶ Conducting predictive analytics using Spark `MLib`

Introduction

In the previous chapter, we talked about how to use Mahout and R to solve machine learning problems. In this chapter, we are going to talk about the latest sensation in the Big Data industry called Apache Spark. By now, everyone is aware, and has acknowledged the power of Apache Spark. This is a general and fast engine that processes large-scale data. It provides high-level APIs in Java, Scala, Python, and R. Spark can perform batch processing as well as stream processing. In this chapter, we are going to explore certain important topics related to Apache Spark such as batch processing, Spark SQL, streaming processing, machine learning with `MLib`, and graph processing using Spark's `GraphX` library. So, let's get started.

Running Spark standalone

Spark can be executed in various modes. To get started, we are going to take a look at how to install Apache Spark on a standalone machine.

Getting ready

To perform this recipe, you should download the latest version of Spark. For this recipe, I am using Apache Spark 1.6.0. You can visit the download page at `http://spark.apache.org/downloads.html`.

How to do it...

Apache Spark is a computation engine. It has a built-in cluster manager. It can also use other cluster managers such as YARN/Mesos and so on. In this recipe, we are going to use the built-in resource manager that's provided by Spark:

1. Copy the downloaded Spark binary to a desired location.

2. Extract the tar ball:

   `$sudo tar -xzfspark-1.6.0-bin-hadoop2.6.tgz`

3. Rename the `spark` folder for ease of use:

   `$sudo mv spark-1.6.0-bin-hadoop2.6 spark`

4. Add environment variables in `~/.bashrc`:

   `export SPARK_HOME=/usr/local/spark`

   `export PATH=$PATH:$SPARK_HOME/bin`

5. Source `~/.bashrc` to make the changes effective:

   `$source ~/.bashrc`

6. In case you want to run Spark in cluster mode, you need to repeat the preceding commands on each node. Now, we are all set to use Apache Spark.

   To start the master, use this code:

   `$/usr/local/spark/sbin/start-master.sh`

   To start the slaves, use this code:

   `$/usr/local/spark/sbin/start-slave.sh spark://<masterhost>:<port>`

7. Now, visit `http://localhost:8080/` to take a look at Spark Master's UI and the number of workers that are registered with it.

8. We can now try running one sample Spark application in order to check whether everything is working. The following command will launch a Spark application, which will calculate the value for Pi:

```
./bin/spark-submit --class org.apache.spark.examples.SparkPi \
    --master spark://<master>:7077 \
--deploy-mode cluster \
lib/spark-examples*.jar \
    10
```

9. While the application is being executed, you should be able to take a look at all the stages that are involved as well as other things in the application web UI. To do this, visit `http://localhost:4040`.

How it works...

Spark works in the master-slave architecture. Here, we have started Spark Master and a worker. Spark master acts like a coordinator between the slaves. Once you submit the application, Spark creates a directed acyclic graph of operations. It decides which stages can be executed in parallel and which need to be executed sequentially. Each task is executed by workers, and the status is reported back to the master.

Running Spark on YARN

In the previous recipe, we took a look at how to use Spark's built-in cluster manager; in this recipe, we are going to explore how to use YARN as a cluster manager to execute the Spark application.

Getting ready

To perform this recipe, you should have a running Hadoop cluster. You should also have performed the previous recipe.

How to do it...

As mentioned in the previous recipe, we can either use Spark's built-in cluster manager, or we can use an external cluster manager such as YARN. In order to execute the Spark application on YARN, we need to edit SPARK_HOME/conf/spark-env.sh, and add the following properties to it:

```
export HADOOP_CONF_DIR=/usr/local/hadoop/etc/hadoop
export YARN_CONF_DIR=/usr/local/hadoop/etc/Hadoop
```

Here, /usr/local/hadoop/etc/hadoop is the directory where we have our Hadoop and YARN configuration files.

Now, let's execute the same Spark application on YARN using the following command:

```
./bin/spark-submit --class org.apache.spark.examples.SparkPi \
    --master yarn \
    --deploy-mode cluster \
lib/spark-examples*.jar \
    10
```

Unlike the previous recipe, we don't need to give YARN IP—PORT, but spark will take it from YARN's configuration directory. We need to give YARN the keyword for the master property.

Now, we can use the YARN application UI in order to check the progress of the job so far.

Go to `http://localhost:8088/cluster` for the following output:

How it works...

Working on the Spark application is pretty similar to what was explained in the previous recipe; the only difference is the executors, Resource Manager, and the Node Managers. Spark submits the application to the YARN application master, and the application master then asks the Resource Managers and Node Managers to execute the tasks.

Performing Olympics Athletes analytics using the Spark Shell

Spark supports an interactive Scala-based shell, which can be used to process data as and when we receive actionable commands. In this recipe, we are going to analyze one sample dataset, which contains information about the athletes that have participated in the Olympics.

Getting ready

To perform this recipe, you should have Hadoop and Spark installed. You also need to install Scala. I am using Scala 2.11.0.

How to do it...

First of all, you need to download data from `https://github.com/deshpandetanmay/hadoop-real-world-cookbook/blob/master/data/OlympicAthletes.csv`, and store it in HDFS using the following commands:

```
$hadoop fs -mkdir /athletes
```

```
$hadoop fs -put OlympicAthletes.csv /athletes
```

The following is some sample data from the file for your reference. The data comma-separated file contains various columns in a sequence such as the athlete name, country, year, gold, silver, bronze, and the total number of medals won by each athlete:

```
Yang Yilin,China,2008,Gymnastics,1,0,2,3
Leisel Jones,Australia,2000,Swimming,0,2,0,2
Go Gi-Hyeon,South Korea,2002,Short-Track Speed Skating,1,1,0,2
Chen Ruolin,China,2008,Diving,2,0,0,2
Katie Ledecky,United States,2012,Swimming,1,0,0,1
Ruta Meilutyte,Lithuania,2012,Swimming,1,0,0,1
Dániel Gyurta,Hungary,2004,Swimming,0,1,0,1
Arianna Fontana,Italy,2006,Short-Track Speed Skating,0,0,1,1
Olga Glatskikh,Russia,2004,Rhythmic Gymnastics,1,0,0,1
Kharikleia Pantazi,Greece,2000,Rhythmic Gymnastics,0,0,1,1
Kim Martin,Sweden,2002,Ice Hockey,0,0,1,1
Kyla Ross,United States,2012,Gymnastics,1,0,0,1
Gabriela Dragoi,Romania,2008,Gymnastics,0,0,1,1
Tasha Schwikert-Warren,United States,2000,Gymnastics,0,0,1,1
Yang Yun,China,2000,Gymnastics,0,0,1,1
Sophie Lamon,Switzerland,2000,Fencing,0,1,0,1
Alejandra Orozco,Mexico,2012,Diving,0,1,0,1
Yuliya Koltunova,Russia,2004,Diving,0,1,0,1
Shawn Johnson,United States,2008,Gymnastics,1,3,0,4
Carly Patterson,United States,2004,Gymnastics,1,2,0,3
```

Next, we start the Apache Spark shell using the following command:

```
$cd /usr/local/spark
$./bin/spark-shell
```

This will start the Spark shell, and it will prompt Scala. Now, to get started, we will first initialize the spark context and start with loading files into it from HDFS:

```
scala>valatheletes =
sc.textFile("hdfs://localhost:9000/athletes/OlympicAthletes.csv")
```

Let's check whether the data is loaded properly by executing the following command:

```
scala>atheletes.take(10).foreach(println)
~

    Yang Yilin,China,2008,Gymnastics,1,0,2,3

    Leisel Jones,Australia,2000,Swimming,0,2,0,2

    Go Gi-Hyeon,South Korea,2002,Short-Track Speed Skating,1,1,0,2

    Chen Ruolin,China,2008,Diving,2,0,0,2

    Katie Ledecky,United States,2012,Swimming,1,0,0,1

    Ruta Meilutyte,Lithuania,2012,Swimming,1,0,0,1

    Dániel Gyurta,Hungary,2004,Swimming,0,1,0,1

    Arianna Fontana,Italy,2006,Short-Track Speed Skating,0,0,1,1

    Olga Glatskikh,Russia,2004,Rhythmic Gymnastics,1,0,0,1

    Kharikleia Pantazi,Greece,2000,Rhythmic Gymnastics,0,0,1,1

    ~
```

It will print the first 10 athlete records. Next, let's count the total number of records in the dataset. That can be done by the following command:

```
scala>atheletes.count
~

    16/02/03 13:05:28 INFO DAGScheduler: Job 2 finished: count at
    <console>:30, took 0.188182 s

    res2: Long = 8613

    ~
```

Now, let's filter out athletes from India using the following commands:

```
scala>valindianAthletes = atheletes.filter(_.split(",")(1) == "India").
cache
```

We can print the records using this command:

```
scala>indianAthletes.foreach(println)
    Vijender Singh,India,2008,Boxing,0,0,1,1

    Saina Nehwal,India,2012,Badminton,0,0,1,1

    Sushil Kumar,India,2008,Wrestling,0,0,1,1

    Karnam Malleswari,India,2000,Weightlifting,0,0,1,1

    Abhinav Bindra,India,2008,Shooting,1,0,0,1

    Vijay Kumar,India,2012,Shooting,0,1,0,1

    Yogeshwar Dutt,India,2012,Wrestling,0,0,1,1
```

```
Sushil Kumar,India,2012,Wrestling,0,1,0,1

Gagan Narang,India,2012,Shooting,0,0,1,1

M. C. Mary Kom,India,2012,Boxing,0,0,1,1

Rajyavardhan Rathore,India,2004,Shooting,0,1,0,1
```

Next, we would like to find out the number of athlete records on the basis of their countries; thus, we will need to execute the following command:

```
scala>valatheletesTuples = atheletes.map(line =>line.split(","))

scala>valatheletesKeyValuePairs = atheletesTuples.map(line =>
(line(1), 1))

scala>valgroupByCountry = atheletesKeyValuePairs.reduceByKey(_+_,
1).collect
```

In the preceding commands, we first split each record by a comma and then emit the country as the key and 1 as the value. Next, we execute reduce by operation to get the final results. The output is shown here:

```
groupByCountry: Array[(String, Int)] = Array((Australia,524),
(Brazil,217), (Mexico,38), (Uzbekistan,19), (France,287),
(South Korea,274), (Finland,112), (Germany,552), (Macedonia,1),
(Montenegro,14), (Uruguay,1), (Cuba,188), (Bahrain,1), (North
Korea,21), (Sweden,167), (Vietnam,2), (Serbia,31), (Iran,24),
(Slovakia,33), (Venezuela,4), (Denmark,89), (Chinese Taipei,20),
(Saudi Arabia,6), (Paraguay,17), (Serbia and Montenegro,38),
(Sudan,1), (Botswana,1), (Greece,59), (Italy,307), (Slovenia,24),
(Iceland,15), (Netherlands,286), (Spain,195), (Kuwait,2),
(Hong Kong,3), (Mongolia,10), (Malaysia,3), (Kazakhstan,42),
(Ukraine,137), (Romania,97), (Egypt,8), (Indonesia,22), (Latvia,17),
(Eritrea,1), (Armenia,10), (Norway,158), (Thailand,18), (Poland,73),
(Tajikistan,3), (Afghanistan,2)
```

Similarly, we can also execute commands to get the number of athletes by the sport they play:

```
scala>valsportsWiseKeyValuePairs = atheletesTuples.map(line =>
(line(3), 1))

scala>valgroupBySport = sportsWiseKeyValuePairs.reduceByKey(_+_,
1).collect
```

The output for this is as follows:

```
groupBySport: Array[(String, Int)] = Array((Basketball,287),
(Judo,224), (Football,407), (Modern Pentathlon,24), (Luge,36),
(Table Tennis,67), (Swimming,487), (Synchronized Swimming,109),
(Cycling,261), (Athletics,687), (Baseball,216), (Diving,113), (Cross
Country Skiing,128), (Waterpolo,306), (Equestrian,157), (Skeleton,18),
(Hockey,386), (Alpine Skiing,61), (Rhythmic Gymnastics,84),
(Handball,351), (Softball,134), (Gymnastics,194), (Nordic Combined,39),
(Canoeing,295), (Weightlifting,180), (Wrestling,245), (Sailing,210),
(Taekwondo,112), (Ski Jumping,40), (Trampoline,24), (Short-Track Speed
Skating,96), (Boxing,188), (Biathlon,94), (Tennis,71), (Triathlon,24),
(Figure Skating,54), (Badminton,91), (Curling,82), (Rowing,567),
(Snowboarding,48), (Beach Volleyball,48), (Ice Hockey,384)
```

This way, you can perform various operations to analyze data interactively.

How it works...

The Spark shell gives us interactive ways to analyze data. Internally, it's the same Spark application that gets executed, as explained in the previous recipes.

Creating Twitter trending topics using Spark Streaming

Spark supports various modules. In this recipe, we are going to take a look at its SQL module, which allows the execution of SQL queries through a Spark application. We are going to explore how to access Hive from Spark and perform analytics.

Getting ready

To perform this recipe, you should have Hadoop and Spark installed. You also need to install Scala. I am using Scala 2.11.0. You should also have Hive installed.

How to do it...

To use Hive from Spark, we are going to write one sample spark application in Scala. You can choose an IDE of your choice. Since we are going to write the application in Scala, you will need Scala and SBT installed on your machine.

First of all, I am going to create a folder called `HiveFromSpark`, and add the following files to it:

```
HiveFromSpark\src\main\scala\com\demo\HiveFromSpark.scala
HiveFromSpark\ project\assembly.sbt
HiveFromSpark\build.sbt
HiveFromSpark\src\main\resources\emp.txt
```

Then, we set `build.sbt` to add dependencies, as shown here:

```
name := "HiveFromSpark"

version := "1.0"

scalaVersion := "2.11.7"

libraryDependencies ++= Seq(

  "com.google.guava" % "guava" % "14.0",
  "org.apache.spark" %% "spark-core" % "1.6.0" % "provided",
  "org.apache.spark" %% "spark-sql"  % "1.6.0" % "provided",
  "org.apache.spark" %% "spark-hive" % "1.6.0" % "provided"
)
resolvers += "Akka Repository" at "http://repo.akka.io/releases/"
```

Next, we create the `assembly.sbt` file so that it is able to generate the fat jar:

```
addSbtPlugin("com.eed3si9n" % "sbt-assembly" % "0.12.0")
```

We then add `emp.txt`, which is a simple file that we are going to use during execution:

```
16,john
17,robert
18,andrew
19,katty
21,tom
22,tim
23,james
24,paul
27,edward
29,alan
31,kerry
34,terri
```

Now, we will write a Scala class, which will create a Hive table and load `emp.txt` into the table. Later on, we will perform various operations in this table. The following code is from `HiveFromSpark.scala`:

```scala
packagecom.demo

importcom.google.common.io.ByteStreams
importcom.google.common.io.Files


importjava.io.File

importorg.apache.spark._
importorg.apache.spark.sql._
importorg.apache.spark.sql.hive.HiveContext

objectHiveFromSpark {
case class Record(id: Int, name: String)

  // Copy emp.txt file from classpath to temporary directory
valempStream = HiveFromSpark.getClass.getResourceAsStream("/emp.txt")
valempFile = File.createTempFile("emp", "txt")
empFile.deleteOnExit()
ByteStreams.copy(empStream, Files.newOutputStreamSupplier(empFile))

def main(args: Array[String]) {
valsparkConf = new SparkConf().setAppName("HiveFromSpark")
valsc = new SparkContext(sparkConf)


valhiveContext = new HiveContext(sc)
importhiveContext.implicits._
importhiveContext.sql

sql("CREATE TABLE IF NOT EXISTS empSpark (id INT, name STRING) ROW
FORMAT DELIMITED FIELDS TERMINATED BY ','")
sql(s"LOAD DATA LOCAL INPATH '${empFile.getAbsolutePath}' INTO TABLE
empSpark")

    // Queries are expressed in HiveQL
println("Result of 'SELECT *': ")
sql("SELECT * FROM empSpark").collect().foreach(println)

    // Aggregation queries are also supported.
```

```
val count = sql("SELECT COUNT(*) FROM empSpark").collect().head.
getLong(0)
println(s"COUNT(*): $count")

    // The results of SQL queries are themselves RDDs and support all
normal RDD functions.  The
    // items in the RDD are of type Row, which allows you to access
each column by ordinal.
valrddFromSql = sql("SELECT id, name FROM empSpark WHERE id < 20 ORDER
BY id")

println("Result of RDD.map:")
valrddAsStrings = rddFromSql.map {
case Row(id: Int, name: String) =>s"Key: $id, Value: $name"
    }
    // You can also register RDDs as temporary tables within a
HiveContext.
valrdd = sc.parallelize((1 to 100).map(i => Record(i, s"val_$i")))
rdd.toDF().registerTempTable("records")

    // Queries can then join RDD data with data stored in Hive.
println("Result of SELECT *:")
sql("SELECT * FROM records r JOIN src s ON r.key = s.key").collect().
foreach(println)

sc.stop()
    }
}
```

In order to execute the preceding code, we run the following commands to create the assembled fat jar of this application:

sbt compile

sbt package

sbt assembly

This will create a fat jar, called HiveFromSpark-assembly-1.0.jar, in the target\
scala-2.11 folder.

Now, we take this jar and copy it in a Spark cluster. Execute the following command to start the Spark application:

```
/usr/local/spark/bin/spark-submit \
   --class "com.demo.HiveFromSpark" \
   --master yarn \
   HiveFromSpark-assembly-1.0.jar
```

If you want to run this on the Spark default master slave, then you will have to execute the following command:

```
/usr/local/spark/bin/spark-submit \
  --class "com.demo.HiveFromSpark" \
  --master spark://admin1:7077 \
  HiveFromSpark-assembly-1.0.jar
```

This will start the Spark application in YARN. This will create a table in Hive, called `empspark`, where data from `emp.txt` will be loaded into it.

You can go to the Hive prompt and check whether this table, called `empspark`, exists:

```
hive>descempspark;
hive>select * from empspark;
```

How it works...

Spark SQL is an interpreter between the underlying technology and Spark. It sends queries and accepts results. All the features of Spark RDDs are available here.

Twitter trending topics using Spark streaming

In the previous recipe, we took a look at the SQL integrations of Spark. In this recipe, we are going to explore yet another powerful module called Spark Streaming. As the name suggests, Spark Streaming can listen to a stream of events and process data as and when it arrives.

Getting ready

To perform this recipe, you should have Hadoop and Spark installed. You also need to install Scala. I am using Scala 2.11.0. You should also have a Twitter account and some keys and tokens.

How to do it...

Spark streaming supports input from various sources such as Flume, HDFS, Kafka, Twitter, and so on. In this recipe, we are going to use Spark Streaming's Twitter source where we will be listening to streaming tweets and compute the top trending topics on Twitter.

To perform this recipe, we are going to write one Spark Streaming application in Scala.

In order to create the application, I am creating a folder called `TwitterSpark`, and it will have the following files in it:

```
TwitterSpark\build.sbt
TwitterSpark\src\main\scala\com\demo\TwitterPopularTags.scala
TwitterSpark\project\assembly.sbt
```

The contents of `build.sbt` are as follows:

```
name := "TwitterSpark"


version := "1.0"


scalaVersion := "2.11.7"


mergeStrategy in assembly <<= (mergeStrategy in assembly) { (old) =>
    {
casePathList("META-INF", xs @ _*) =>MergeStrategy.discard
case x =>MergeStrategy.first
    }
}


libraryDependencies ++= Seq(

 "com.google.guava" % "guava" % "14.0",
 "org.apache.spark" %% "spark-core" % "1.6.0" % "provided",
 "org.apache.spark" %% "spark-streaming" % "1.6.0" % "provided",
 "org.apache.spark" %% "spark-streaming-twitter" % "1.6.0"
)


resolvers += "Akka Repository" at "http://repo.akka.io/releases/"
```

Here, we need to add dependencies for Spark Streaming and Spark Streaming Twitter.

Next, `assembly.sbt` will show you the following:

```
addSbtPlugin("com.eed3si9n" % "sbt-assembly" % "0.12.0")
```

We need to add a Scala class, which fetches Twitter streams and performs computations on them:

```
packagecom.demo


importorg.apache.spark.streaming.{Seconds, StreamingContext}
importorg.apache.spark.SparkContext._
```

```
importorg.apache.spark.streaming.twitter._
importorg.apache.spark.SparkConf

objectTwitterPopularTags {
def main(args: Array[String]) {


valconsumerKey = "XXXX"
valconsumerSecret = "XXXX"
valaccessToken = "XXXX"
valaccessTokenSecret = "XXXX"
val filters = args.takeRight(args.length - 4)
    // Set the system properties so that Twitter4j library used by
twitter stream
    // can use them to generat OAuth credentials
System.setProperty("twitter4j.oauth.consumerKey", consumerKey)
System.setProperty("twitter4j.oauth.consumerSecret", consumerSecret)
System.setProperty("twitter4j.oauth.accessToken", accessToken)
System.setProperty("twitter4j.oauth.accessTokenSecret",
accessTokenSecret)

valsparkConf = new SparkConf().setAppName("TwitterPopularTags")
valssc = new StreamingContext(sparkConf, Seconds(2))
val stream = TwitterUtils.createStream(ssc, None, filters)

valhashTags = stream.flatMap(status =>status.getText.split("
").filter(_.startsWith("#")))

valtopCountsInOneMinute = hashTags.map((_, 1)).reduceByKeyAndWindow(_
+ _, Seconds(60))
                    .map{case (topic, count) => (count, topic)}
                    .transform(_.sortByKey(false))



    // Print popular hashtags
topCountsInOneMinute.foreachRDD(rdd => {
valtopList = rdd.take(10)
println("\nPopular topics in last 1 minute (%s total):".format(rdd.
count()))
topList.foreach{case (count, tag) =>println("%s (%s tweets)".
format(tag, count))}
    })
```

```
ssc.start()
ssc.awaitTermination()
  }
}
```

Now, we build an assembly jar for this project by executing the following commands:

sbt compile

sbt assembly

This will create a fat jar with the name `TwitterSpark-assembly-1.0.jar`. To execute it, we copy it into a Spark cluster and execute the following commands.

Here is the code to execute it:

```
/usr/local/spark/bin/spark-submit \
  --class "com.demo.TwitterPopularTags" \
  --master local[2] \
  TwitterSpark-assembly-1.0.jar
```

Here is the code to execute it on the Spark default master:

```
/usr/local/spark/bin/spark-submit \
  --class "com.demo.TwitterPopularTags" \
  --master spark://host:port \
  TwitterSpark-assembly-1.0.jar
```

Here is the code to execute it on the YARN cluster:

```
/usr/local/spark/bin/spark-submit \
  --class "com.demo.TwitterPopularTags" \
  --master yarn \
  TwitterSpark-assembly-1.0.jar
```

As a result you should see the top trending hash tags of every minute:

```
#style (1 tweets)
#followmejp (1 tweets)
#amateur (1 tweets)
#VotaSebastianVillalobos (1 tweets)
#poem (1 tweets)
#followme (1 tweets)
#thoughtoftheday (1 tweets)
#followcircle (1 tweets)
```

How it works...

Spark Streaming internally receives live data streams from the source. It then divides data into batches and processes these batches one by one. These streams are called `DStreams`. Along with the streaming context, we also need to provide the time slot that Spark needs in order to wait for a batch. In the preceding code, the time period needed is 2 seconds. Once the batch has been received by the spark engine, the rest of the processing is similar to what has already been explained in the previous recipes. You can read more about this at `http://spark.apache.org/docs/latest/streaming-programming-guide.html`.

Analyzing Parquet files using Spark

Parquet is columnar data file format, which is being used extensively. In this recipe, we are going to take a look at how to access this data from Spark and then process it.

Getting ready

To perform this recipe, you should have Hadoop and Spark installed. You also need to install Scala. I am using Scala 2.11.0.

How to do it...

Spark supports the accessing of Parquet files from the SQL context. You can read and write Parquet files using this SQL context. In this recipe, we are going to take a look at how to read a Parquet file from HDFS and process it.

First of all, download the sample parquet file, `users.parquet`, and store it in the HDFS / `parquet` path `https://github.com/deshpandetanmay/hadoop-real-world-cookbook/blob/master/data/users.parquet`.

We will create a Scala project with the following files:

```
SparkParquet\build.sbt
SparkParquet\project\assembly.sbt
SparkParquet\src\main\scala\com\demo\SparkParquet.scala
```

The contents of `build.sbt` are as follows:

```
name := "SparkParquet"

version := "1.0"

scalaVersion := "2.11.7"
```

```
libraryDependencies ++= Seq(

  "com.google.guava" % "guava" % "14.0",
  "org.apache.spark" %% "spark-core" % "1.6.0" % "provided",
  "org.apache.spark" %% "spark-sql"  % "1.6.0" % "provided"
)


resolvers += "Akka Repository" at "http://repo.akka.io/releases/"
```

The contents of `assembly.sbt` are as follows:

```
addSbtPlugin("com.eed3si9n" % "sbt-assembly" % "0.12.0")
```

Then, we write a Scala class, which reads the parquet file stored in the given HDFS location and creates another file from it, `.SparkParquet.scala`, as follows:

```
packagecom.demo


importorg.apache.spark._
importorg.apache.spark.sql._

objectSparkParquet {


def main(args: Array[String]) {
valsparkConf = new SparkConf().setAppName("SparkParquet")
valsc = new SparkContext(sparkConf)
valsqlContext = new org.apache.spark.sql.SQLContext(sc)
val users = sqlContext.read.load("/parquet/users.parquet")

users.select("name", "favorite_color").write.save("/parquet/
namesAndFavColors.parquet")

users.registerTempTable("userParquetFile")
users.map(t => "Name: " + t(0)).collect().foreach(println)
sc.stop()
    }
}
```

We build an assembly jar for this project using the following commands:

sbt compile

sbt assembly

Then, we execute the application using the following commands:

We use this code for local threads:

```
/usr/local/spark/bin/spark-submit \
--class "com.demo.SparkParquet" \
--master local[2] \
SparkParquet-assembly-1.0.jar
```

We use this code for YARN:

```
/usr/local/spark/bin/spark-submit \
--class "com.demo.SparkParquet" \
--master yarn \
SparkParquet-assembly-1.0.jar
```

This will start the application and print something like this:

```
~
Name: Alyssa
Name: Ben
~
```

I will also create another parquet file called `namesAndFavColors.parquet` in the `/parquet` HDFS path.

How it works...

The Spark SQL context has features to serialize and deserialize Parquet files. The preceding code makes use of this feature to read the data and print it. We can also register a temporary table and use SQL to analyze the parquet file data using its schema.

Analyzing JSON data using Spark

JSON is one of most frequently used data storage and exchange formats in use these days. In this recipe, we are going to take a look at how to access the JSON file data from Spark and process it.

Getting ready

To perform this recipe, you should have Hadoop and Spark installed. You also need to install Scala. I am using Scala 2.11.0 here.

How to do it...

Spark supports the accessing of JSON files from the SQL context. You can read and write JSON files using the SQL context. In this recipe, we are going to take a look at how to read a JSON file from HDFS and process it.

First of all, download the `people.json` sample JSON file and store it in the `/json` HDFS path using this link:

https://github.com/deshpandetanmay/hadoop-real-world-cookbook/blob/master/data/people.json.

We will create a Scala project using the following files:

```
SparkJSON\build.sbt
SparkJSON\project\assembly.sbt
SparkJSON\src\main\scala\com\demo\SparkJSON.scala
```

Here is the content of `build.sbt`:

```
name := "SparkJSON"

version := "1.0"

scalaVersion := "2.11.7"

libraryDependencies ++= Seq(

  "com.google.guava" % "guava" % "14.0",
  "org.apache.spark" %% "spark-core" % "1.6.0" % "provided",
  "org.apache.spark" %% "spark-sql"  % "1.6.0" % "provided"
)

resolvers += "Akka Repository" at "http://repo.akka.io/releases/"
```

The contents of `assembly.sbt` are as follows:

```
addSbtPlugin("com.eed3si9n" % "sbt-assembly" % "0.12.0")
```

Then, we write a Scala class, which reads the JSON file stored in the given HDFS location and process it. `SparkJSON.scala` is as follows:

```
packagecom.demo

importorg.apache.spark._
importorg.apache.spark.sql._
```

```
objectSparkJSON {


def main(args: Array[String]) {
valsparkConf = new SparkConf().setAppName("SPARKJSON")
valsc = new SparkContext(sparkConf)
valsqlContext = new org.apache.spark.sql.SQLContext(sc)
val users = sqlContext.read.json("/json/people.json")

users.map(t => "Name: " + t(0)).collect().foreach(println)
users.show()

        // Print the schema in a tree format
        users.printSchema()

        // Select only the "name" column
        users.select("name").show()

        // Select everybody, but increment the age by 1
        users.select(users("name"), users("age") + 1).show()

        // Select people older than 21
        users.filter(users("age") > 21).show()

        // Count people by age
        users.groupBy("age").count().show()

sc.stop()
    }
}
```

We build an assembly jar for this project using the following commands:

```
sbt compile
sbt assembly
```

Then, we execute the application using the following command:

First on local threads

```
/usr/local/spark/bin/spark-submit \
--class "com.demo.SparkJSON" \
--master local[2] \
SparkJSON-assembly-1.0.jar
```

For YARN, we use the following code:

```
/usr/local/spark/bin/spark-submit \
--class "com.demo.SparkJSON" \
--master yarn \
SparkJSON-assembly-1.0.jar
```

This will start the application and print something like this:

```
+----+-----+
| age|count|
+----+-----+
|50|      1|
|  19|    1|
|  30|    1|
+----+-----+
```

How it works...

The Spark SQL context has features that are used to serialize and deserialize JSON files. The preceding code makes use of these features to read the data from the files and then print it. We can also register a temporary table and use SQL to analyze the JSON file data using its schema.

Processing graphs using Graph X

A graph is combination of vertices and edges. Spark provides a module to define a graph and then process these graphs in real time. In this recipe, we are going to look at a social graph example and process data using Spark.

Getting ready

To perform this recipe, you should have Hadoop and Spark installed. You also need to install Scala. I am using Scala 2.11.0 here.

How to do it...

Take a social networking site that has users and other users such as the activities of a user. Based on the likes, we can conclude who is connected to whom. Consider the following data:

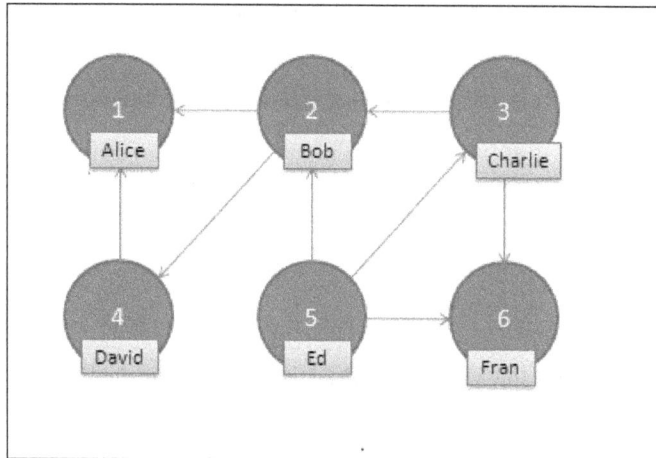

Now, we have to analyze this graph based on the likes that are provided. In order to do so, we start the Spark Shell, and run the following commands:

Import graph libraries like this:

```
scala>import org.apache.spark.graphx._
scala>import org.apache.spark.rdd.RDD
```

Next, we define vertices and edges:

scala>valvertexArray = Array(

```
(1L, ("Alice", 28)),
(2L, ("Bob", 27)),
(3L, ("Charlie", 65)),
(4L, ("David", 42)),
(5L, ("Ed", 55)),
(6L, ("Fran", 50))
)
```

Here, we have a username and age as the properties of each vertex:

```
scala>valedgeArray = Array(
Edge(2L, 1L, 7),
Edge(2L, 4L, 2),
Edge(3L, 2L, 4),
Edge(3L, 6L, 3),
Edge(4L, 1L, 1),
Edge(5L, 2L, 2),
Edge(5L, 3L, 8),
Edge(5L, 6L, 3)
)
```

Every edge displays the link between the vertices and the number of likes that are given to various activities.

Now, we create RDDs of given arrays and orders in order to distribute data in parallel:

```
scala>valvertexRDD: RDD[(Long, (String, Int))] =
sc.parallelize(vertexArray)
scala>valedgeRDD: RDD[Edge[Int]] = sc.parallelize(edgeArray)
```

Next, we need to build a graph out of these vertices and edges, as shown here:

```
scala>val graph: Graph[(String, Int), Int] = Graph(vertexRDD, edgeRDD)
```

Now, we are ready to process this data. First of all, let's try to print all the users who are more than 30 years of age:

```
scala>graph.vertices.filter { case (id, (name, age)) => age > 30
}.collect.foreach {
case (id, (name, age)) =>println(s"$name is $age")
}
```

The output for this is as follows:

```
David is 42
Fran is 50
Charlie is 65
Ed is 55
```

We want to print the relationship between the users. We can do this as follows:

```
scala> for (triplet <- graph.triplets.collect) {
println(s"${triplet.srcAttr._1} likes ${triplet.dstAttr._1}")
}
```

The output for this is as follows:

```
Bob likes Alice
Bob likes David
Charlie likes Bob
Charlie likes Fran
David likes Alice
Ed likes Bob
Ed likes Charlie
Ed likes Fran
```

We can conclude that if a user likes another user's activities more than five times, then they are in love. This can be represented through the following command:

```scala
scala>for (triplet <- graph.triplets.filter(t =>t.attr> 5).collect) {
println(s"${triplet.srcAttr._1} loves ${triplet.dstAttr._1}")
   }
```

The output for this is as follows:

```
Bob loves Alice
Ed loves Charlie
```

This way, you can analyze various datasets that are available in the graph format.

How it works...

Spark GraphX is used for the parallel computation of graph datasets. GraphX extends the Spark RDD by introducing a directed multi-attribute graph with vertices and edges. To support graph processing, it exposes sets of APIs such as subgraphs, join vertices, and so on. It also includes a set of algorithms, which will be helpful in graph computations such as the Page Rank Algorithm.

> You can read more about Graphx at `http://spark.apache.org/docs/latest/graphx-programming-guide.html`.

Conducting predictive analytics using Spark MLib

Spark has a very rich machine learning library called `MLib`. This is a collection of various algorithms that are used for classification, clustering, recommendations, and so on. In this recipe, we are going to take a look at how to build a predictive model using `MLib`.

Getting ready

To perform this recipe, you should have Hadoop and Spark installed. You also need to install Scala. Here, I am using Scala 2.11.0.

How to do it...

For this recipe, we are going use the classic example dataset of iris flowers; you can find out more about this at `https://en.wikipedia.org/wiki/Iris_flower_data_set`.

Here, based on the petal length and width and the sepal length and width, we need to classify the flowers into species. First, we build a model, and then run tests on it to predict the output.

To start with, we first download `iris.txt` from `https://github.com/deshpandetanmay/hadoop-real-world-cookbook/blob/master/data/iris.txt`.

Next, save it in HDFS.

We start the Spark Shell, and run the following commands:

```
scala>import org.apache.spark.mllib.classification.NaiveBayes
scala>import org.apache.spark.mllib.linalg.Vectors
scala>import org.apache.spark.mllib.regression.LabeledPoint
```

This will import the required libraries. We are going to use Naïve Bayes classifiers in this case.

First, we create a class to define the file data model:

```
scala>case class Iris(
id:java.util.UUID,
sepal_l:Double,
sepal_w:Double,
petal_l:Double,
petal_w:Double,
species:String
)
```

Next, we load data from HDFS and parse it:

```
scala>val data = sc.textFile("iris.txt")

scala>val parsed = data.filter(!_.isEmpty).map {row =>
valsplitted = row.split(",")
val Array(sl, sw, pl, pw) = splitted.slice(0,4).map(_.toDouble)
    Iris (java.util.UUID.randomUUID(), sl, sw, pl, pw, splitted(4))
}
```

We can check whether the data is loaded properly by executing the following command:

`parsed.take(10).foreach(println)`

It would print something like this:

```
Iris(006f1567-e7ad-4e2a-8519-45272a66ce9b,5.1,3.5,1.4,0.2,Iris-setosa)
Iris(9ddd68aa-46f4-4d92-8de7-3c783bb5fd2b,4.9,3.0,1.4,0.2,Iris-setosa)
```

Here, we are going to use `LabledPoint`, which contains labels and features. The labels need to be in the Double format, and features need to be in the Vector format. Our label is a string in this case, so in order to convert it to the Double format, we create a map of unique values and then reverse them:

```
scala>val class2id  = parsed.map(_.species).distinct.collect.
zipWithIndex.map{case (k,v)=>(k, v.toDouble)}.toMap
scala>val id2class = class2id.map(_.swap)

scala>valparsedData = parsed.map { i =>LabeledPoint(class2id(i.
species), Vectors.dense(i.petal_l,i.petal_w,i.sepal_l,i.sepal_w)) }
```

Next, we train the model using the sample data we have:

```
scala>val model = NaiveBayes.train(parsedData)
```

Now, the model is ready to predict the species of the given flower on the basis of its features. Here is an example of this:

```
scala> id2class(model.predict(Vectors.dense(5, 1.5, 6.4, 3.2)))
res19: String = Iris-versicolor
```

This way, you can perform predictive analytics using Spark MLib.

How it works...

Spark `MLib` provides a huge list of supported algorithms. In the preceding example that uses a training dataset, Spark builds a model that has probability data. So, once the model is built, we can start predicting the output for certain given features. There are various classification algorithms available, so you can choose any of them.

10

Hadoop Use Cases

In this chapter, we'll take a look at the following recipes:

- ▸ Call Data Record analytics
- ▸ Web log analytics
- ▸ Sensitive data masking and encryption using Hadoop

Introduction

Throughout this book, we have been discussing Hadoop and its real-world use cases. In this final chapter, we are going to discuss the end-to-end implementation of a few such use cases. The motivation for this chapter is to apply the learning you've gathered from the earlier chapters. We will discuss use cases related the telecom, finance, and e-commerce domains. So, let's get started.

Call Data Record analytics

Call data records is data that is gathered by telecom operators that are specific to individual customers. We are going to take a look at telecom domain-specific use cases in this recipe.

Getting ready

To perform this recipe, you should have an up and running Hadoop cluster. We need some sample data for these use cases; I have written a data generator, which can used for your reference. You can find it at `https://github.com/deshpandetanmay/cdr-data-generator`.

How to do it...

Before jumping into the solution let's first try to understand a problem statement.

Problem Statement

Telecom companies keep records of each and every call made by their subscribers. They also keep information such as when a call was made, who it was made to, the start time, end time, and so on. Detailed information, such as SMSes, data sessions, and so on, is also stored by these companies. Here, the problem statement is how we can use this data to make company operations run smoother and help them generate valuable information about their customers.

Solution

Take a situation where a telecom company stores its data in RDMBS such as MySQL or Postgres. So, our solution flow diagram will look like this:

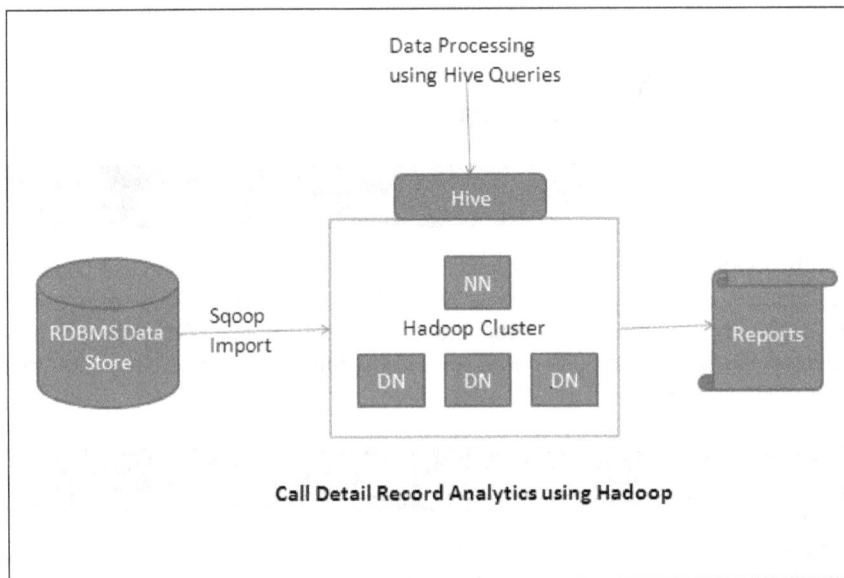

Call Detail Record Analytics using Hadoop

Now, let's assume that we have our data already present in the MySQL database in the `abctelecom.cdr` table:

```
mysql> desc abctelecom.cdr;
```

Field	Type	Null	Key	Default	Extra
id	varchar(50)	NO	PRI		

caller	varchar(20)	YES		NULL		
calling	varchar(20)	YES		NULL		
start_time	varchar(20)	YES		NULL		
end_time	varchar(20)	YES		NULL		
type	varchar(20)	YES		NULL		
charge	double	YES		NULL		
result	varchar(20)	YES		NULL		

```
8 rows in set (0.00 sec)
```

Now, let's execute the Sqoop command to import this data into HDFS.

First of all, make sure that the data directory is created, and then execute the Sqoop `import` command:

```
$ hadoop fs -mkdir /data
$sqoop import --connect jdbc:mysql://localhost:3306/abctelecom
--username root --password password --table cdr --target-dir /data/cdr
--fields-terminated-by '|'
```

This will import the data from the MySQL table to the HDFS `/data/cdr` directory.

Next, we start the Hive prompt and create an external Hive table pointing to the preceding directory:

```
CREATE EXTERNAL TABLE cdr (
id STRING,
caller_num STRING,
called_num STRING,
start_time STRING,
end_time STRING,
call_type STRING,
call_charge DOUBLE,
call_result STRING
)
ROW FORMAT DELIMITED
FIELDS TERMINATED BY '|'
    LOCATION '/data/cdr';
```

We can confirm whether the data load is as expected by executing the following commands:

```
hive> SELECT * FROM cdr LIMIT 2;
OK
02240095-bc62-4973-a143-710a5fb3509a 0989256849    1238082266
     2016-01-19T11:01:14.        2016-01-19T11:01:14.        SMS
0.35525125
     ANSWERED
30d73a30-6e93-472a-82cb-b1e53c94d1cb 5564259141    0537330705
     2016-02-15T00:56:17.        2016-02-15T00:58:53.        VOICE
     0.29876852    ANSWERED
Time taken: 1.387 seconds, Fetched: 2 row(s)
```

Now, let's start analyzing this data. Let's say we want to know how many calls and SMSes subscribers are making. To know this information, we can execute the following query:

```
SELECT caller_num, call_type, COUNT(*)
FROM cdr
        GROUP BY caller_num, call_type;
```

The result for this is as follows:

```
0537330705        SMS 53
0537330705        VOICE 59
0989256849        SMS 59
0989256849        VOICE 53
1238082266        SMS 55
1238082266        VOICE 56
5314043825        SMS 56
5314043825 .      VOICE 55
5564259141        SMS 55
5564259141        VOICE 56
```

Next, we want to find out the total duration of time for which a subscriber is making voice calls:

```
SELECT caller_num, SUM(UNIX_TIMESTAMP(end_time , "yyyy-MM-
dd'T'HH:mm:ss.SSSX") - UNIX_TIMESTAMP(start_time, "yyyy-MM-
dd'T'HH:mm:ss.SSSX"))  as duration
FROM cdr
group by caller_num, call_type
HAVING  call_type = 'VOICE';
```

This will give us information on how much time each subscriber has spent on voice calls. Now, we can filter out the subscribers who make voice calls for more than a specific amount of time and offer them a voice call-specific package.

The result of the preceding query is as follows:

```
0537330705        8698
0989256849        7929
1238082266        8554
5314043825        7988
5564259141        4007
```

Next, we can find out the customers who spend the most amount of money and offer them better packages. In order to find the top five billed customers, execute the following query:

```
SELECT caller_num, sum(call_charge) AS bill
FROM cdr
GROUP BY caller_num
ORDER BY bill DESC LIMIT 5;
```

The result is as follows:

```
5314043825        58.67936635200001
0537330705        56.971656405699996
1238082266        56.0622671385
0989256849        53.69393956600001
5564259141        42.46016877900002
```

We can round off the bill as follows:

```
SELECT caller_num, round(sum(call_charge)) AS bill
FROM cdr
GROUP BY caller_num
ORDER BY bill DESC LIMIT 5;
```

The result of this is as follows:

```
5314043825        59.0
0537330705        57.0
1238082266        56.0
0989256849        54.0
5564259141        42.0
```

We can also find out how many times a call was placed but the called number was busy:

```
SELECT call_result, count(*)
FROM cdr
GROUP BY call_result;
```

The result of this is as follows:

```
ANSWERED    527
BUSY        29
```

This way, the more data you have, the more analysis you can do with it.

How it works...

We have already taken a look at how Hadoop, Sqoop, and Hive work in the previous chapters, so in case you need more details on any of these, refer to the respective chapters.

Web log analytics

Web logs is data generated by web servers running a website. This use case is applicable to domains where companies have their websites hosted and want to know more about their website performance and customer behavior on the website.

Getting ready

To perform this recipe, you should have an up and running Hadoop cluster. I have uploaded the data of some sample web logs from

```
https://github.com/deshpandetanmay/hadoop-real-world-cookbook/blob/
master/data/mylog.txt.
```

How to do it...

Before jumping into the solution, let's first try to understand the problem statement:

Problem statement

Many companies run businesses on their websites. Their website performance decides the sales or profitability. Web servers generally log information about the user, browser, IP address, and so on. We can use this information in order to make the website browsing experience smoother for users, which would help increase profitability.

Solution

Here, we assume that a company hosting its website on an Apache server and we will be listening to the logs generated by the server. We will use Flume to copy the logs to the HDFS folder, and then use Apache Hive to process the data.

To import data into HDFS from web servers, we have to install the Flume agent on each web server instance. The following is the configuration that we have to use for the Flume agent configuration:

```
flume1.sources  = weblogs-source-1
flume1.channels = hdfs-channel-1
flume1.sinks    = hdfs-sink-1

# For each source, channel, and sink, set
# standard properties.
flume1.sources.weblogs-source-1.type = exec
flume1.sources.weblogs-source-1.command = tail -f /path/to/log/file.
log
flume1.sources.weblogs-source-1.batchSize = 100
flume1.sources.weblogs-source-1.channels = hdfs-channel-1

flume1.channels.hdfs-channel-1.type    = memory
flume1.sinks.hdfs-sink-1.channel = hdfs-channel-1
flume1.sinks.hdfs-sink-1.type = hdfs
flume1.sinks.hdfs-sink-1.hdfs.writeFormat = Text
flume1.sinks.hdfs-sink-1.hdfs.fileType = DataStream
flume1.sinks.hdfs-sink-1.hdfs.filePrefix = test-events
flume1.sinks.hdfs-sink-1.hdfs.useLocalTimeStamp = true
flume1.sinks.hdfs-sink-1.hdfs.path = /logs/web/%y-%m-%d
flume1.sinks.hdfs-sink-1.hdfs.rollCount=100
flume1.sinks.hdfs-sink-1.hdfs.rollSize=0

# Other properties are specific to each type of
# source, channel, or sink. In this case, we
# specify the capacity of the memory channel.
flume1.channels.hdfs-channel-1.capacity = 10000
```

This would be listening to the given log file path. Here, we are using the exec source, which executes the given command after a certain time interval.

The source is the output of the exec command that we have provided. The channel transfers the data to Sink, which writes it to HDFS.

To execute the preceding configuration, we have to run the following command:

```
/usr/local/flume/bin/flume-ng agent -n flume1 -c /usr/local/flume/conf
-f /usr/local/flume/conf/weblogs.conf -Dflume.root.logger=INFO,console
```

Now, as and when the log file is updated, the data will be written to HDFS as well.

The data we get is as follows:

```
103.22.239.216 - - [10/Feb/2016:23:05:30 -0800] "GET / HTTP/1.1" 304 0
"http://www.google.co.in/url?sa=t&rct=j&q=&esrc=s&source=web&cd=5&cad=
rja&uact=8&ved=0ahUKEw
js6N3jku_KAhXFkI4KHbRKBOwQFghGMAQ&url=http%3A%2F%2Fhadooptutorials.co.
in%2F&usg=AFQjCNEnec258W4qoaZBxqTY1SxCekMBtw&sig2=GUz56esk1WQ9ga
H6IoKBFA" "Mozilla/5.0 (Windows NT 6.1; Trident/7.0; rv:11.0) like
Gecko"
202.183.129.168 - - [10/Feb/2016:23:03:24 -0800] "GET /js/freelancer.
js HTTP/1.1" 304 0 - "Mozilla/4.0 (compatible;)"
202.168.90.179 - - [10/Feb/2016:23:03:06 -0800] "GET /tutorials/
hadoop/images/understanding-map-reduce-programming/map-reduce-flow.PNG
HTTP/1.1" 304 0 - "Mozilla/4.0 (compatible;)"
115.249.142.9 - - [10/Feb/2016:23:02:54 -0800] "GET /tutorials/
hadoop/images/big-data-analytics-what-is-that/3Vs_of_big_data.png
HTTP/1.1" 200 0 "http://hadooptutorials.co.in/tutorials/elasticsearch/
install-elasticsearch-kibana-logstash-on-windows.html" "Mozilla/5.0
(Windows NT 6.3; WOW64) AppleWebKit/537.36 (KHTML, like Gecko)
Chrome/48.0.2564.97 Safari/537.36"
115.249.142.9 - - [10/Feb/2016:23:02:54 -0800] "GET /tutorials/
sqoop/images/apache-sqoop-advanced-features/apache-sqoop-advanced-
features.png HTTP/1.1" 200 0 "http://hadooptutorials.co.in/tutorials/
elasticsearch/install-elasticsearch-kibana-logstash-on-windows.html"
"Mozilla/5.0 (Windows NT 6.3; WOW64) AppleWebKit/537.36 (KHTML, like
Gecko) Chrome/48.0.2564.97 Safari/537.36"
```

Next, we start the Hive prompt and create a table in Hive using `RegexSerde`:

```
CREATE TABLE apache_combined_log (
    host STRING,
    identity STRING,
    userid STRING,
    time STRING,
    request STRING,
    status STRING,
    size STRING,
    referer STRING,
    agent STRING)
ROW FORMAT SERDE 'org.apache.hadoop.hive.serde2.RegexSerDe'
WITH SERDEPROPERTIES (
    "input.regex" = "([^ ]*) ([^ ]*) ([^ ]*) (-|\\[[^\\]]*\\]) ([^
\"]*|\"[^\"]*\") (-|[0-9]*) (-|[0-9]*)(?: ([^ \"]*|\"[^\"]*\") ([^
\"]*|\"[^\"]*\"))?",
    "output.format.string" = "%1$s %2$s %3$s %4$s %5$s %6$s %7$s %8$s
%9$s"
)
STORED AS TEXTFILE;
```

Load the data to this table from HDFS.

Now we are all set to start our analytics.

First of all, let's try to find the most popular pages on the website by executing the following query:

```
SELECT request, COUNT(*) AS page_view_count FROM apache_combined_log
GROUP BY request
ORDER BY page_view_count DESC
LIMIT 5;
```

The output will be shown as follows:

```
"GET /font-awesome-4.1.0/css/font-awesome.min.css HTTP/1.1"    409
"GET /css/freelancer.css HTTP/1.1"    405
"GET /js/classie.js HTTP/1.1" 402
"GET /js/cbpAnimatedHeader.js HTTP/1.1"    400
"GET /js/freelancer.js HTTP/1.1"    396
```

Next, we want to know the most number of hits from the referral page, and for this, we need to execute the following command:

```
SELECT referer, COUNT(*) AS referer_count FROM apache_combined_log
GROUP BY referer
ORDER BY referer_count DESC
LIMIT 5;
```

The output for this is as shown here:

```
-   1374
"http://hadooptutorials.co.in/"       1096
"http://hadooptutorials.co.in/tutorials/spark/install-apache-spark-on-
ubuntu.html"      1029
"http://hadooptutorials.co.in/tutorials/elasticsearch/install-
elasticsearch-kibana-logstash-on-windows.html"      848
"http://hadooptutorials.co.in/tutorials/hive/hive-best-practices.html"
573
```

Next, we want to know which server threw an error for which pages during browsing. We can work on such pages in order to improve the site performance. Here, an error occurs when the HTTP status is not 200:

```
SELECT request, status FROM apache_combined_log
WHERE status != 200;
```

The output for this is as follows:

```
"GET /js/contact_me.js HTTP/1.1"        304
"GET /js/jqBootstrapValidation.js HTTP/1.1" 304
"GET /js/freelancer.js HTTP/1.1"        304
"GET /tutorials/spark/images/install-apache-spark-on-ubuntu/WordCount_
Demo.PNG HTTP/1.1"        304
```

Next, we want to do analysis based on location. But in our data, we don't have any such information; however, we can find this information using an IP address.

To do this, we are going to use a UDF, as shown here:

```java
package in.co.hadooptutorials.ip.location.hive.udf;

import java.io.BufferedReader;
import java.io.IOException;
import java.io.InputStreamReader;
import java.net.HttpURLConnection;
import java.net.URL;

import org.apache.hadoop.hive.ql.exec.UDF;
import org.apache.hadoop.io.Text;

public class LocationFinder extends UDF {

    public Text evaluate( Text inputIp) throws IOException{
        URL url = new URL("http://freegeoip.net/json/"+inputIp.
toString());
        HttpURLConnection conn = (HttpURLConnection) url.
openConnection();
        conn.setRequestMethod("GET");
        conn.setRequestProperty("Accept", "application/json");

        if (conn.getResponseCode() != 200) {
            throw new RuntimeException("Failed : HTTP error code : "
                    + conn.getResponseCode());
        }

        BufferedReader br = new BufferedReader(new InputStreamReader(
            (conn.getInputStream())));

        String output = br.readLine();
        return new Text(output);
    }


}
```

First, we take out unique IPs:

```
CREATE TABLE unique_ips as
SELECT DISTINCT(host) FROM apache_combined_log;
```

Then, we use the UDF to find details about each IP:

```
ADD JAR ip-location-hive-udf-1.0.jar;
CREATE TEMPORARY FUNCTION get_details AS 'in.co.hadooptutorials.
ip.location.hive.udf.LocationFinder' ;

CREATE TABLE location_details ( data string) ;
INSERT INTO location_details
SELECT get_details(host) FROM unique_ips;

Next we create table with JSON SerDe.
ADD JAR json-serde-1.1.9.9-Hive1.2-jar-with-dependencies.jar;

CREATE TABLE ip_location_details (
ip STRING,
country_code STRING,
country_name STRING,
region_code STRING,
region_name STRING,
latitude DOUBLE,
longitude DOUBLE,
zip_code STRING,
time_zone STRING,
city STRING,
metro_code INT
)
ROW FORMAT SERDE 'org.openx.data.jsonserde.JsonSerDe'
LOCATION '/user/hive/warehouse/location_details';
```

We are all set to use the location details by joining the tables. For example, to get the number of sessions per country, we need to execute the following command:

```
SELECT ild.country_name, COUNT(*) FROM
ip_location_details ild JOIN apache_combined_log acl
ON (ild.ip = acl.host)
GROUP BY ild.country_name;
For City,
SELECT ild.city, COUNT(*) FROM
ip_location_details ild JOIN apache_combined_log acl
ON (ild.ip = acl.host)
GROUP BY ild.city;
```

We can also create reports in order to visualize the results of these queries.

How it works...

We have already seen how Hadoop, Flume, and Hive work in previous chapters, so in case you need further details on any of these, refer to the respective chapters.

Sensitive data masking and encryption using Hadoop

A lot of companies handle sensitive information such as SSN numbers, names, credit card numbers, and so on. In this recipe, we are going to take a look at how to use Hadoop to mask or encrypt this data in order to secure it. This recipe can be referred to by various domains, such as finance, retail, telecom, and those people who handle critical information.

Getting ready

To perform this recipe, you should have an up and running Hadoop cluster.

How to do it...

Before jumping into the solution, let's first try to understand the problem statement.

Problem statement

Handling sensitive information is a critical part of today's data operations. Here, the problem statement is to transform critical information into masked data or completely encrypted data.

Solution

Here, we assume that we already have data with us in flat files and it has been loaded into HDFS.

Let's say we have some sample data, as shown here, which has the name and credit card number of a person:

```
Ryan Levine|4716840526341330
Erika Smith|4539326321106479
Brooklyn Sloan|4916571896673675
Karen Mayer|5428124448681073
Eddie O'neill|5374594066409623
Nancy Stevens|5390742852412406
Chasity Conway|378238168241362
```

```
Aaron McCray|374762693530829
Kendra Allen|374606063397725
Jenna Burns|535512655184557
Jane Mayo|343637926486924
George Suarez|347956127969751
Janet Abbott|6011345775765400
Steven Marshall|6011414499816624
Shane Heath|6011322907488797
Unborn Vega|6011417989731237
Kaitlyn Wilder|6011055063404451
Donald Morgan|5140126646868581
```

First of all, we will create a Hive table, and then load data into it:

```
CREATE TABLE personal_details(
name STRING,
ccnum STRING
)
ROW FORMAT DELIMITED
FIELDS TERMINATED BY '|';

LOAD DATA LOCAL INPATH 'personal_details.txt' INTO TABLE personal_
details;
```

Now, we can write Hive UDFs to mask the name as well as the credit card number. Credit card numbers are not random numbers, but they are generated through an algorithm called Luhn's Algorithm, which can be found at `https://en.wikipedia.org/wiki/Luhn_algorithm`.

We can write algorithms based on our complexity but for the purposes of demonstration, I am using a simple algorithm, which subtracts each number from 9 and returns it. Before starting anything, make sure that you add the required dependencies in `pom.xml`:

```
<dependency>
    <groupId>org.apache.hive</groupId>
    <artifactId>hive-exec</artifactId>
    <version>1.2.0</version>
</dependency>
<dependency>
    <groupId>org.apache.hadoop</groupId>
    <artifactId>hadoop-common</artifactId>
    <version>2.7.1</version>
</dependency>
```

Our CC number masking UDF code is as follows:

```java
package in.co.hadooptutorials.hive.udf.masking;

import java.io.IOException;

import org.apache.hadoop.hive.ql.exec.UDF;
import org.apache.hadoop.io.Text;

public class CCMasker extends UDF {
    public Text evaluate(Text ccNumber) throws IOException {
        String[] num = ccNumber.toString().split("");
        StringBuilder sb = new StringBuilder();
        for (String c : num) {
            if(!("".equals(c))){

                int i = 9 - Integer.parseInt(c);
                sb.append(i);
            }
        }
        return new Text(sb.toString());
    }

}
```

Our name masking UDF code is as follows:

```java
package in.co.hadooptutorials.hive.udf.masking;

import java.io.IOException;
import java.util.Random;

import org.apache.hadoop.hive.ql.exec.UDF;
import org.apache.hadoop.io.Text;

public class NameMasker extends UDF {
    public Text evaluate(Text name) throws IOException {

        return new Text(mask(name.toString(), 0));
    }

    char randomChar(Random r, String cs, boolean uppercase) {
        char c = cs.charAt(r.nextInt(cs.length()));
        return uppercase ? Character.toUpperCase(c) : c;
    }
```

```
String mask(String str, int seed) {

    final String cons = "bcdfghjklmnpqrstvwxz";
    final String vowel = "aeiouy";
    final String digit = "0123456789";

    Random r = new Random(seed);
    char data[] = str.toCharArray();

    for (int n = 0; n < data.length; ++n) {
        char ln = Character.toLowerCase(data[n]);
        if (cons.indexOf(ln) >= 0)
            data[n] = randomChar(r, cons, ln != data[n]);
        else if (vowel.indexOf(ln) >= 0)
            data[n] = randomChar(r, vowel, ln != data[n]);
        else if (digit.indexOf(ln) >= 0)
            data[n] = randomChar(r, digit, ln != data[n]);
    }

    return new String(data);

    }
}
```

We build the project and copy the JAR file to the Hadoop cluster:

```
ADD JAR masking-udf-1.0.jar;

CREATE TEMPORARY FUNCTION ccmask AS 'in.co.hadooptutorials.hive.udf.
masking.CCMasker';

CREATE TEMPORARY FUNCTION namemask AS 'in.co.hadooptutorials.hive.udf.
masking.NameMasker';

And then we execute the query to start masking name and cc number.
CREATE TABLE personal_details_masked AS
SELECT namemask(name), ccmask(ccnum) FROM
personal_details;
```

Once the execution is complete, you can see these results:

```
hive> select * from personal_details_masked;
    Buek Typozi      5283159473658669
    Aleky Rpozs      5460673678893520
    Bleytryc Zsyyr   5083428103326324
    Bumyt Ryoos      4571875551318926
```

```
Almyy Y'poosw      4625405933590376
Bumky Rpoziww      4609257147587593
Blekyry Coswyy     621761831758637
Aumyt RpCziy       625237306469170
Bumkty Ycziw       625393936602274
Bumky Ryczs        4664873448815442
Bumy Tyyo 656362073513075
Buekty Poosyw      652043872030248
Bumyt Ypcosw       3988654224234599
Blekyr Pozswyrd 3988585500183375
Bleky Ryozs        3988677092511202
Almytr Pozi        3988582010268762
Buektyp Coswyr     3988944936595548
Bumytr Pozsyw      4859873353131418
```

This way, you can use Hadoop to mask or encrypt sensitive information.

How it works...

We have already taken a look at how Hadoop and Hive work in previous chapters, so in case you need further details, refer to the respective chapters.

Index

A

access log, formats
  %b 39
  %h 39
  %l 39
  %r 39
  %>s 39
  %t 39
  %u 39
  referrer 39
  user agent 39
Apache Spark
  about 221
  URL 222
Area Under a Curve (AUC)
  reference 206
atomic export
  performing, Sqoop used 154, 155
Avro format
  Hive data, processing in 116-118

B

balancer command
  executing, for uniform data
      distribution 14-16
benchmarking
  performing, on Hadoop cluster 19-22

C

Call Data Record analytics
  defining 249-253
  performing, Hive used 130, 131
  problem statement 250

  solution 250-253
  URL 249
Call Data Records (CDR)
  about 129
  reference 129
Change Data Capture (CDC)
  implementing, Hive used 135-138
CLI
  Hbase operation, performing in 97-103
combined access logs
  reference 38
command options, Hadoop
  reference 9
compressed data
  saving, on HDFS 34, 35
configuration parameters, Hadoop
  core-site.xml 4
  hadoop-env.sh 4
  hdfs-site.xml 5
  mapred-site.xml 5
  yarn-site.xml 5
Confusion Matrix
  about 207
  reference 207
context Ngram
  performing, in Hive 127-129
custom SerDe
  reference 113

D

data
  exporting, from HDFS to local machine 25, 26
  exporting, from HDFS to RDBMS 148-151
  importing, from Hadoop cluster 31, 32